"Whether you're a writer, development executive, or anyone in or outside the business who wants to master script evaluation and screenwriting, you've got to read this book! It's packed with insights on writing, analyzing, and marketing scripts (and marketing yourself)!"
— Lisa Gooding, Head of Development, Capital Arts

"There's nothing more frustrating, or satisfying, than writing a good script. But, to make it great, everyone needs a little help. Derek's book shows you, in step-by-step detail, exactly how to give and get that help."
— Jason Blumenthal, producer, *The Weather Man*, *The Pursuit of Happyness*

"With great clarity, Mr. Rydall celebrates those unsung hero and heroine script consultants who, from the sidelines, can make the difference between a sale or not. Finally, a smart, comprehensive guide that demystifies the mystifying process of getting and giving professional feedback on a screenplay."
— Devorah Cutler-Rubenstein, CEO, The Script Broker

"I see dozens of books of this type, and my attitude going in was, 'Well, how is this one different?' You know what? It is different. Derek Rydall's emphasis of two vital issues — strategic analysis of the art of writing and competitive analysis of the business of advertising and marketing a script — make this much more valuable than the usual 'how-to' books."
— Barbara Hiser, Emmy Award-winning producer

"Writing is a real job. And so is script consulting. Every writer needs that 'traffic cop' who can read their screenplay and tell them when it's full speed ahead, when to proceed with caution, when to come to a stop, backup, and proceed down an alternate road. After you read Derek Rydall's wonderfully insightful book I guarantee you'll be ready for your badge and nightstick!"
— Ken Rotcop, award-winning writer and author of *The Perfect Pitch: How To Sell Yourself and Your Idea To Hollywood*

"This is a great book! It breaks down the process of evaluating a script so clearly, it should be required reading for anyone reading, writing, developing, or producing film and TV. And for those who want to make a good living consulting on scripts, they should memorize this book!"
— J. P. Farrell, producer, *Enterprise, Star Trek: The Next Generation*

"Derek's book will give you the skills you need and show you, step-by-step, how to build your business and launch your new career. You will be happy to be in Derek's company as he leads you through the ins and outs of this fulfilling and creative profession!"
— Linda Seger, best-selling author of *Making a Good Script Great*

"Just when you thought you knew everything about Hollywood, along comes a book like this! It's incredibly useful on so many levels, from screenwriting to development to production! I just can't imagine anyone in this business not getting something valuable out of it!"
— Gloria Fan, V.P. Production and Development, Mosaic Media Group

"The art of evaluating scripts is in direct relation to your ability to evaluate the world around you. If you have a specialty in life which gives you a direct insight into that specific world then you have an unexploited talent that can help the film industry. Mr. Rydall's book gives the so-called outsider an entree into the film industry. Whoever finds this book first dive in, because the door has just opened."
— Allan Katz, award-winning writer

"A great reference and straightforward approach to analyzing and developing screenplays."
— Jake Wagner, Head of Development, Avatar Entertainment

"If you love movies, and have the talent and analytical skills for evaluating screenplays, Derek Rydall's book will be one of the most valuable references on your shelf. But it's more than a reference book — it's a manual that clearly illuminates the fundamental building blocks necessary to make a living as a scriptwriter or consultant."
— Tony Savant, director, playwright, screenwriter, script consultant

"The sheer amount of information and experience packed into these pages is incredible! An invaluable resource for aspiring and professional script consultants, development execs, producers, and screenwriters everywhere!"
— Jed Strahm, Head of Development, Raw Nerve Films

"This book taught me quite a bit about script analysis. And as a producer, I've been developing scripts for 15 years! After finishing the book, I felt like I could have a career as a script consultant if I got tired of producing. The book really was so comprehensive. This book is all you need!"
— Joel Rice, producer

"Derek Rydall is a man who walks his talk as a conscious individual who's developed brilliance in his career as a script consultant. For him to share his gift and inspire others to do the same is a testament to his character. As a TV host/producer/writer I'm always looking to expand my craft and this book has had a huge impact. Grab it! Read it! And inhale it! It's complete in every sense of the word."
— Paul Ryan, author of *The Art of Comedy* and director of the CBS Comedy & TV Hosting Workshop

"One of the most informative, easy to follow, and, most importantly, accurate books on script consulting I have read. Rydall blends industry savvy with humor in an uncondescending way in this step-by-step book, perfect for anyone looking to break into script consulting or any current consultants and executives who are looking for tips on how to analyze a script better."
— Danny Manus, Head of Development, Sandstorm Films

"Derek knows how to take scripted material to the next level. 'Good' isn't good enough. For a script to be in demand and catch the attention of the industry, it needs to be engaging, powerful, cutting edge, a step above the rest. Derek's insights in this book on how to bring scripts to that level is remarkable."
— Fran Montano, Emmy Award-winning director, actor, acting coach

I COULD'VE WRITTEN A BETTER MOVIE THAN THAT!

How to Make Six Figures as a Script Consultant
Even If You're Not a Screenwriter

DEREK RYDALL

Published by Michael Wiese Productions
11288 Ventura Blvd., Suite 621
Studio City, CA 91604
T: 818.379.8799
F: 818.986.3408
mw@mwp.com
www.mwp.com

Cover Design: Michael Wiese Productions
Layout: Gina Mansfield
Editor: Paul Norlen

Printed by McNaughton & Gunn, Inc., Saline, Michigan
Manufactured in the United States of America

Library of Congress Cataloging-in-Publication Data

Rydall, Derek, 1972-
  I could've written a better movie than that! : how to make six figures as a script
consultant even if you're not a screenwriter / Derek Rydall.
      p. cm.
  ISBN 1-932907-07-6
  1. Motion picture authorship. I. Title.
  PN1996.R94 2005
  808.2'3--dc22

                                                        2005007311

Table of Contents

Acknowledgments

This book (and just about everything else in my life) would not have been possible without the unflagging support of my wife and kids, who cheer me on — then leave me alone — when I start a new project. And are there to curl up with, make a batch of Newman's Own, and watch the latest episode of *Extreme Makeovers*, when I invariably crash into a wall. Second only to God (and it's a close second), they are my greatest source of inspiration, motivation, and regeneration. Thanks, guys, I love you like a rock.

Many friends have helped me and offered feedback and support along my path, but one individual deserves special thanks — Allan Katz. Writing can be a lonely pursuit. Having a confidante on that journey, in the middle of those dark creatively barren nights — someone to brainstorm ideas with, get blistering feedback from, or just vent about the latest deal that bit the dust — is an invaluable gift. Allan's support and belief in me all these years, I believe, saved me (at least once) from strangling myself with printing ribbon. You're a true friend, Allan, and if I haven't told you lately — Thanks, man, I really appreciate you (and you better give me a cool thanks in one of your books!).

A very special thanks to Michael Wiese and Ken Lee, two creative, innovative, and sincere guys who had the insight, foresight — and all the other sights you need to publish great books — to recognize the unique opportunity this book presented and take a chance on me. They've been nothing but supportive. Let's do it again soon!

I want to extend my heartfelt gratitude to all of my writing mentors and teachers, especially Linda Seger, Michael Hauge, Syd Field, and Robert McKee, whose books and classes truly fed and sustained me when I began this journey (and still do).

Oh, and thanks to Kraft Macaroni & Cheese, which also sustained me.

Of course, I must thank my mom and dad, without whom I would've had to channel this book from another dimension. And let's not forget all the pain and suffering they provided, without which I would've never been forced to find a creative outlet for my neuroses. (Never underestimate the value of a good trauma.) Seriously, my mom has been one of the biggest champions of my artistic endeavors. And my dad has given me the tools and teaching to turn my creative contortions into cash. What more could I ask for — except maybe reimbursement for therapy bills.

Thanks Bill Lae, Katie Lippa, and Johnny Cho, for being the first people to read early drafts of this book and provide incredible feedback. Thanks to all my clients who have provided the raw experience that became this book. And a big thanks to all the script consultants who contributed to this book: Linda Seger, Michael Hauge, David Freeman, Rachel Ballon, Kathie Fong Yoneda, Judith Searle, Dave Trottier, Chris Vogler, Jeff Freeman, Richard Krevolin, and Pamela Jaye Smith.

Thanks to the producer (you know who you are) who bought a script of mine, strung me along, then let the deal crash and burn — which prompted me to finally write this book. If it wasn't for you, I might be sitting on the veranda of some sun-drenched villa in Italy, drinking cappuccino, tearing my hair out over script rewrites for tomorrow's shoot, rather than sitting in a noisy, sterile Starbucks writing this acknowledgment. So there! And to all the agents, publishers, executives, producers, and everyone else who has ever rejected me or my work — Thank you! Thank you! Thank you! You've been my greatest teachers.

There are so many others who have contributed to this tapestry called my creative life: my spiritual community (Agape), Rev. Michael Beckwith, Rev. Nirvana Gayle, my agent, Barry Perelman, Amanda Moore, Matt Siegel, Johnny Griggs....

For anyone I'm forgetting, thank you (*insert your name here*)!

Thanks, God.

And last, but certainly not least, I want to thank myself. That's right. Thank you, Derek. Without your workaholism and willful, stubborn tenacity, none of this would have been possible. Without you... I wouldn't be here.

Foreword

Before 1981, there were no script consultants. There were development executives at studios and production companies who chose material, developed it, and then produced it. There were story analysts who wrote synopses of the material and short comments, either recommending the project to the executive, or suggesting that the executive pass on it. There were some teachers of screenwriting, such as the renowned Syd Field, working at colleges or independently to teach screenplay writing and to help writers develop their scripts. But the independent, entrepreneurial script consultant did not yet exist.

Since 1981, however, this industry has begun to grow, with many script consultants now in practice around the world. There are different ways to define this job, but most script consultants see themselves as the objective professional eye, helping writers identify and solve script problems and helping them shape, craft, and structure the script into a workable, professional product.

Although most of us work mainly with screenwriters, many of us also have clients who are producers, directors, editors, and executives, and sometimes fiction writers who want to turn their novels into screenplays. We have become an important part of the industry, some even say an essential part of the industry. Our work not only has helped create better scripts, but also helped these writers find agents, and get their work optioned and produced. At our best, we make sure that the wonderful films that you see are well crafted, without holes and confusion. We help make sure that the themes come through, the characters are strong, and the story is focused.

As this position has evolved, consultants have found their own niches. Some are writing coaches, holding the hand of the writer through the various drafts. Others are experts on military or investigative procedures, there to help make sure the writer gets the crime scene right and the technology accurate. Some are psychologists, specializing in making sure the characters ring true. Then there are the legal and medical authorities, and those who know how to research and guide the writer through a period piece.

This is not only one of the newest careers in the film industry, it is also one of the most creative and exciting. Consultants and writers work together collaboratively — and the script reaches a new level of meaning and artistry.

Derek Rydall understands this business, having worked in it and studied it. He introduces the reader to the approaches and vast amount of knowledge that make up this business. If you've ever thought of hiring a script consultant, this book will give you an overview of what we do and the variety of services that make up this job. He introduces you to some of the top people in the field and shows the different methods that script consultants use to achieve results.

If you already have skills in script analysis, this book can help you refine those skills, market yourself, and find your niche within the script consulting profession. And if you've yet to embark on this journey of script consulting, Derek's book will give you the skills you need and show you, step-by-step, how to build your business and launch your new career.

In the 1980s, this business was known as a "well-kept secret" since few writers wanted to admit that they needed help on their script. Now it's a well-respected and well-established business; many writers now consider it a part of the process to seek out the help of a script consultant to help make their script better. In this book, Derek has helped raise the profile of this job, clarified the complexities, and articulated the knowledge required to be good at this work.

And he's done this in an easy, nurturing, and accessible way. Derek is thorough and fair, and helps the reader understand that this job demands integrity, knowledge, and people skills. And he's done this with a generous spirit and an entertaining wit. As a reader, you will be happy to be in Derek's company as he leads you through the ins and outs of this fulfilling and creative profession!

Dr. Linda Seger
Script Consultant

Introduction

How many times have you watched a movie or TV show and thought you could write it better — or at least tell the writer (or filmmaker) how they could?

How would you like to have that conversation for real?

How would you like to make a living doing it?

In *I Could've Written a Better Movie Than That: How to Make Six Figures as a Script Consultant — Even If You're Not a Screenwriter*, you'll learn how.

The field of professional screenplay consulting officially began back in the early 1980s when Linda Seger, considered the "mother of script consulting," developed a method for diagnosing and treating script problems. She started out charging $70 for a complete script evaluation, and within two years was able to turn it into a full-time business. (She now receives thousands for this service.) At the time, it was considered taboo to have a script consultant or "script doctor" on your project. No writer wanted to admit his script was ailing and needed a "check-up from the text up." Nowadays, this attitude has reversed. In fact, it might even be considered irresponsible *not* to have a professional give you an objective evaluation of your script. It would be like knowing you have a potentially fatal disease and not seeking a medical opinion.

Linda Seger was one of the pioneers who paved the way. But since those first steps on the frontier, many more have followed. Today, script consulting has become a respected field, attracting talented and passionate people, from diverse backgrounds, who bring a variety of specialties. And it's only the beginning. The art and craft of story analysis is still in its infancy. While we already have great thinkers who have transformed the way we look at screenwriting (and storytelling in general), the greatest ideas, the ones that will take this art to new heights, have yet to be articulated.

If you're a writer, producer, executive, or director working in the entertainment industry — or aspire to be one — becoming a script consultant may not seem like such a leap. Besides the obvious benefit of extra income, it will also enable you to grow your analytical and writing skills, and strengthen your ability to recognize and develop great scripts. But the exciting news is that *you don't have to live or work in Hollywood at all to become a script consultant*. Linda Seger lives in Colorado, isn't a screenwriter, and has consulted on over 2,000 screenplays, written many books, and traveled the world teaching the art and craft of screenwriting. "At this point, my clients now come from six continents," Seger says. "I'm still waiting for that first script from Antarctica, even though they're not writing scripts there yet."

As the field matures, more and more individuals from non-entertainment backgrounds are becoming consultants, bringing with them a whole new array of services to upgrade the quality of writing and the quality-of-life of the writer. Just as doctors can specialize in various body parts or health issues, script consultants (or "Script Doctors") have also created their own specialties. There are consultants who specialize in everything from the "mythological," "psychological," and "spiritual" aspects of story and character, to the "criminal," "legal," and "relationship-focused" films. If you're a doctor, lawyer, teacher, police officer, politician, psychologist, minister, comedian, relationship coach, weapons expert, soldier, or just about anything else, and you have a love of movies and an understanding of story, you could create a niche business consulting on films that fit your unique knowledge base.

For example, let's say you're a history teacher with a passion for historical accuracy in films. Just add a solid understanding of screenwriting and *voila!* You're on your way to being a script consultant specializing in historical pieces. Get the picture? And if you're a retired professional, this offers a whole new way to use your life's worth of knowledge, and a whole new world of adventure.

So the big question is, can *you* make six figures as a script consultant? Are there enough people out there in need of such services? Every year thousands of new screenplays, treatments, and outlines are written by professional and aspiring writers. (The WGA reports that over 50,000 new screenplays are registered annually — and what about all the ones that aren't registered?) Thousands more are conceived of by professionals in other fields — doctors, lawyers, mobsters (we'll get to my mob story later) with private dreams of making movies and dining with the Hollywood Elite. (A partnership I have with a neurosurgeon has led to some of my most exciting projects. And as an added bonus, if I develop a brain tumor from banging my head against the wall, I can barter my services for his.)

Add to this number the thousands of aspiring producers (with ideas they're sure will be blockbusters), and the truckloads of novels sitting in desk drawers (whose authors have dreams of seeing them adapted to celluloid) and you start to realize just how big a market there is. (Over 200,000 new books are published in the U.S. and U.K. alone each year, and it's estimated that well over a million are written with hopes of seeing the inside of a Barnes & Noble. That's a lot of potential adaptations!) If that doesn't convince you of the immense opportunity out there, you can also throw in the thousands of scripts that circulate through talent agencies and production companies that need "Readers Coverage," and are frequently outsourced to script consultants. And I haven't even mentioned the multi-billion dollar video game market! Video games are becoming increasingly story-driven — especially with the growing trend of turning video games into movies and movies into video games. Do you think there might be some opportunity here for story consultants? You bet there is.

While some of these scribes will seek feedback from their agent (hopefully one who's not charging them), their friend (if they don't mind risking their friendship), or their grandma (if they want a pat on the head and a warm cookie with milk), many more will need to hire a script consultant to give their ailing material a complete physical. And even the ones who get granny's seal of approval will oftentimes need a "second opinion" to save their baby from suffering a stillbirth. What's more, some of these consulting jobs can turn into writing assignments, where you are hired to polish, rewrite, or completely develop a script — at a substantially higher price.

Finally, if you think it's too late to "get into the market," because there are already too many script consultants out there, think again. The fact is, many of the above referenced individuals — especially those in other professions — don't even know these services exist yet.

And with over a million potential clients, there's enough to go around!

In *I Could've Written a Better Movie Than That*, I'll show you how to tap into these markets and let these prospective clients know you've hung your shingle out. Utilizing over a hundred years of combined experience from the top script consultants in the business (including Yours Truly), you'll be led through a step-by-step process where you'll learn how to:

○ Hone your reading, writing, and analytical skills
○ Do "Story Analysis," "Book Analysis," and "Coverage"
○ Become a Script Doctor
○ Market your clients' material for sale — and even be attached as a partner
○ Create the perfect advertising and target the right venues
○ Master client communication and feedback skills
○ Negotiate the deals, create the contracts, and collect payment
○ Clarify your mission and compose a plan of action
○ Maintain balance and passion

And much more!

How I Got Started

About a decade ago, I was a steadily working actor. But, despite making a nice living, I was tired of waiting by the phone, beholden to someone else for my job opportunities — and decided to start creating my own.

Enter the world of screenwriting.

At first I thought I would write the perfect script for me to star in (every actor's dream). But I soon realized I actually loved writing, and wanted to be more than just a wannabe. I took some screenwriting classes, read some books, and wrote several scripts. But something was missing. I just wasn't getting the kind of hands-on guidance that I really needed to succeed. I needed a mentor....

Enter the script consultant.

His name was Allan Katz. He came from an acting background (as I had), and was now working full-time as a writer—script doctor—stage director (he was directing my soon-to-be wife in an award-winning play when we met). We really hit it off, and I decided to hire him to evaluate all the scripts I'd written so far.

I was a novice, of course, so those scripts were destined to be quartered and used as scratch pads and flip-books by my son. But getting together over coffee, hashing out my work page-by-page, line-by-line, and having revelations about my stories and my craft, was great fun. Equally important was having a mentor, a creative collaboration with someone who knew more about writing than I did. I looked forward to our meetings almost more than I did the writing itself. Writers tend to be a lonely bunch. Most of us need to come out of our caves and dwell amongst the living on a regular basis, or we start growing hair in strange places and craving raw animal flesh.

I grew tremendously as a writer during this "apprenticeship." And one day, Mr. Katz looked at me and said he could no longer work for me — because I knew as much as he did. (That's integrity, huh? Surely, he could've squeezed a few more bucks out of me.) And soon after this "graduation," he started asking me to read his scripts and give him feedback. Needless to say, I was flattered — and nervous. But I did it.

He liked what I had to say.

And so began my journey as a script consultant....

Opportunity Knocks — And I Look Through the Peephole
I began offering to read other people's scripts and, as word spread of my "insightful" and enthusiastic feedback, the phone started ringing. It was a great learning (and ego-boosting) experience, allowing me to hone my analytical and writing skills. Then, one day, while I was giving my usual brilliant, witty, and "humble" feedback on a script — and the writer was slipping me two other scripts to read *for free* — it suddenly dawned on me:

"Hey, maybe I could actually get paid for this."

Thus began my "professional" career as a script consultant.

And as more opportunities came my way, I started to think: "You know, if I actually took this seriously, I might be able to keep myself in clean socks all year!" So I decided to take the leap and make it an "official business." I registered by DBA (Doing Business As) under the name "*The Script Doctor*," took out ads, printed up business cards and brochures, rented an office, and officially hung out my shingle. Word-of-mouth spread, and soon I had a full-time gig telling other people how to write better.

Things were rolling along.

Then something unexpected happened....

A client was so "impressed" with my feedback on his script that he didn't think he could pull off the rewrite — and asked *me* to do it. At first I wasn't sure if that was ethical, or if it really served the client (since he was a writer himself). But he insisted and asked how much I would charge. I took a deep breath, authoritatively allowing the question to hang in the silence like I'd done this many times before — as my mind frantically groped for a clue of what the heck to say. Then I gathered myself, leaned forward confidently, and laid out the "deal points" in such savvy fashion that Mike Ovitz would've been impressed.

Actually, I asked him how much he could afford — he threw out a number that was somewhere north of a high-priced typist — and I shook his hand like an eager kid getting his first job working for daddy.

But hey, I had my first "script doctoring" deal.

When the project was completed, he liked it so much that he hired me again. This time, however, I was the wiser. I had him pay me part of my high-priced typist fee *before* I did the work.

Ha-ha! I was becoming a regular mover-and-shaker.

It's true that "like attracts like," because soon other clients began showing up who wanted me to not only analyze their material, but rewrite or polish it as well. They were writers, executives, producers, directors, grandmas (I know, don't hate me), and professionals from other fields. I found myself consulting on every aspect of story — from choosing the right idea, to outlines, treatments, pitches, synopses, book adaptations, and more!

And within two years I was earning six figures consulting for clients around the world!

But being a script consultant has brought me many rewards beyond merely the monetary. Helping people realize their story's potential, watching them pop into a whole new level of understanding and artistry, and celebrating their successes (including selling, producing, and starring in their award-winning films) brings with it a special satisfaction that remains long after the deal is done.

And the friendships and colleagues I have met along the way are, as the credit card commercial says, "Priceless."

A Final Introductory Thought

You might think you're not qualified. And you might be right... for the moment. That's what this book is for — to get you qualified. All the tools you need to become a success are here.

Just add sweat.

But let me remind you again that some of the top script consultants aren't screenwriters, don't live in L.A., and initially came from completely different professions. And many who *are* screenwriters haven't sold a screenplay in a long time (if ever) or made much money writing — but are making a nice living helping others do it. I don't say this with any disrespect. In fact, many script consultants can write and do sell their work. The point is, you don't need to be an A-list writer living in the Hollywood Hills to be a successful script consultant.

Do you love movies? Do you have the drive to be part of the magic? Do you believe you can, with the proper training, offer something of value to others with a similar passion — perhaps specializing in scripts that deal with your professional background? And are you willing to roll up your sleeves, push away the excuses, and do what it takes to succeed?

Then you, my friend, might just have what it takes.
The question is, will you take what you have — and get to work?

Good luck!

How to Read This Book

I suggest you read the whole book through first.

Once you have an idea of what this work entails, do the section on creating your Script Consultant Credo and business plan. Then go back to the chapters that deal with areas you are weak in, and develop the necessary skills to succeed.

As you work your business, you can use this book as an "owner's manual," referring back to specific sections as needed for a refresher.

Act 1

The Set-up

ᴑ What is a Script Consultant

ᴑ Why We Need Script Consultants

ᴑ Your Market

ᴑ Fifteen Reasons to Become a Script Consultant

ᴑ Do You Have What It Takes?

ᴑ The Challenges of Script Consulting

Chapter One

"I always knew that one day
I would take this road but
Yesterday
I did not know today
Would be that day."
——— *Nagarjuna*

Getting Started

What is a Script Consultant?

There are many types of script consultants with many techniques and specialties, but the following covers the basic job description:

Script Consultant: *Someone who analyzes and offers varying depths of feedback on screenplays at all stages (concept, query, pitch, outline, treatment, completed script, and even finished film), as well as evaluating books and stage plays for adaptation to the big or small screen. Services can also include "script coverage," "coaching," "teaching," and "script doctoring" (rewriting and polishing scripts).*

A script consultant works for writers, directors, producers, studio executives, and just about anyone else who has a story and a need to develop it. Script consultant fees vary, depending on the person, their resume, or their whim. Some charge by the hour, others by the project. Some even partner up and assist in the marketing. Some script consultants focus more on typos and grammatical errors than story and structure. Others utilize ancient tools and techniques, mythological maps and sacred mandalas. Some script consultants are ex-agents or studio executives, and will focus more on the commercial elements of the material. Others are psychologists or therapists and will diagnose the writer as well as what's written!

Sometimes their feedback is so brilliant you'll want them to write the script. Other times, it's like taking a trip to hell — development hell. But mostly, script consultants are hardworking, intelligent, thoughtful, creative, disciplined, caring professionals that will give you a fresh perspective on your material, and offer guidance to take it to the next level.

Every major field has consultants that help diagnose problems and create innovative solutions. The entertainment industry is no different. Script consultants, therefore, deserve the same level of respect given to consultants in all fields. But they also deserve the same level of scrutiny to determine if they are qualified and the right fit for the client.

This is the profession you are about to embark on.

Which kind of script consultant will you be?

Why We Need Script Consultants

If you were developing a business that would require an investment of tens of millions of dollars and have a possible return of hundreds of millions, would you invest a few hundred or even a few thousand to make sure your business plan was the very best it could be? If you were designing a building that would cost millions to build and could yield future contracts worth millions more, would you invest in having the blueprints evaluated to make sure that building would stand? If your answer to these questions is "yes" (and I sure hope it is), is it unreasonable to expect a writer, who has created a blueprint or business proposal (the script) for a multimillion dollar enterprise (the movie) to invest some money in making sure it's as good as possible?

I don't think so.

And I put my money where my mouth is by hiring script consultants myself.

Writers need to invest in themselves and their business — which is the script. Every successful company hires consultants to diagnose problems, create solutions, and gain a competitive edge. Screenwriters (and all who broker scripts) need to look at their business in the same fashion. Hiring a script consultant is an excellent way to give their script that extra advantage in a highly competitive marketplace.

That's what you're here to do.

And that's the attitude you need to project to your potential prospects.

As a script consultant, you're offering an incredibly important service that not only helps the writer create a better, more marketable script, but ultimately increases the potential of better movies being made — movies that have a more powerful impact on the global audience. In other words, the work you do can ultimately affect millions.

Yes, I'm a major optimist. But what I'm saying still has validity. It isn't going to happen tomorrow. It may not even happen in our lifetime. But every quality note we give that inspires a writer, producer, executive, or director — and improves the project — is a seed being planted that, over time, could reap a harvest of better, richer entertainment.

So be bold.

Know the value of your work and of yourself.

And when the opportunity presents itself, accept it — and the check — with quiet confidence, knowing that you're adding real value to your client's life, the entertainment community — and potential audiences around the world.

Your Market

The obvious prospects for your business are screenwriters (aspiring and professional) across the planet. Next would be the novelists and playwrights who want feedback on their material, or need it analyzed for its potential to be adapted to the screen. Then there's everyone else in Hollywood with a script — from talent and literary agencies (who need script "coverage"), to executives, producers, actors, directors, grips, drivers, make-up artists, caterers, and their second cousins.

But it doesn't end there.

Not by a long shot.

There are the thousands of professionals in other fields (doctors, lawyers, invest-ment bankers, entrepreneurs) who have scripts, books, or ideas they want devel-oped into polished screenplays — and have the money to pay for it. What's more — and this is a big one — most of these people aren't jaded, cynical, or paranoid.

Everyone has at least one great story in them. At any moment, your neighbor could decide their life is worthy of the big screen and seek help in turning it into the next Great American Screenplay.

Bottom line: *Everyone is a potential client.*

Fifteen Reasons to Become a Script Consultant

Just in case you're not totally convinced about the prospects of becoming a script consultant, here are a few more reasons to whet your appetite:

1. **A love of stories.** I've listed this as the number-one reason because I honestly don't see how you could do this work without a love of stories — or at least movies. This is what it's all about. If you don't get that tingling feeling in the pit of your stomach every time the lights go down in the theatre — and I'm not talking about the popcorn, sour gummy worms, and diet Mr. Pibbs creating nuclear fusion in your gut — you might want to reconsider your career path.

2. **Creative Collaboration.** For me, this was a major reason for becoming a script consultant. What I crave most is the creative interplay with like-mind-ed individuals. It's the process that really turns me on. If you're a writer, this gives you the opportunity to be part of the process whether or not your scripts are selling. Another reason this is crucial is that if you don't like, or have, the skills to collaborate, you're going to have a tough time in show business. Filmmaking is a collaborative medium. A screenplay is just a blueprint. It takes a whole crew of dedicated individuals to build that house.

I've made some lasting friendships doing this work. And I've learned a lot about life through my interactions with so many different people. If you like people and enjoy interacting with them, this will add richness to your life. If you don't like people, however, you might want to consider a job in the fine art of embalming. Those clients rarely talk back.

3. **The magic.** Let's face it, there's just something magical about "the movies." If you're already a part of the industry, you know what I'm talking about. If you're not, this is an excellent way to participate in the process, to have a creative hand in what may become the future stories that shape our industry and culture.

4. **Arrogance.** In other words, you think you can do it better. Be honest, you've said it many times, "God, I could write a better movie than that piece of *&^%$!" And you know what, you might've been right. Of course, you can't judge a script by the movie. The script might have been brilliant or at least really good. The fact is, there are so many elements that go into the process of making a movie — pleasing an actor or director, fulfilling a preexisting deal with them, getting a movie in the can for a certain release date, or just too many cooks in the kitchen. By the time the script reaches the big or little screen, instead of bearing the screenwriter's unique fingerprint, it looks more like the result of a bunch of kids fingerpainting.

5. **Telling others what to do.** Admit it, you're better at telling others what they need to change then you are at telling yourself. It's always easier to see what's wrong with someone else, isn't it? The same seems to be true with screenplays.

6. **Using your expertise.** If you have a unique perspective or field of knowledge that could be useful in screenplay development, this could be an excellent way to put your wisdom to work. Categories like medicine, military, martial arts, and magic — just to name some of the M's — have become genres in and of themselves. If you have a specialty, and a solid understanding of screenwriting, you could create a potentially profitable niche — and help create better, more innovative stories in these areas. Or if you just hate seeing movies in

your area of expertise portrayed inaccurately, this could be your chance to finally change that!

7. **Cash flow.** If you're an aspiring writer (or aspiring anything), you probably often find yourself with "more month at the end of the money." Trying to work on your projects and pay your bills at the same time is particularly challenging — and if you have a family, it's exponentially more difficult. You work a full-time job so you can pay the bills and squeeze in some time to write your script, book, play, or shoot your short film (to keep from shooting yourself). Often you're too tired to do it, or just plain uninspired after serving lattes to people all day long. And you look back after months — or years of this — to discover that you haven't really accomplished all that much and are still living on mac & cheese. Don't get depressed. Becoming a script consultant is a way to pay your bills (and much more), and be involved in work that inspires and expands you at the same time.

8. **Greed.** Not about money, but about movies. If you're like me, you want to see really good movies (TV shows, plays). I hunger for them. I'm greedy for them. This is your way to have some control over the quality of material that gets made in the future.

9. **Education.** This is a great way to hone your skills and become a master writer, reader, story analyst, filmmaker, or just moviegoer — and get paid along the way! It's important to stay a student of your life and work. All truly successful people know that life is about constant growth. If you're not growing, you're dying. Adopt what Tony Robbins (world-famous motivational speaker) calls CANI — Constant and Never Ending Improvement!

10. **Credentials.** As a writer, being a script consultant can give you more exposure in the business, especially if you break into the studio system and work on bigger projects. But having any experience on your resume can give you more credibility for the next project, that book you're trying to sell, or a seminar you want to teach.

11. **A love of writers.** I really enjoy hanging out with writers — and most other creative people in the arts and entertainment fields. I love talking about philosophy, world affairs, and brainstorming story ideas that connect it all. It feeds my soul. If you enjoy this kind of creative intercourse, then being a script consultant should be a good fit.

12. **Flexibility in your career.** If you're working a 9 to 5 job (or 7 to 7 with traffic), you're already painfully aware of the yearning for more flexibility. You already know the stress of trying to make a living and still have a life *worth* living. You already know the sense of loss of having to do all your chores on the weekend and never really getting a rest.

    I've been fortunate not to work a "regular job" for almost two decades (although I'm still haunted by the ghosts of day-jobs past). Being a script consultant has afforded me a lifestyle beyond what I had ever imagined, not just in terms of income, but in terms of freedom. I make up my schedule. If I want to go on a field trip with my kids, I can do that. If I want to take a vacation during the week, I take one. I'm my own boss. My dress code consists of whatever I happen to go to sleep in the night before. Most days my hairstyle is modeled after Einstein. Rush hour is the walk from my bedroom to my home office — which can be quite precarious, I admit. And my office is totally mobile (read: laptop at Starbucks). That's flexibility, baby!

13. **To add excitement and variety to your life.** Doing the same job day after day can become worse than tedious, it can be downright soul-crushing. One of the greatest things about being a script consultant is that you get to work on different projects about different subjects all the time. And if you end up script doctoring (writing or rewriting scripts), you get to do research and learn about things you'd never normally take the time to investigate. If it wasn't for this work, I wouldn't know about early American bandits, ancient Atlantean customs, the sacred ruins of Angkor, the secret corruption of the social service system, and how many chromosomes a sperm has — and that was just on one project!

14. **Tax advantages**. If you already own a business, you know about this one. If you don't, boy do you need to. Did you know you could save potentially thousands of dollars a year by having your own business? Things you already pay for, such as phones, cars, gas, computers, meals, trips — you name it — can all be partially or completely written off as business expenses. Check with an accountant to make sure everything you're doing is ethical and according to current tax codes — but don't delay in taking advantage of this!

15. **For the fun of it**. Being creative, helping others do the same, working on scripts and playing in all the different worlds they offer — is just plain fun! If you don't think so, you might want to consider a career in the plumbing arts (no offense to plumbers).

Do You Have What It Takes?

Contemplate the following statements, then write *True* or *False* beside each one. This is no Myers-Briggs personality test, so don't take it too seriously. Nonetheless, it should serve to give you some insight into what "type" of script consultant/script doctor you would be.

_____ 1. I have a strong, yet thoughtful point of view.

_____ 2. I am comfortable speaking my mind and directing the conversation.

_____ 3. I believe collaboration can improve the material.

_____ 4. I am able to give and take criticism without taking it personally.

_____ 5. I believe in myself and am not quick to change my stance based on other's opinions.

_____ 6. I have a good command of English and can have an intelligent conversation with just about anyone.

_____ 7. I am not afraid to defend what I believe.

_____ 8. I seek win-win agreements over win-lose or lose-lose.

_____ 9. I know my boundaries and honor them.

_____ 10. I know my value and ask for what I need (including the right price for my services).

_____ 11. I have a good analytical mind, able to dissect things and get to their core.

_____ 12. I am interested in what makes people tick, and what life is really about.

_____ 13. I believe others have a right to their opinions — even when I disagree.

_____ 14. I usually follow my gut, and I'm often right when I do.

_____ 15. I have a good understanding of storytelling in general, and screenwriting in particular.

These statements deal with certain core values, attitudes, and aptitudes a good script consultant — or script doctor — usually has. Add up all the times you answered "*True*," then compare them with the guidelines below. There are no right or wrong answers, but how you responded will give you some idea of where you fall on the scale.

12 or more Trues

You are probably flexible, yet have a strong sense of self that isn't easily trampled on. You possess the outer skills as well as the gut-instinct to make solid judgements. And while being a collaborator, you aren't afraid to have a strong point of view. You should make a good script consultant (if you have or develop the other fundamental skills), but be careful not to be too strong. While it's true that the client is paying you for your expert opinion, they ultimately have the final word and must be honored — at least if you want to keep working.

8 to 11 Trues

You probably have a pretty strong point of view and a healthy dose of head and heart intelligence. But you might find yourself struggling when push comes to shove. Maybe you're a little stubborn, or maybe you're not willful enough. Make sure you clearly communicate your needs and practices in a professional manner up front, honor your boundaries, be bold in your point of view, and remain flexible.

7 or less Trues

You probably tend to be more sensitive. That will serve you as an artist and overall human being, but if you want an enduring business as a script consultant, you might want to beef up your boldness and bone up on your communication skills. Don't worry though, your passion and commitment should compensate for any "seeming" lack of other traits.

The Challenges of Script Consulting

While there are many reasons to become a script consultant, there are also a few challenges you might face along the way.

○ **Being Your Own Boss.** I know this was also one of the "pros." But the truth is, there's more security (or at least the perception of security) in a regular job. There's a weekly paycheck, a place to go every day, a routine to allow you to go on auto-pilot, free coffee (usually), someone else keeping you in line, and a host of other possible "perks."

Being your own boss, running your own business, can be a challenge of Sisyphean proportions. It's up to you to be a self-starter, to put together a plan (which we'll talk about in Part III), and to implement it — without someone else looking over your shoulder all the time, telling you what to do. In other words, if there are problems or screw-ups, you can't pass the buck to anyone else — the entire burden of responsibility rests upon your shoulders.

Still up for the task? Read on.

○ **Dealing with People.** I know I already said you need to love people. But the fact is some people are really hard to love. Remember when I mentioned my run-in with the mob?

Well, I once had a client with a friend in that aforementioned group. He was a tough guy to please. And by tough, I mean impossible. And when he was ultimately, and expectedly, unsatisfied with my work, he demanded I redo it or he would have one of his "boys" pay me a visit to collect. (Collect what exactly, I wasn't sure. Nor was I eager to find out.)

I'm a lover, not a fighter. But I have a family and I was, and still am, quite fond of all my limbs. So I faced my fears, calmly but firmly chastised him for using cheap threats, and told him that if he wanted to resolve this in a mature and professional manner, I would be more than happy to accommodate him. If he didn't, however, I would not type another word on his behalf. Obviously, I wasn't fitted with size 10 cement shoes. And I can confidently confess that I no longer have to cringe when I start my car. He got the message and we resolved it. In fact, he became a long-term client who learned to respect my boundaries.

I had another client who would only pay me in cash, which isn't so bad on the surface, except that he would only deliver it through drive-by drop-offs in strange locations. I knew I was in trouble when I found myself wrapping the script pages in unmarked butcher paper.

Bottom line: It takes all kinds. And if you're at this long enough, you'll probably meet them all. Remember, this is show biz, folks. Just be ready to communicate your boundaries clearly, and stick to them. And you'll do just fine.

◦ **Quitting Your Day Job.** My advice — don't. At least not until you have a growing business and some cushion in the bank (at least six months is preferred). It takes time to develop a presence in the marketplace, and credibility as a trusted and capable script consultant who delivers the goods. So give yourself the time, and relieve yourself of the unnecessary stress.

On the other hand, you need to believe in yourself and your vision, have the courage of your convictions, and be willing — if the opportunity presents itself — to take a "leap of faith" even when the outer conditions don't seem to warrant it. This requires real inner strength. Something that needs to be developed. Until then, it's a good idea to apply your practical skills. Keep your day job — if you have one — and build your script consultant business on the side.

So that's the list. Short, but potent.

If you feel the need to go a little deeper, take an honest inventory of yourself and your situation, write out your fears and fantasies, and create your own list of "pros" and "cons." Then give yourself the time to let it all soak in before you jump in.

Now let's get to the good part — the work of script consulting.

Chapter Summary

() The role of a script consultant is diverse, including script, play, and book analysis, "coverage," coaching, teaching, script doctoring, and many possible specializations or "niches."

() A script is a "blueprint" or "business proposal" for a multimillion dollar business, and having it evaluated is as important and necessary as any professional business endeavor.

() Everyone is a potential prospect — doctors, lawyers, teachers, authors, screenwriters, playwrights, even your next-door neighbor — because almost everyone has a story to tell.

() Fifteen reasons to become a Script Consultant — a love of stories, creative collaboration, arrogance, telling others what to do, using your expertise, cash flow, greed (for better movies), education, credentials, a love of writers, flexibility in your career, to add excitement to your life, for the tax advantages, and for the fun of it!

() To be a great script consultant, strive to be flexible, yet have a strong point of view; be generous and collaborative, yet unafraid to defend your ideas; stand for what you believe, and ask for what you need.

() The challenges of being a Script Consultant — being your own boss, dealing with people, quitting your day job.

Chapter Two

"There is no royal path to good
writing; and such paths as do exist
do not lead through neat critical
gardens, various as they are, but
through jungles of self, the world,
and of craft."
— Jessamyn West

"The words 'Kiss Kiss Bang Bang,'
which I saw on an Italian movie
poster, are perhaps the briefest statement imaginable of the basic appeal
of movies."
— Pauline Kael

Analyzing the Material

Putting Their Money Where Your Mouth Is

Why do some stories make you sit up and pay attention, while others make you want to lie down and go to sleep? Why does one movie put you on the edge of your seat, white knuckled, while the guy behind you is more interested in checking his cell phone messages?

As a professional script consultant, you won't be able to just say "That was a great film!" or "I could've written a better movie than that!" You'll have to support your responses with rational reasons and practical solutions. If you want to analyze material, you'll need to develop a critical eye for evaluating. If you want to suggest improvements, you'll need to develop a strong story-sense. Your mission – should you choose to accept it — will be to guide your client's material through the mysterious, often treacherous, *'jungles of self and craft,'* find the buried treasure, and bring it safely back to the page.

Are you ready for an adventure?

In the Beginning There Was the Word

So what makes a great screenplay — or at least a good one? I could tell you all the "rules" and "principles" that underlie what are believed to be great scripts, but in William Goldman's infamous words — nobody knows anything. If they did, wouldn't we have more consistently good movies? The problem is, it's not a science. No matter how many mathematical, mythological, or mystical techniques we come up with to create that magic alchemy which will turn ink into gold — we still get *Gigli*. And these weren't first-timers turning out a student film. These were seasoned pros with some serious cash to blow. They probably thought they had something special. Certainly, many people had to give the "thumbs up" for this movie to get made. Nobody sets out to make a bad film. So what happened?

What happened is, "nobody knows anything."

On the other hand, if someone had brought me *Being John Malkovich* as a script, I probably would have encouraged them to reconsider their career path. I mean, come on — a movie about John Malkovich? That sort of limits the playing field, don'tcha think? And worse yet, a movie about a hole in a wall that leads inside Malkovich's head! Gimme a small break! Has this writer ever seen a Hollywood movie before? Has this writer cracked a single book by Syd Field? Who in the heck wants to see a movie about John Malkovich's big noggin? Well, obviously a few did — including yours truly. Not only did the film make a few bucks and garner critical acclaim, it established the career of Academy Award winner Charlie Kaufman, one of the most talented and innovative writers to come to Hollywood in a while.

The fact is, some of the greatest movies of all time almost never got made because people didn't "get it." And I guarantee you there are profoundly great scripts (that could become profoundly great movies) sitting on shelves right now, collecting dust, because someone just didn't "get it."

So how can you be sure, as a script consultant, that the advice you give your hungry clients — scratching around for a crumb to feed their ravenous muse — doesn't poison a potentially staggering talent and kill what could be the next great film? The honest answer is, you can't. Not entirely. Your best intentions could be taken the wrong way. Your brilliant ideas could be poorly executed. Jeff Kitchen, a script consultant who's been at this for over two decades says "I still have to start from square one with each new script. Often, I'm just feeling my way around in the dark." Ultimately, all you can do is master the craft as best you can, trust your gut, and render an "educated opinion."

That's show biz, folks.

If you already have a solid understanding of screenwriting, that's great. If, on the other hand, you don't know the difference between plot points and brownie points, please put down this book and pick up one of the numerous tomes available on the craft. And don't forget to watch lots of movies and read lots of actual scripts too!

Developing a Clear Point of View

"If you don't have anything nice to say, don't say anything at all." "Don't rock the boat." "Fit in." Do these sound familiar? Many of us were brought up to not have our own voice, but someone else's (our parents, our religion, society). When it comes to honestly evaluating a piece of material, however, you can't simply "be nice," and you just might have to "rock the boat." You must be constructive, but you can't pull any punches. If they want a hug and a cookie, they can visit grandma. They come to you to get real-world feedback. And you're doing them a disservice if you don't give it to them.

But developing your own "voice" goes beyond merely giving your "opinion" or personal "preference." Your client doesn't need to know if you "like" their script — although they'll certainly *want* to know — they need to know if it *works*. And you should be able to tell them, whether or not you would plunk down eighty bucks to see it (two tickets, $20; popcorn and soda, $10; dinner, $25; babysitter, $25). "The first thing most writers will ask is 'Did you like it?'" says Allan Katz, professional screenwriter and script consultant. "But this is the wrong question. The only opinion they should be concerned about is the buyer's. Everyone else should stick to objective feedback."

This requires a bit of that "backbone" we touched upon earlier. As you educate yourself and develop a sense of what works in stories (movies, books, etc.) and what doesn't, you need to be willing to put your mouth where *their* money is. That's what you're getting paid for. So many people in this town are "yes men and women." That's one reason bad movies get made by otherwise talented and intelligent people. The fact is, our ability to formulate an objective — and hopefully constructive — critique of a piece of material, and have the courage to express it, is a necessary set of skills if we're going to be of use to anyone.

Developing Analytical Skills

As script consultants, we can't be lazy. Reading the script quickly, allowing it to "wash" over us, then giving feedback based on such a casual glance is not only unprofessional, it's ineffective. We must take the material in, massage it, ponder it, ask questions, and seek answers. In other words, really stretch that space between our ears. As Galileo said, "I do not feel obliged to believe that the same God who has endowed us with sense, reason, and intellect has intended us to forgo their use."

If you don't think you've got the intellectual chops to pull this off, do whatever you can to beef up your brain. In this information age, with most of the world's knowledge and resources only a mouse-click away, there's just no excuse for being mediocre. As Woodrow Wilson said, "I not only use all the brains that I have, but all that I can borrow." You're actually a whole lot smarter and wiser than you think. You've probably seen hundreds of movies, read dozens of novels, articles, and scripts. You've already got an innate sense of what works and what doesn't.

Trust that.

One of the challenges in analyzing material is staying objective. There are so many factors that can impede or skew our judgment — from our unconscious dreams and desires, to the weather and world events — that we must be vigilant in our efforts to remain unbiased. Of course you can never completely avoid your "hidden agendas" — they're so close to you that you're often unaware of their impact on your opinion — but you can mitigate their limiting influence by becoming aware of them before, during, and after you read the material.

What follows are some basic questions to keep in mind as you approach a new project. Considering these will help you eliminate some of your subjective filters and allow you to gain a more objective perspective.

What is your first impression of the work?

- ○ What expectations or preconceptions do you have before you begin reading?
- ○ Do you have any prior knowledge of the writer, this work, or similar works?
- ○ Could previous scripts, movies, reviews, story meetings, articles in trade papers be influencing your expectations and assumptions about the material?
- ○ Have any comments the client made about herself or the material, or the client's appearance or demeanor had an effect on your expectation of the work?

Do you enjoy reading this type of story?

- ○ Why or why not?
- ○ What motivates you to read through to the end or reread it (besides a paycheck)?

What is your initial impression of the work's purpose / writer's intent?

- ○ Is it entertaining, informative, didactic (teaching a lesson), philosophical, violent, or some combination of these?
- ○ Does the title set an expectation? Is it the right expectation in regards to the type of material?

Is the work difficult to read?

- ○ If so, why?
- ○ Does it go against your own values and beliefs?
- ○ Does it go against your own tastes?
- ○ Does it anger, disgust, or repel you in any way?
- ○ Does it attract, intrigue, or compel you in any way?

Do your first impressions change as you go through the material? Upon subsequent readings?

- ○ If so, why?

Reading the Script

This seemingly simple act can be deceptively difficult. In addition to preparing your mind, it's also important to prepare your space for the act of reading. Many script consultants have a special "reading chair" they can sink into. Others meditate, light candles or incense, or simply close their office door to set the tone. Whatever reading ritual you develop, the key is to create a quiet, receptive atmosphere, free of distractions.

So now that you're cuddled up in that cozy chair, the question arises: *"How should I read the script to get the best evaluation?"*

Reading Rule #1 — Read the entire script in one sitting. Some script consultants are more interested in "finishing" the script than they are in actually "reading" it. They'll whip through it once, and give feedback based on that superficial glance. Others will read the script like it's the latest edition of *People* magazine — a little while they're sitting in the "smallest room in the house," a little while they're sucking back their morning java and Krispy Kreme, and a little while they're burning the calories off on the treadmill. If the writer is lucky, he'll get a few tasty morsels to chew on, but more often the feedback he feasts on will be empty calories.

The problem with this, besides being disrespectful, is that the reader can't possibly get a real sense of the story's flow this way. Some will argue that they're "professionals," and they can read the first word of a script — heck, they can just look at the title page — and know everything they need to know to give feedback. I don't buy it. A script, like a movie, is meant to be experienced in its entirety *in one sitting* — unlike a book, which can be picked up and put down more easily. Not only is it difficult to track with the emotional through-line of a script by reading it piecemeal, but a good story has many set-ups and payoffs that are easy to miss — or misunderstand — if you don't read it straight through.

"You only get a first read once," says Jeff Kitchen. "So I read it in one sitting. Then I write down my first impressions, just dump whatever I'm feeling without having to be polite or tactful — because 99% of it the client will never see. I've written notes like 'This is the foulest piece of garbage I've ever read, I wanted to slit my wrists. This person should move back to Iowa and become a pig farmer.' Then once I get that out of my system, I'll start dealing with the real diagnostic stuff — you know, there's no dilemma, the characters are weak, it's flat dramatically."

Ouch.

But at least it's honest. And by purging these knee-jerk reactions, a consultant is more readily able to render objective, constructive feedback.

The next obvious question to ask is: *"How many times should I read the script?"*

Reading Rule #2 — Read the script until you really know it. Some consultants read the script the first time as if they're the audience — to get a real feel of the movie. During this read, they'll usually jot down "first impressions," but won't get into too much detailed analysis. Most consultants will read the script a second time, and write more specific notes (which will eventually end up in a written or oral report). And a select few will even read the script a third time to make sure they really know it inside and out. I've worked with consultants who analyzed my material so thoroughly they knew it better than I did. You know you're in the hands of a real pro when they can refer specifically to even the smallest story beat — and know what page it occurs on! When you sense that kind of commitment, it's easy to relax and be open to their feedback.

Bottom line: Read it enough to know how it's built and to be able to talk intelligently about its construction. It's like "reverse engineering." You're deconstructing the script to see what its guts are and how it was put together. Then you can more easily diagnose what parts are missing, where the design flaws are, and how to build a better one. "Open it up the same way a watchmaker does a broken watch," says Jeff Kitchen. "He didn't make that watch, but he can take it apart and see how it works, see what makes it tick."

Next question, please... *"Should I make notes directly on the script?"*

Reading Rule #3 — Make all notes written on the script legible. Some consultants feel it's unprofessional to write their ramblings directly on the screenplay.

I personally like making notes on the script page — and I like having them done by other consultants analyzing *my* material. The only criterion is that they be "readable." If your client needs to hire an Egyptologist to decode your hieroglyphics, you'd probably be better off typing them.

The Basics of Script Evaluation

Okay, so you have an idea of *how* you're going to read the script, meaning the physical act of sitting there and turning the pages. And you have a sense of *how many times* to read the script to gain a thorough understanding of it. Now we're going to talk about how to *read* a script. In other words, what to look for and where to look for it in order to begin breaking it down and analyzing it.

Says Linda Seger, author of the classic *Making a Good Script Great*, "In working with the script I take the parts out, look at them separately — like a doctor looks at an x-ray — then put them back and ask, 'What's the connection between all the parts?' How are the subplots informing the 'A' story? How does the character arc interrelate to the 'A' and 'B' story? After I pull it apart, sometimes I find that there's a second turning point missing, or maybe the 'B' story is ended at the midpoint, and isn't integrated with the overall script, then I'll begin making some suggestions about how to create or strengthen the second turning point so it pushes the story into the third act. I'm always looking at the details and asking, 'How does this all work together?'"

"My process is to try and get back to the beginning," says Chris Vogler, author of another classic, *The Writer's Journey*. "That's sort of a mythological principle, to go back to Creation. A lot of the myths, when you unravel a thing, go back to the beginning. I like to get the writer or whoever I'm consulting with to explain to me how the idea was generated. What's the genesis of it? I try to get to the initial spark so that I can then understand how it's developed and where they may have lost sight of that original idea. That involves drawing out of the client some of the background and history of the thing. I try to cherish that, keep that initial impulse planted in mind."

Remember, a movie is a series of "moving pictures." It's just images and sound, put together in a way that tells a story — hopefully a compelling one. Let me repeat

— a movie is just *images* and *sound*. So a script should be filled primarily with only those two things — because that's all we can see on the screen. I know Shane Black became famous for his clever quips in the descriptive passages of his screenplays — but it's been done to death and readers don't find it funny anymore. And I know that some writers feel the need to embellish, even slip in a few character "thoughts," for fear that the reader won't "feel" their movie. Done well, this can actually be effective. But the operative phrase here is "done well."

In other words, these rules can be broken if they're broken brilliantly. If it works, it works, who cares what the rules say. But usually it doesn't work. Usually, it makes the writer look like an amateur who is trying way too hard. So keep an eye out for it — and nip it in the bud. Otherwise, the "reader" will (the person evaluating scripts at the studio, production company or agency) — and that will be the end of your client's chances there.

So let's break down the evaluating process in stages, from first read to last:

The First Read
Read it like an audience member. At this stage, it's okay to let the story just "wash over you." Don't look for problems. But if problems occur, if you get bored, bogged down, or hit a moment you don't buy — make a note of it — and continue on. The point of this read is to get an overall sense of the story, its structure, and its general impact. Once you're finished, make some more notes from memory about the script. Jot down whatever stuck with you — problems and high points. Then put the script aside.

Some consultants like to take a day or two off in between the first and second read of a script, to give their unconscious a chance to begin working. (In the meantime, you can start another script — or go grass skiing — whatever turns you on). I think taking a break is a good idea, if your schedule permits it. If not, consider changing your schedule. At the very least, try to split up the first and second read with a good nap.

The Second Read
Time to get a bit more analytical. Some consultants, especially those who read the

script three times, will still let the process be "loose" at this point. Instead of looking hard for problems, they'll allow the deeper layers to reveal themselves organically. This is a great approach, if you're willing to make that kind of commitment to the material. It's definitely the least invasive — and probably the most respectful — method. Story, after all, is a living thing. It's meant to be experienced in all of its aliveness — not broken down, dissected, and analyzed to death. It's like trying to really "know" a person by cutting them open, laying all their parts out on a table, and studying each organ individually. Obviously, the "conversation" in that relationship will be pretty one-sided. The same is true of story. You need to enter into a dialogue with the story and its inhabitants.

Let it speak to you long enough and it will reveal its secrets.

Whichever way you choose to approach the second read, the ultimate goal here is to begin recognizing and articulating the areas where the story *isn't working* (as well as where it *is working*, because you'll need those positive points to set a receptive tone with the writer). You'll also want to begin organizing your notes, starting from the larger issues, such as structure, story, and character problems, and working your way down to the smaller issues such as dialogue, description, and theme. (I call these "smaller" issues, because if your structure, story, and characters are flawed, critiquing the dialogue and description would be like commenting on the decorating in a house with a bad foundation. You're going to have to take a wrecking ball to the place anyway, so who cares about the crooked crown molding and hot-pink carpeting.)

The Most Important Issue. The first and most powerful principle to address is:

"Thou Shalt Not Bore Thy Audience."

Did you hear the heavenly organ music on that one? You should have. This is the cardinal rule of screenwriting. If the story is flowing and you're turning pages, don't get caught up in "formulas." But if you find yourself getting fidgety, irritated (and not because you're having caffeine withdrawal), or more interested in seeing if you can catch your reflection in those shiny little brads holding the script together — pay close attention to what's going on at that point in the script.

It doesn't matter how "brilliantly" the prose is written — *if it bores you it's bad writing*. (If, however, you find yourself getting jealous and envious, you may just have something worthwhile in your hands.) Of course, being "boring" is just a symptom of a much deeper problem. Don't leave it at that and tell the writer his script really helped you quit sleeping pills.

The Overall Look and Feel of the Script

I know this sounds trivial, but it's true. The title page, the font, the white space on the page, even the weight of the script — all of these factors go into creating a first impression with the reader, an impression that can color the rest of the read. It's so much easier for a reader to write "pass" on the coverage than "recommend." In fact, they have a better chance of keeping their job if they reject the script (if they put themselves on the line and the project fails, they'll get the blame).

Your task as the script consultant, therefore, is to help the writer eliminate everything that gives the reader a reason to say "no." Of course the actual story is most important, but you want to make sure the reader gets to the story, and gets to it free of any negative prejudgments because of an unprofessional presentation. (These considerations are not as important if you're working on scripts that have already sold and are in development.)

So how should the "overall look and feel" look?

In a word, professional.

Hopefully, most clients will take the time to format their script correctly. But occasionally you'll get a script where the margins are two wide or too narrow, the font is Old English, the character headings are in the left margin like a play, the script is bound by metal bolts, and the cover page is in full color with newspaper clippings inserted. In this, or lesser cases, you'll have to address the issue of proper format. If you don't know what that is, there are books on script formatting with your name on them, not to mention plenty of professional scripts. To get free downloadable screenplays, go to *www.scriptwritercentral.com* and click on the "links" page.

Signs of an Amateur

There are several red flags that let you know you're working with an amateur —
and in the beginning, that's probably what you'll be working with most:

- A confidentiality clause that you must sign before reading (Don't sign it. We'll talk more about protecting yourself later.)
- Magazine or newspaper clippings attached
- Pictures or drawings on the cover
- Fancy bindings (anything other than two #5 brass brads)
- More than 125 pages (nowadays, 110 is optimal)
- A character list or synopsis inserted into the script
- Lots of camera angles
- Lots of parenthetical phrases (those emotive words in parentheses under the character name, like "sadly," "angrily," "furtively")
- Too many scene transitions, such as CUT TO, FADE TO, DISSOLVE TO, or my favorite, SMASH CUT. What the heck is a SMASH CUT really? It's a cut, plain and simple. Maybe there's a sound effect or another visual attached to it, but it's still just a "snip-snip" on the negative. What's more, you really don't need CUT TO between any slugline (scene heading), because it's implied.

As far as novels are concerned, you can usually tell by the length and appearance.
Many novice novels are either too short or dreadfully too long. You receive this
"monster in a box," as the late Spalding Gray called his own work. When the man-
uscript pages are stacked so high you can't see the person sitting across from you
at the desk, then odds are it's a novice at work. As far as charging to read this mam-
moth tome, you should have a base reading fee, plus a per page cost after a certain
page count. (You also might want to allocate a budget for alcoholic beverages,
chocolate, Starbuck's, or whatever your fix of choice is — because unless you are a
Zen monk, you're going to need it.)

Signs of a Pro

Obviously, the overall writing will be the surest sign of a pro, but there are a few
other things that will clue you into what kind of writer you're working with:

- Plain script covers, fastened with two #5 solid brass fasteners

- Pages typed neatly, not handwritten, and without coffee stains on them
- Pages in the right order
- Correct script format
- More white space than black ink on the page
- Minimal to no camera or actor directions
- Basically, if all the things mentioned about the amateur script are *missing*, and there's still a coherent, clean script left, you can rest assured you're at least working with someone who has read a screenplay or two.

"Page One" Analysis

So you've made it past the title page. Congratulations! But the first script page is even more important, and requires greater scrutiny. The first page — even the first sentence — sets the tone of the story, and the opinion of the reader. You're being paid a lot more than a "reader" to evaluate this script (unless you're doing script "coverage"), so you're (hopefully) going to finish it and give the writer the benefit of the doubt. A reader won't. And a reader is influenced before they even read "FADE IN."

Ideally, the first page will "hook" the reader, establish the "feel" of the piece, the visual style, and generate anticipation for the story to come. The best scripts open with a key image that embodies most of these elements. In some cases, this opening imagery creates a motif that is woven through the rest of the story, expanding and illuminating the deeper thematic meaning of it.

A perfect example of this is discussed in Linda Seger's classic book, *Making a Good Script Great*. In it, she describes how the "rolling wheat fields" in the beginning of *Witness* established the idea of the peaceful Amish world and their philosophy of living in harmony with the earth, in contrast to the violence of city life as personified by John Book, a police officer. This motif was further developed, as Book's gun is hidden in the flour jar, then ironically paid off at the end when the grain in the silo kills the bad guys.

Your challenge is to help your client identify the themes, motifs, and overall tone of her script, and craft an opening image or sequence that represents this and launches the story in a way that compels the reader to turn the page.

"Ten Page" and "Last Page" Analysis

The first ten pages and the last page (or last few) are critical parts of a screenplay — in terms of getting the reader to invest in it and paying the story off in a satisfying way. A great beginning can give the script enough momentum to push through a less-than-stellar first half. But if the first ten pages don't hook the reader, she'll probably toss the script in the "round file" and start on number two of the twenty scripts she brought home for the "weekend read." Likewise, a great ending can make up for a less-than-brilliant second half. But if an otherwise strong script falls flat in its finale, the reader is unlikely to recommend it to his boss.

So let's take a closer look at what makes up these crucial elements:

The Beginning. In the first ten pages, pay special attention to how the story is set up. Are you pulled into it immediately, introduced to the main character, the main problem, the basic question or theme, and a compelling antagonist? Like good foreplay, are you revved up for some serious action after reading those ten pages, or are you ready to call it a night?

If you're into a more formulaic structure (where the inciting incident comes around page 10-15, the first turning point around page 25-30), try not to be too dogmatic. Don't just get to page ten or fifteen and go "No inciting incident! This script doesn't work!" If the story has real problems, then clearly articulating the inciting incident — or lack of one — is a good first step to solving them. But if things are flowing, who cares what the structure is. Movie goers don't view movies with a stopwatch in their hands and go, "Uh-oh, it's past the ten minute mark and no inciting incident. I'm outta here!"

Think more in terms of *what must happen before the inciting incident can occur*. In other words, we need to know certain information about character, plot, and theme in order for the inciting incident to be meaningful enough to launch the story. The real inciting incident of *Back to the Future* didn't occur until the end of the first act, because there was a lot that needed to be set up for the rest of the script to work.

The Ending. There are essentially four kinds of endings:

- Happy Ending: The protagonist achieves the "outer" and "inner" goal. In other words, the hero gets the gold *and* becomes a better person.
- Bittersweet: The protagonist achieves the "inner" goal, but fails to get the "outer" goal. In *Rain Man*, Charlie doesn't get "ownership" of his brother, but he does grow from a self-centered narcissist to a more selfless brother.
- Cautionary Tale: The protagonist gets the "outer" goal, but fails to achieve the "inner" transformation. In *Citizen Kane*, Charles Foster gets the power and wealth (outer), but dies empty and unfulfilled ("Rosebud" represented the innocence and joy of his childhood).
- Tragic: The protagonist achieves neither the "inner" nor the "outer" goal. *Leaving Las Vegas* was, in my opinion, a tragedy (although, you could argue that the protagonist's goal was to "drink himself to death" — which he did accomplish).

The "ending" should fulfill several other things in order to be considered complete:

- Answer the Main Question posed at the beginning of the story. In *Jaws*, "Will the shark be destroyed and the beach made safe again?" In *Finding Nemo*, "Will Nemo's dad find him?"
- The Protagonist's "inner problem" is resolved (positively or negatively), completing the "arc" of the character. In *Star Wars*, Luke learns to fully trust the Force, and becomes a full-fledged Jedi.
- Connect the inner and outer problems in a singular climax. In solving the "inner problem," the protagonist is usually able to fulfill the "outer problem" simultaneously. In *Star Wars*, when Luke finally trusts the Force, he is able to destroy the Death Star.
- The overall "meaning" or "message" of the piece is illuminated, usually through an emotional catharsis. The audience can't always articulate it, but they know when they "feel" it. "Love conquers all," "Forgiveness heals," "Good overcomes evil."

◊ Ideally, the "motif" is used to create a final image which gives a richer meaning to the overall theme. In *Star Wars*, the danger of creating a hi-tech, low-touch society devoid of real humanity was a theme that represented the "Dark Side." Hence, Darth Vader, being half-man, half machine, was a motif that embodied this. And in the end, when Luke pushes aside the viewfinder — rejecting technology in favor of "intuition" or the Force — and succeeds in destroying the Death Star, the motif/theme is driven home in a powerful way.

A truly great ending is tough to pull off. Even if all of the above criteria have been met, a straight-ahead resolution (unless it's a great drama and makes us cry) just doesn't seem to be enough anymore (at least in Hollywood). Check out the last five box office successes — or better yet, the last five major script sales — and you'll probably find that a large percentage of them had endings with a Big Twist, Reveal, or Reversal.

Buyers are constantly looking for that *Sixth Sense* ending. Your client's script may not seem to lend itself to this kind of "cleverness," but look closely — and step back far enough — to see if there isn't another, deeper, or larger, perspective that can give the story a greater meaning or context.

Here are some questions to ask when contemplating a "bigger" ending:

◊ What if nothing is as it really seems? (*Sixth Sense*, *Identity*)
◊ What if the characters reveal themselves to be completely opposite of who or what we thought they were? (*What Lies Beneath*, *The Usual Suspects*)
◊ What if the whole story was a set-up for a larger situation? (*Matchstick Men*, *Anger Management*)
◊ What if what the characters are going for turns out to be completely different than what they thought it was? (*The Da Vinci Code*, *Pirates of the Caribbean*)

Asking yourself (or your client) these questions might stimulate the creative juices, resulting in an ending that is bigger and better than what's currently on the page — and increasing the chances of a sale.

Character vs. Plot Driven

Some believe character is everything; that plot is character and character is plot. Others believe plot is king; that character grows out of plot, and a compelling plot can make up for a weak character (this is pretty much the summer movie axiom in Hollywood). I think there's only one thing that matters: *Does the story fly?*

There are many theories on plot and structure, from Syd Field (who articulated a particular construction inherent in many films which, unfortunately, has led to more formula than art form) to Robert McKee (who speaks more to the underlying principles of good storytelling). I encourage you to read these, and as many other theories as you can stomach.

Then take what works and discard the rest.

Character

There are a few key things you want to look for when evaluating this aspect of story:

- Protagonist's Goal
- Universal Appeal
- Stakes
- Obstacles
- Antagonist

Protagonist's Goal. Your main character fuels the forward momentum and emotional involvement of the story. And what motivates her is the "goal." In most mainstream movies, the hero has a concrete external objective; to "get the boy," "stop the bad guy," "find the treasure," "climb the mountain," etc. (Some dramas have goals that are harder to define — they're more qualitative than quantitative — but we should still be clear what they're going for.)

Some say the goal should be introduced by page 10 (the inciting incident), and completely defined by page 30 (the first act turning point). I say just tell us as quickly as possible so we know what we're rooting for, but not so quickly that we don't care.

Universal Appeal. The protagonist's goal must be something that a majority of us can relate to. If it's not obviously universal, it can be made more so by attaching a recognizable human need and emotion to it. For example, most people can't relate to a character's obsessive drive to raise alpacas, but they can relate to having a dream, wanting to make money, or a love of animals — so these qualities must be the emphasis of the character's motivation.

Remember, most of your clients want their films to be seen by more than their mom, dad, and high school English teacher. So if they give you a script about how their great grandma Marge loved to milk cows, you might want to help them find a more universal angle. You'll also want to address the next key issue....

Stakes. Creating a character who wants a concrete goal — and even a universally appealing one — is still not enough. The main character must want it more than anything; it must be as close to life and death as the writer can make it. So Grandma Marge doesn't just love to milk cows, she's in *love* with a cow — because it's the reincarnation of her long-lost lover! And if the cow doesn't produce for the farm, it'll be sold off, or turned into a Big Mac — and she'll never see her beloved again!

Obstacles. Unlike life, you want as many obstacles thrown in the character's path as possible — and the more difficult the better. Nobody wants to go see a movie about the Village of the Happy People. If the script is bogging down, lagging, or getting boring, ask yourself if the main character is facing sufficient challenges in attaining his goal. How many boulders are blocking the hero's path? Help your client create more — and bigger — ones. And the closer they are to crushing the hero to death, the better!

Antagonist. The worse the bad guy acts, the better the good guy looks. A powerful antagonist forces the protagonist to dig down deep and pull out her greater potential. If the script has a weak villain, it won't demand much from the hero. So make sure the antagonist is beating the heck out of the hero at every possible turn!

This is easiest to do when the antagonist is an external force — a shark, a mobster, a criminal, a monster. But in many stories, the antagonist is a part of the hero's psyche. In that case, help your client personify that "dark" characteristic — then magnify it. If the hero is struggling against his own greed, think of this trait like a monster trying to devour him. If it's a love story and the hero's greatest foe is her inability to commit, think of that part of her as a "wild stallion" that won't be broken. Get the picture?

Always be fighting the war on clichés. The day of pure evil, mustache-twirling bad guys is largely over. We don't live in a world of black and white anymore. The lines of good and evil are blurry at best and invisible at worst. Help your client find the ambiguities and paradoxes in the bad guy — or gal. Help them craft a villain with a compelling motivation that grows organically out of a real need — a motivation that might even, under certain circumstances, not seem so insane.

Other "Character" Questions to Ask About Your Client's Script

- Are the characters believable (round and complex, like real people) or are they flat stereotypes? Can you feel their history bleeding through the plot, or do they feel like their lives began when the script did? Do they all sound different; have different quirks, character flaws, idiosyncrasies?
- Is there one protagonist (main character) or many? Is it clear who the story is about? Does the story have traditional heroes or heroines (protagonists) and villains (antagonists)? Are the characters simple archetypes or more complex combinations?
- How does the writer reveal character — through dialogue, description, action, a combination of all three, or through the dialogue of other characters? Is it heavy-handed exposition, or subtle and story-driven?
- Is the main character sympathetic? Even if we don't like him, do we relate to him, do we care enough to follow his journey?
- How has the writer drawn the secondary and minor characters? Are they simply "functions" in the story (in other words, they just exist to fulfill a certain need), or do they feel like real people with complexities of their own? Do they offer comparisons and contrasts to the main character, thereby expanding our understanding of the main character and the overall theme of the material?
- Does the main character grow or have a "character arc" through the story? If so, is it believable and meaningful? If not, why? Does the story lack because of it?

Plot

If you've read this far, I'm assuming you already have a basic understanding of screenwriting. This is, therefore, meant to be a "refresher" on things you already know, and to whet your appetite for further study in areas you're less familiar with. There are several ways to look at the plot and structure of your client's material. But here are a few key components to consider when evaluating this aspect of the story:

- Proper Diagnosis
- Dilemma
- Plot Points
- Value Changes
- Plain Old Story Sense

Proper Diagnosis. A potential mistake in diagnosing a plot problem is to deal with it only at the point in which it impedes the story — especially in the second half of the script — when in fact it usually began much earlier, most likely in the set-up. If a script is sagging in the middle or falls flat in the end, it probably has to do with the "stakes" not being high enough, or the "goal" not being compelling enough — all of which is established in the beginning. It's like the analogy of a house with a furnace in the basement. If the attic gets cold, the problem is often not in the attic, but in the basement. If you only treat the symptom, you might end up with a better attic, but it'll still be cold.

Dilemma. Jeff Kitchen considers "dilemma" the core to a compelling story, and uses it as a key diagnostic tool in his analyses. Dilemma is defined as "(a) a situation that requires one to choose between two equally balanced alternatives; (b) a predicament that seemingly defies a satisfactory solution; (c) an argument in which a choice of two or more alternatives, each being conclusive and fatal, is presented."

It's "Sophie's Choice." It's like that moral question they give in philosophy class, where they ask what you'd do as the captain of a lifeboat that was going to sink if you didn't throw some people overboard. The choices are: (a) sacrifice a few innocent people for the good of the rest, or (b) let everybody, including you, die. That's a problem that would compel the main character into action, right? You could imagine him trying everything in his power, every trick up his sleeve, every clever gambit he could think of, to get around it. Well, there's your plot, compelled by a life-or-death goal with life-or-death stakes, and enough dramatic juice to carry you to the climax. (Hitchcock's *Lifeboat* is one version of this dilemma.) As Jeff Kitchen says, "One good dilemma can fuel an entire story." Of course, it doesn't have to be literally life-and-death, but it should "feel" like it is.

Plot Points. Because so many Hollywood movies can be broken down using the "plot point" theory (as described in Syd Field's perennial classic, *Screenplay*), I think understanding it can be very useful. Does the story hook and turn into another direction — the main body of the story — at the end of act one? Does the protagonist make a decision or encounter a circumstance that creates a "no turning back" around the midpoint of the story? Does the protagonist encounter a situation that creates an "all is lost" moment around the end of act two? (In stories that end tragically, the act two turning point tends to be an "up" moment where the problem seems solved, only to later take a turn for the worse.)

Value Changes. Looking at a story as a series of "value changes," with a rising line of action and importance, is another valuable tool to use in analyzing a piece of material. (Robert McKee's teachings deal in-depth with this concept.) From this perspective, you recognize that a story is basically about "one grand value change" — from life to death, falsehood to truth, adolescence to manhood, etc.

In this model, the smallest measurement of story would be the "beat," in which a minor value change occurs. These beats add up to a larger change in a "scene." The scenes build to a greater value change in the "sequence." The sequences evolve to an even larger value change at the end of the "act." And each act builds upon another to bring us to the ultimate value change in the climax — which, hopefully, illuminates the meaning and intent of the story.

This diagnostic technique is useful in that it allows you, the consultant, to look at each building block within a script and determine if there is real "movement." In other words, there might be a lot going on, but nothing really happening. You might wonder why it's not working when there are all these great action sequences or witty dialogue. Or you might think that the lack of these kinds of scenes is what's bogging it down — and prescribe "more action" to get things moving. But if you haven't diagnosed the underlying "value change" (or lack of one) all you would be doing is adding gratuitous material that amounts to nothing more than rearranging deck chairs on the Titanic.

When you begin looking at the script from the point of view of creating value changes, however, it suddenly opens up a world of possibilities for reworking beats, scenes, sequences, and acts. You might even find that your client can cut a lot of the action — and the script becomes a faster, more exciting read.

Plain Old Story Sense. As you read scripts, watch movies, and study screenwriting from a variety of sources, you'll develop your own story sense. You'll begin to "just know" when a story is or is not working (at least for you), and be able to offer sound advice. (You might even come up with your own screenwriting technique like many of this book's contributing script consultants.) You may not have fancy terms to color your feedback, but you'll know what you're talking about. Remember, it doesn't have to be complicated.

Good story is simple: "Kiss Kiss Bang Bang."

Other "Plot" Questions to Ask About Your Client's Script

- ◊ How are the actions of the story presented? Is the structure traditional or does the writer "break the rules"? Is it successful? Are there major and minor events in the story? How are the major and minor events related? Do they flow as one story or feel like two stories running parallel?
- ◊ How does the passage of time function in the plot? Are the episodes in chronological order? If not, why not? Is the time clear or confusing? Is the time-span too long? Does it feel episodic? Could the story be told in a shorter time period?
- ◊ Are later incidents foreshadowed early in the story? Are the set-ups and pay-offs clear? Are the set-ups too heavy-handed (in other words, do they give away what's going to happen)? Are flashbacks used to fill in past events? If so, why? Can the points be made without them? If so, how?

○ What elements create suspense in the plot? Is the suspense maximized or is there room for more? Is it plausible?

○ Where is the climax? Is it too early or too late? Does it resolve not only the main character's goal, but also her inner need/motivation?

Theme / Premise / Message

Plot tells us "what" happens. Theme tells us "why" — hopefully in a way that has some meaning to our own lives. When done well, good writing can be both fictional and "true" because it expresses real human emotions and makes valid comments on human experience.

Some separate "theme" and "premise." In this model, a film's theme might be described as "exploring issues such as greed, morality, and self-destruction" and its premise stated as "greed, unchecked by morality, leads to self-destruction." Which one is more effective in developing a script? The first statement is an abstraction with very little practical use, whereas the second one gives you an arc that can be dramatized. You can even begin to see potential scenes, right?

In helping a client develop the theme or premise of their piece, it's important to let the work reveal what it wants to be about, rather than imposing some arbitrary idea on it. Likewise, when developing a project from scratch, I never recommend starting with the theme or premise. When you begin with a theme, you are more likely to create something that is didactic at best and preachy at worst. Or as fellow writer Bill Lae says, "You have to keep rebuilding the house to fit the furniture."

Encourage the writer (or yourself, if you're script doctoring it) to start with the story, or some aspect of story — such as a compelling character — that they're really passionate about. The writer's passion or interest is the key. Within it is the seed of meaning that can, when cultivated, grow into a full-blown theme or premise that comes directly out of them. In other words, the stories that interest us do so because they are resonating with the deeper thematic part of our nature already. We don't have to create themes and premises, we're living them — and our stories tell us what they are if we'll pay close attention and follow the clues.

Other "Theme" Questions to Ask About Your Client's Script

◊ Does the title indicate the theme? Could it be clearer?

◊ Are the themes revealed in direct dialogue by the characters? If so, is it too heavy-handed? Could it be subtler?

◊ Are the themes revealed through actions, or the results of those actions? Could the theme be magnified more by the actions or consequences?

◊ Do different characters stand for different thematic points-of-view, thereby creating a collective "message" through their conflicts, compromises, and conclusions? Could the writer make better use of the characters and their conflicts in this way?

◊ Are character names, locations, or the names of other things in the piece (such as the books, plays, or movies the characters indulge in) symbolic clues to the theme?

◊ Are there other symbols, images, motifs, or descriptive details (sometimes repeated for effect) that suggest themes?

◊ Are there characters or other information that seem to have no relation to the themes? Could they have hidden meanings the writer intended, or are they superfluous?

◊ What themes does the whole work suggest? What impressions are you left with? How does it make you feel? What does it make you think about in your own life? Sometimes these signs can help us clue in to the work's underlying meaning.

Setting

In some pieces, *where* the story takes place is almost as important as *what* takes place. The location, itself, becomes another character. Think of the house in Haunted House movies. Some stories couldn't be told independent of their settings. Could you tell *Star Wars* in the ocean? How about *Jaws* in the desert? (That's called *Tremors*.)

Sometimes a writer hasn't chosen the setting that best suits the story. Maybe they've created a generic *city*, when the material clearly calls for a more specific locale. A tale that takes place in sunny Beverly Hills is quite different than one unfolding on the mean streets of New York.

Has the writer selected the most appropriate or dramatic setting possible? Is the setting believable? In other words, is it clear the author is an "authority" on the place? The first sign of the wrong setting or a writer who's just using a generic location is *clichés*. Fight the war on cliches and encourage the writer to ask the question, "What is the *most* dramatic and evocative setting that my story could believably take place in?" Then tell her to do her homework!

Other "Setting" Questions to Ask About Your Client's Script

◊ Why has the writer chosen this setting? And why has she chosen to empha-size certain details in it? Is it just to make it a believable backdrop or does it contain other symbolic / thematic meaning?

◊ Are the social class and occupations of the characters significant? Are they appropriate for this setting? Does the social, economic, political, or religious environment affect the lives of the characters and help to shape the story and theme? If not, why not?

◊ What mood is created by the location and the details of it? Is it the right mood for the story? Is there a better place to set the story that will evoke a more powerfully appropriate mood?

Dialogue

The characters should sound like *real* people, but not like real people. If your client is writing the way people actually speak, it will be both boring and incoherent most of the time. On the other hand, some writers have memorized too many Quentin Tarantino movies and (misunderstanding what Mr. Tarantino was really doing) are now deluded by the idea that good dialogue is long-winded, talking about mostly trite, meaningless trivia.

Your job is to slap them upside the head and tell them to snap out of it!

Dialogue that is short and crisp tends to be best (unless your client is the next Paddy Chayefsky, in which case encourage them to write lots of long speeches). When in doubt, cut it out. Push the client to say the same thing with a third less words. It's amazing how often they're able to do it. Of course there will be times when a monologue is necessary. In most of these cases, however, you can at least break up the dialogue with actions or description. This is advisable, as most readers upon seeing a block of black ink will either resort to scanning the script or get a sudden case of narcolepsy.

Good dialogue illuminates the desires, drives, and demons of a character — hopefully more by what is *not* said than what is (good action does the same). It also gives us enough information to follow the story, and propels the plot forward. Good dialogue has each character talking in their own rhythms, with their own unique phraseology. If Dr. Phil (the TV therapist) were in the script, he might say, "You talk more than a jackrabbit in a spelling bee!" (Whatever the heck that means). Whereas a New Yorker might just say, "Shut your big fat mouth!" One test of clear character voices is to cover up the character names and see if you can tell the difference between them.

Other "Dialogue" Questions to Ask About Your Client's Script

◦ Does the dialogue serve multiple functions — revealing character, giving exposition, moving the plot forward? If not, could it?
◦ Are the characters saying what they mean (called "on-the-nose" and considered bad writing) or is the dialogue layered with subtext (what's being said between the lines)?
◦ Is the dialogue actable? Will it "play"? Will it attract a star?
◦ Do the characters have their own distinct "voices"?
◦ Is the dialogue crisp? Does it crackle off the page?
◦ Does the dialogue sound like "reel" people or real people? (As I've already stated, the fine art of dialogue is to create characters who sound real — but not really — because real people's conversation is usually repetitive, circular, and uninteresting.)

Description

This area has been corrupted by the likes of Shane Black and William Goldman (not so much *by* them, but by everyone trying to be *like* them). If you read their scripts, you might get the idea that writing pithy comments — the equivalent of winking at the reader — makes for good description. It doesn't. And this kind of cleverness mostly turns readers off. Likewise, if you read some of Ron Bass's scripts, like the opening to *My Best Friend's Wedding*, you might get the idea that writing blocks of novelistic prose that goes on and on is the way to paint a powerful picture for the reader. The fact is, Ron Bass is Ron Bass, and his scripts will be given the benefit of the doubt. If your clients do the same, however, their scripts will be given the benefit of the boot.

Good description creates a mental movie in the reader's mind. That's its purest purpose. It's not the place to include all of the character's thoughts, motivations, and history. It's not the place for the writer to show off their Hemingway-inspired prose. If your client wants to be a novelist, encourage them to write a book. But if they want to write — and sell — screenplays, they need to think "haiku." They need to ask themselves, "How can I describe in visceral, emotional, colorful terms what the reader will see and experience on screen — *with the least possible words?*"

So, like the dialogue exercise, encourage your clients to cut their description by a third. They will be shocked at how much clearer and cleaner their writing gets. Then if they have to throw in a few bits of cleverness — or maybe, God forbid, even a character thought here and there — it won't be so bad.

Other "Description" Questions to Ask About Your Client's Scripts

- Does the writer convey a "style"? Does their style draw attention to itself, or does it enhance the mental movie in the reader's mind?
- Is the style or tone of the piece consistent from beginning to end?
- Is the style suitable for the subject and theme of the work? Does it contribute to the meaning of the whole or hinder the reader's understanding?
- Are the descriptive passages kept to four lines or less (as a general rule)? Is there plenty of white space on the page?

Other Script Questions to Consider

Besides the basic script issues, there are several more elements to consider when evaluating a piece of material:

- Is there enough in this script — or any individual scene — to attract a good actor or even a star?
- Is there enough in this script to attract a good director?
- Are all the minor characters drawn well enough to attract strong character actors?

- Does each scene start as late as possible and end as quickly as possible?
- Are the scenes connected with creative transitions?
- Are there characters, scenes, or subplots that could be cut out — and not be missed?
- Is it clear that the main character could not have made the climactic choice at any earlier point in the movie?
- Does the climax answer all questions that need to be resolved? Is it fulfilling, surprising? Could it be set up better? Could it resolve better? If so, how?

The Analysis Report

The exact form you put your analysis in is up to you, as long as it provides all the information your client needs to fix their script.

Here are some of the basic services that can be mixed and matched to create analysis "packages" of varying prices:

- Notes directly on the script
- Typed reports, ranging from two to 20 pages or more, and sometimes put into nice binders broken down by categories
- Story meeting, to discuss notes (over the phone or in person), lasting from half an hour up to eight hours or more
- Story coaching: hands-on work with the client over a period of time, reading and re-reading the script, offering various levels of notes
- Script Coverage: consisting of a synopsis of the script, a basic evaluation, a "grade" in each major category, and a "pass," "consider," or "recommend"

Sample Analysis Report

What follows is an example of an in-depth script analysis I did, mixing critical feedback with fundamental teaching. (Not every client needs — or wants — to be taught. As you read more scripts, and interact with more clients, it becomes evident which ones these are.) Because there isn't room to include the script that this evaluation is based on, many of the details won't have meaning to you. That's okay. The point of this example is to give you the look and feel of a real report, so that you can write one in a similar — yet unique — fashion.

Pay particular attention to the hierarchy of notes, starting with the overview, then going deeper into character, and finally page-by-page notes. Also be aware of the page number the notes refer to for more insight into the specific types of notes that might occur at key points in a script's three-act structure.

For more analysis examples, check out *www.scriptwritercentral.com*.

THE SCRIPT DOCTOR
SCRIPT ANALYSIS

Script: MagicLand
Writer: I. M. Righter

OVERVIEW:

First of all, and this is no small thing, you can write. By that I mean that you have a certain passion, style and, in my opinion, an appreciation of the written word.

I also think you have several cool story ideas here, and some nice visual and dramatic moments... however...

These ideas ultimately aren't of a whole cloth. Some of them start out well, then dissolve (Alice's journey). Others are interesting, but never fully develop (Simeon/Roderick sibling rivalry). And finally, your core concept is never made clear. I don't understand what it is, what the point of it is, or why Alice is pursuing her goal.

I think you need to get very clear about what story you want to tell, and who the main characters are. You might want to consider the following, as you redesign your characters:

PROTAGONIST. A strong, usually empathetic character, with a clear visible goal, who drives the story forward. And an inner problem that gets solved through the struggle of the journey. Ideally, it's a problem that MUST be solved for the protagonist to be able to complete the mission. (Luke Skywalker could not defeat the Dark Side until he learned to "trust the Force.")

ANTAGONIST. An equally strong character who we love to hate, with a clear visible goal — in total opposition to the protagonist. The Antagonist could be doing something the Protagonist must stop (Darth Vader taking over the Universe for his dark purposes, and

Luke Skywalker trying to save the galaxy). Or the Antagonist and Protagonist could be after the same Treasure, but for different purposes. (*Indiana Jones and the Lost Ark*).

The following are ARCHETYPES that can be broken into individual characters or combined to create more complex characters. Ideally, all of these qualities will be represented in your mythic-structure story in some way.

GUARDIAN. This is your hero's conscience. (Think OBI WAN in *Star Wars*). This could be Merlin, if he is more actively involved in the story. This character would be the one helping Alice (if she is your heroine) to understand the Talisman and to build the necessary skills to fulfill the journey. This character could also voice the other side of the Thematic Argument. In *Star Wars*, Obi Wan's argument was "Trust the Force." Luke's was, "I Do It My Way." Ultimately Obi Wan's premise prevailed, and Luke changed.

TEMPTER (also Temptress). This character, if present, represents the temptation to sell out to the dark side, or the lower common denominator. Darth Vader was actually part antagonist and part Tempter. Remember his invitation to Luke to "join the dark side." It was tempting to Luke, especially when he discovered it was his dad talking. The Guardian character usually counters this temptation. And sometimes even confronts the tempter to help the hero (in *Star Wars*, Obi Wan ultimately sacrifices his life for Luke by fighting Darth).

SIDEKICK (FAITH). Think C3PO in *Star Wars*. This is the faithful dog, or best friend, who is rooting the hero on. When all seems lost, this character says, "You can do it, Master Luke!" This character can also serve as a Confidante, allowing our hero a sounding board to express their feelings. And this character usually counters the negative influence of THE SKEPTIC.

SKEPTIC. I'm sure you're sick of hearing about *Star Wars*, but it's as good as any to explain the archetypal relationships of a mythical story structure. In that flick, Han Solo was the skeptic. He never thought anything was going to work. This character is sometimes helpful though, and saves lives, if they are right in their skepticism.

LOGIC. This is the rational thinker. Princess Leah in *Star Wars*. This character always has the logical solution. Which sometimes helps. But as you know, sometimes you must ignore the head, and listen to the heart. That's where the next character comes in...

EMOTION. This character shoots from the gut. He makes decisions based on emotion. Passion, anger, fear. Sometimes he's right, and his energy helps to propel the story or convince the hero of much needed information. Other times though, his impulsive behavior gets them in trouble. Chewbaca filled this role in *Star Wars*.

To better understand how these qualities interact with the hero, think of the story as one person's dream — where every character represents an aspect of the Dreamer (or Protagonist) who is trying to solve a problem.

Better yet, think of it like the problem-solving process that goes on in your own head. When you're trying to achieve a goal, you usually have all these "voices" inside giving you their opinion of how to go about it (some people have an entire Board of Directors between their ears). You want to accomplish some goal, and the skeptic in you says, "What, are you crazy, you can't write a script! Who do you think you are?!" But the Faith part of you says, "Don't listen to him, you can do it! Remember how you won that second grade story contest, you've got real talent!" Then the logic part of you says, "Just follow these rules and guidelines, write a little every day, and you'll eventually have a script." And the emotional part cries out, "I don't care what it takes, I just have to follow my heart!"

That's how characters interact with the protagonist, at every stage of the journey. The story is essentially peopled with the personifications of the protagonist's unresolved issues, and the drama forces these elements to the surface for the protagonist to confront, resolve, and grow through, in order to achieve her outer goal — and transform her inner nature.

These are the questions you must sufficiently answer to create your story...

◊ Who is the Protagonist? What do they want and why? (And it must be as close to life or death as possible in this kind of story.) What must they learn, or how must they grow to complete this journey?

◊ Who is the Antagonist? (And all of the above questions. Although you probably won't reveal this character in the same depth as your hero.)

◊ What is the Objective Story, the Plot? This can be summed up in a sentence like, "It is a story about a girl who must save her father before he is fed to a dragon." There must be a clear problem, clearly defined as early as possible.

◊ What is the Subjective Story? This is the thematic argument, or the internal struggle. And it usually fulfills the story's "premise." In *Star Wars*, it was something like, "In order to defeat Evil, we must let go of our ego and trust a Higher Power (The Force)." This is then dramatized by the Hero's point of view coming into conflict with the opposing side of the argument, and testing his thesis as he tries to accomplish his mission. In *Star Wars*, Luke kept trying to stay ego-based, and kept getting his clock cleaned. But as he began to let go, and trust the force little by little, he saw results in the world that built his faith, and ultimately convinced him to take the leap and "trust the Force."

This is by no means intended to be a complete course in screenwriting. But hopefully these points will give you some framework to begin looking anew at your story.

SPECIFIC COMMENTS:

SET-UP

Your set-up isn't clear. Or paid off. Why does this story take place? What purpose does it serve the Heroine's life? If she fails, what will be the consequence? If she succeeds, how will it dramatically alter her life? Set up the world of your hero so that we can clearly see that THEY MUST GO ON THIS JOURNEY. It must seem inevitable.

For example, a father's child is dying of some disease, and he's heard that there is a half-mad doctor in the treacherous rain forest who has discovered a cure. Now the father has two choices — let his daughter die, or go on a journey to get that cure. He doesn't have much of a choice. We know he MUST go in search of the cure.

In your story, you could set it up that Alice's mother is dying or they're about to be put on the streets unless they can come up with some large amount of money (these are just random suggestions to make the point). Then Alice finds some scrap of paper her father left behind that speaks of a great treasure. This is her last chance. She must go in search of it. And the clock is ticking (always a nice device to create tension, where you have a limited amount of time before the hero must accomplish his task — or face certain doom).

Like I said, this is just a random idea, and not a very good one. The point is, you must clearly set up a world where our hero is in need of something and out of options. Then the door opens and they see one last chance at redemption — but it will pose great risk. At this point, we need to know what the hero wants and why. And we have to have sufficient empathy with the hero to be rooting for them to get it. (You can create empathy by having the hero, or their loved ones, in jeopardy, or by making the hero a victim of something. You can also create identification by having the hero really good at what she does, such as a great detective or fighter, etc.)

INCITING INCIDENT

This is what gets the story going. In Hollywood terms, it usually happens by page 10 or 15. I hate to give page numbers, but at this stage I think it will be helpful. The idea is that you want to have your reader hooked within the first ten pages or so, otherwise they might put the script down. The key is that your set-up needs to create a sufficient emotional/physical need so that the inciting incident offers the promise of fulfilling it — and emotionally involves us.

Right now, the inciting moment is not adequately set up. I don't feel a real stake in Alice's discovery of the Talisman (beyond simple fascination) and thus I am not involved in her journey. We haven't been given any time with Alice and her father to build a sense of how important they are to each other, or how tight this family is.

For example, what if we saw how much he adores her, and how beautiful and powerful she feels in his presence? Then when he vanishes, her life crumbles. We understand why she MUST find him; we project our own desire for a loving father-figure. Then when she finds the Talisman and the possibility of finding him, we are emotionally involved in her goal.

FIRST ACT TURNING POINT

This is where the script needs to really kick into gear (usually around page 25-30). Something should happen that spins the tale into another, larger direction — the body of the story. Our hero's goal becomes clear. Our emotional involvement increases. And we again question whether or not our hero will accomplish her goal. (Again, these are not hard and fast rules. They are tools to help understand why a story isn't working, and how to get it back on track. The truth is, if your story is cranking along, nobody cares where your "plot points" are.)

In your story, the first act turning point is somewhat convoluted. You have something new occurring when Alice arrives at the castle and meets the Princess and King, but it doesn't really up the stakes or involve us more. Part of the problem is that the story isn't clear, and our hero's goal isn't clear. This is really at the heart of the problem.

If the story was structured so that Alice doesn't go through the portal until this point, it would be on the right track. However, I think the story demands that we get through that portal much quicker, like on the inciting incident.

In that case, the First Act Turning Point could be something like this: Let's suppose that Alice's father disappeared years ago, and is believed dead. She and her mother are on the verge of being put on the streets, where her mother, who is ill, will surely die. A series of things leads Alice to discover what her dad was working on before he died – a great treasure. She sets out to find it, goes through the portal (the inciting incident), and meets Merlin, who gives her some advice and begins to argue with her about how she needs to grow, etc. She meets a couple other folks along the way who fill the roles of the archetypes (ala *The Wizard of Oz*, *Star Wars*). Then she discovers that her father isn't dead, he's a prisoner of some evil ruler in a dark kingdom deep in the heart of this mystical land. And not only is he scheduled to be executed in three days, but only he knows the location of the great treasure. This turns the story in a new direction (First Act Turning Point). Now she isn't just here to get the treasure, but to save her daddy! And, as a team, they can get the treasure – which fulfills her lifelong dream of going on an adventure with her father. Thus begins the real descent, into a dark land of monsters and magic, trials and treasures beyond her wildest dreams.

This is a total spitball version, which needs to be massaged and fleshed out a lot, but hopefully it will get your juices flowing in the right direction.

MIDPOINT

Ideally, at this point, the hero is having a lot of problems and feeling a lot of pressure to turn back. But at the same time, there is greater promise than ever to achieve the goal. The hero must make a decision, a total commitment. She must burn the boats, blow up the bridge, allow the portal to seal shut, etc. – so there is NO TURNING BACK. Sometimes this is a conscious choice. Other times, it just happens. This is where the hero enters the "belly of the beast." And once this commitment is made, things really start heating up, the stakes get higher, and the obstacles become harder and harder. This is where Luke and Team journey to the Death Star, where he will ultimately confront his father/Vader. And where Pinocchio confronts the whale to save his father.

In your current script, there's no clear midpoint. Again, this is because there's no clear protagonist. (I know this is sounding like a broken record.)

In your new version, it could be where Alice finds the Dark Castle and decides to enter into the labyrinth of terror to find her daddy and rescue him. You might want to look at *Star Wars* or *Spy Kids* (two films reflected in your script) to get a structural idea of how to plot this.

ACT TWO TURNING POINT

This is the all-is-lost moment. The lowest point for your hero. All options seem exhausted, or the hero seems dead. Biblically, it's where Christ is crucified. In *Star Wars*, it's where Luke drowns in the trash compactor — but then ends up surviving. (Interestingly, in films that end tragically, this is usually an "up" moment.)

In your current draft, this is where Simeon and Bryan (and the rest of the good guys) are captured and sentenced to duel to the death in the tournament. But we don't feel a great stake in this because we haven't clearly established Alice as the protagonist, or her relationship with her father.

In the new version, it could be that Alice finds her dad in the dark castle, breaks him out, and just before they make it — they're caught. She escapes, but he is dragged away. She finds out that the execution date has been moved up   to tomorrow at sunrise! And the castle security has been beefed up so much that the Navy Seals couldn't penetrate it. (Not too different than your current story, but more meaningful because of the new structure.)

THIRD ACT

Right now, your third act feels like it should end at the tournament, but it just keeps on going. It's anticlimactic. This is because you have more than one story going on (Simeon/Roderick and the Alice/Malick plotlines), and they are not of the same cloth — therefore you need different endings.

Structuring your story along the lines I've been discussing (not necessarily doing it my way, but applying these structural guidelines to your own vision) could solve this problem. Once Alice frees her father — and they defeat the evil ruler — the story is basically over. It's a foregone conclusion that they'll get the treasure. You can just cut from the final climax to them opening the treasure chest (or whatever). It won't feel anticlimactic.

One other thing to consider when writing the climax: you want to try and create a final twist where it looks like all is lost for our heroine, and then she pulls something out of her hat at the last moment — and saves the day. (But make sure whatever it is, you have set it up earlier so that it doesn't feel like a cheat.)

Can you see how the story starts to feel clearer this way? It's not radically fresh, but that can be helped through the execution of it. *Shrek* was fresh not because the story was so different, but because they put a lot of twists on familiar plotlines, had plenty of funny moments, and created interesting characters. This is all within the scope of your story.

I don't usually go into this much "teaching" or outlining, but I felt it would help get you on the right track. There is still much work to be done in outlining this story.

(Note: If you find the need to create a new outline for the story, with every beat reworked in a structurally sound, dramatically fulfilling way, I offer that as a service.)

Page-by-Page Notes:

Pg. 1 — Write in Courier Font only. What year is this? Break up your descriptive passages to no more than four lines. And be careful to not give us information that we can't see on screen. Show, don't tell.

Pg. 2 — I would eliminate things like "INSERT" and "BACK TO SCENE" and "POV" unless it is absolutely essential to the story beat. Try to make it as reader-friendly as possible. At this point in the script, I'm not sure where we are in the world.

Pg. 3 — The cut to six years later was odd for me. I had a hard time understanding what had happened. There wasn't enough information for me. I didn't get that he was in danger, just that he left his family — and I hated him for that. And it also seemed like after all this time, they would be starving to death or darn close.

Pg. 8 — This chase feels cliché. We've seen it before. Try and strive for as much originality as possible. If you've seen it, don't use it.

Pg. 11 — I didn't understand how they afforded a house.

Pg. 12 — I'm wondering at this point where dad is. What does Alice want? We need to be further into the heart of the story. We need to know who our hero is, what they want, and why. And we need to CARE.

Pg. 14 — This doesn't sound like Alice talking. Too mature. This stuff with Malick feels a little too easy.

Pg. 15 — Why didn't she find the stone years ago? Why now? What's the significance of the six years of time passed? Is there really a monster lurking in the deep? At this point, I don't know enough info. I don't care about Alice's journey, even though I feel like I should with her dad gone. It hasn't been emotionally set up between them. It's too coincidental that he would go through this portal, and then she could find it this easily. You need to build up a series of clues that lead her to this great discovery.

Pg. 16 — Set up Malick's ability to hypnotize earlier.

Pg. 17 — You need to set up the creature steering the boat. The whole fog-covered dock with the boat that crosses the foggy river — feels a bit cliché. We've seen it many times before. It would be great if you could find something fresh to show us, some unique way to either twist this scene, or get your characters through in a different way.

Feels too easy that Malick is led right to the open book. Having him hit her over the head with the pistol struck me as being too violent for a kid's movie. I'm not sure why, maybe because she's a librarian. Why not just hypnotize her?

Pg. 18 — I find it odd that anybody can enter this portal so easily. It seems too easy for Malick to enter.

Pg. 19 — The talking dragon felt like a cartoon. The tone was different than the rest of the movie. It might work if it's executed in a tonally consistent manner.

Pg. 23 — I don't believe Alice could outsmart these dragons so easily, or that she's greater than all the warriors whose bones now litter the area.

This is a general note: throughout the piece you let your characters off the hook too easily. The enemy seems kind of dopey oftentimes, like bumbling buffoons. I don't think that's the tone you're going for.

Pg. 26 — The Eel creature is cool. There are some really nice moments in your writing, great visuals, and a definite passion and style to it all.

Pg. 28 — Hard to believe a little pistol would stop a giant dragon.

Pg. 29 — These dragons are way too easy to kill.

Pg. 34 — I didn't understand why they saw Alice as dangerous. And if they did, why would they let her stay even another second?

Pg. 35 — At this point, I'm really asking myself, "What is the story?" I'm not clear what Alice wants or why. I don't feel any real desire to have her save her father because I don't have any feeling about how much their relationship meant. So it's adding up to me not caring much about these people or their story. (I know this sounds harsh, but it's important for you to know how a reader might react.)

Act II is too late to introduce Eleanor if she's going to become a major character. Your leads should be introduced in Act I.

I also feel like Alice is taking this all too matter-of-factly. Like she goes through time portals every day. Wouldn't she be in total awe and wonder at this strange new world? And wouldn't they be equally awestruck by this modern creature entering their lives?

Pg. 36 — Did they have "minutes" in the same way we refer to them now?

These guys would frisk, and disarm, Malick. They saw him reaching for something, which caused them to draw their swords.

I was a little confused about who these knights were. I thought they were the good guys.

Pg. 37 — Again, not to sound like a broken record, but at this point I have no sense of a clear protagonist (hero). And now you are setting up a second Antagonist. That is problematic, in that it will diminish the strength of both.

Pg. 40 — I don't believe Roderick would feel so defenseless against the gun. He could easily send all his men after Malick. Sure, a few of them might get shot. But they'd definitely subdue him. And Roderick doesn't seem like the kind of ruler who would mind losing a few men for his cause.

You make Eleanor and Alice talk like they're friends all of a sudden. But we haven't seen them develop this relationship. It takes some pretty significant beats to build this kind of trust and intimacy between complete, and unique, strangers.

The Simeon/Roderick story seems like a whole different movie than what you've set up. Any story about Alice finding her father has disappeared.

Pg. 41 — The way the King gives the kingdom to Simeon doesn't feel very dramatic. In *Gladiator*, the Emperor is going to give Rome to the Soldier, who is like a son to him. When the Emperor's son finds out, he kills his own father and claims the rule. It would be great if you could find something as dramatic as that to create the rivalry.

Pg. 44 — I find it hard to believe that Simeon would consider giving the crown away. Not in a million years. You need a lot more development to make this moment believable.

Pg. 47 — You have some nice bits of dialogue. You clearly have talent with words. There is a need for more subtext, but you're off to a good start.

Pg. 48 — I don't understand Simeon here. Either he thinks Alice is an enemy or not. If he does, then he wouldn't be nice to her. If he doesn't, he wouldn't have her taken away. Something about this feels off. Also, I don't understand why he would care about her anyway. You haven't developed a real relationship between her and these people.

Pg. 49 — I don't understand why Roderick is allowing Malick to have so much power. Why isn't Roderick plotting to kill him, or at least steal his gun? It's not making sense.

Pg. 50 — At this point, I'm starting to get frustrated with Alice's character. Why hasn't she said a word about her father? What is she doing here? What does she want? All of these other subplots don't mean that much to me. I want to care about Alice and her journey, but it's becoming increasingly difficult to do so.

Pg. 52 — Isn't Malick concerned about running out of bullets? His few remaining shots are no match for the hundreds of arrows and swords. Also, what is Malick's goal? To get Alice? Become king? And why? I've lost his thread.

Why is Alice held captive in a room, instead of the dungeon?

Pg. 53 — I don't believe this beat with Eleanor and the guard. I don't think they'd send her to relieve him, and he knows that. He wouldn't leave his post, under threat of being imprisoned for it.

Pg. 54 — Why is Eleanor her friend? Alice hasn't earned this. Maybe in the beginning, Alice could save her life. This might earn the king's favor, and make it more believable that they treat her this way.

Pg. 55 — Why did Eleanor come into Alice's room? Nothing of substance occurs. Eleanor could have gone straight to her father instead.

Pg. 56 — This scene with the guards feels kind of silly. As I said earlier, they all feel like buffoons. It's way too easy for Malick to infiltrate this place. Especially when they're in a crisis mode. They'd have the place beefed up, with hundreds of guards on the lookout.

Pg. 64 — I didn't understand what the big deal over the crown was. If he captures their king and their castle, doesn't that make him the new king? Isn't the crown just a formality at that point?

Pg. 65 — Paul says to Alice, "After so many years, you've come back." I don't understand what he's talking about.

Pg. 68 — I didn't understand why Alice was so happy here.

Pg. 69 — Would they really let her go? Maybe they don't need to see her. Maybe she hides out in some bushes and eavesdrops — hearing about the wedding plans.

Pg. 70 — Where is Alice going now? What is her goal, her story? I have totally lost her character's thread at this point.

I find it odd that Paul is laughing at her. It feel like you put that there just to match the previous moment.

Pg. 71 — It's strange that Paul finds this funny. It's scary and dangerous, not funny.

Pg. 72 — Paul's character seems suddenly much bigger. You can't do that three quarters through. Once you establish the roles, you have to remain true to their scope.

Paul refers to her "Quest." What quest? And why wouldn't Roderick think to interrogate her? Also, I agree with Paul's question, "Why are you risking it all to help us?" I was asking the same thing myself. And what is her personal score with Malick?

Pg. 73 — I find it strange that this is the first time she really talks about her father.

As a general note: Several scenes feel like pure exposition. In other words, they are scenes where you fill us in on information (history, inner feelings, background, etc.) but there is no real dramatic thrust to the scene, no action. The "value charge" at the beginning of the scene is the same as the end of the scene — which renders the scene a "non-event." Always try to find active ways to reveal information, ideally in the middle of some conflict.

Pg. 76 — I find it too easy for the Peddler's family to get through the gauntlet. Wouldn't they be hyper-sensitive with the current situation?

Pgs. 77 to 80 — I'm having a hard time buying much of this action. The same general note applies: you're making it too easy for the characters to accomplish their goals. And you're making the opposition seem stupid. Constantly strive for the truth of a situation, as opposed to "movie truth."

Pg. 81 — Why is Roderick still in his own castle? Wouldn't he overtake and move into Simeon's castle?

You're trying to keep the identity of the OUTSIDER a mystery, but it's obviously her father. Who else?

Pg. 82 — Why does Robert tell the men not to harm them?

Alice and Eleanor's escape feels way too easy.

Pg. 83 — Wouldn't Robert order the gates closed, and have guards posted everywhere immediately upon learning of their escape? It seems delayed.

Pg. 85 — It weakens Alice's position with Malick by the fact that she stole from him. She's not a complete victim here, and I think she should be.

Pg. 88 — It's way too late for Eleanor to ask her where she comes from. This needs to happen when they first meet.

Pg. 89 — It seems strange that the Outsider wouldn't know Paul is talking about his daughter. How many Alices could there possibly be? I'm also finding it odd that they haven't hooked up yet.

Pg. 91 — I didn't understand Roderick's speech at the top. How did Simeon give his daughter up to the devil?

Pg. 92 — I don't believe Simeon would trust Roderick at all. This is another one of those movie conventions. It makes Simeon look stupid, because the audience already knows Roderick is going to double-cross him. And the minute your audience gets ahead of you and your characters, you're in trouble.

Pg. 94 — You act like Alice isn't sure that's her father. I don't see how she would doubt it for one moment. And he would certainly recognize her.

Pg. 95 — One core problem is that this story has little to do with Alice, who you've set up as your protagonist. This story would have happened without her. You need to create a story that could not happen without your protagonist.

Pg. 97 — You need to make this event very fresh, since *A Knight's Tale* recently did all this.

Also, I don't believe Malick would let Alice move about freely — not for a second.

Pg. 98 — Why doesn't Malick just tie Eleanor up, instead of trying to hold her?

Way too easy for Alice to get Malick's gun. How could she get that close to him? He'd never allow it.

Pg. 99 — Why doesn't Alice just shoot him?

Pg. 100 — I don't understand Malick's speech on this page. I never thought they were "running back to their world."

It's anticlimactic to have Alice kill Roderick. If anybody does, it should be Simeon. That's the sibling rivalry.

Pg. 101 — Why doesn't Malick shoot Alice? He surely would.

Pg. 102 — I thought Malick only had four bullets. And by my count, he should be out. Yet, you say he's still got one left. Double-check this.

Pg. 103 — I can't believe Alice and her father haven't reconciled yet.

Pg. 104 — I didn't see how Simeon was such a "wise and just King." You need to show us more to make that credible.

Pg. 105 — Bryan says they can't allow him to go back to their world and do what he's done here. What could he do back in their world? He has no special power there.

This resolution with Alice and Bryan doesn't feel nearly fleshed-out enough to satisfy what you set up. I suggest you rethink this relationship/subplot so that it pays off emotionally.

Pg. 110 — Why don't they just kill Malick? What are they waiting for?

Pg. 111 — Malick's death felt anticlimactic. And I really didn't understand what was going on here.

Pg. 112 — I didn't understand what her journey was, or how she had completed it.

Pg. 113 — I didn't understand why Merlin "put her through this." I'm not tracking with the whole Talisman concept.

Pg. 114 — I liked the family photo at the end. Touching.

CLOSING COMMENTS:

These notes might sound harsh at times, but I wanted to include my honest "first impressions" as well as in-depth suggestions. This is an important perspective, since it simulates what a reader will experience when they look at your script. It allows you to see where they get lost, where they get frustrated, where they get confused, etc.

Try not to let it be discouraging, although that's a very normal reaction. I have had my scripts shredded beyond recognition many times. But the resulting rewrites were always better — and always made me a better writer.

As I already stated, you are ahead of the game with your strong use of the written word. You have style and passion — and that's a lot. Now, the challenge is to really hone your "story sense." To really grasp an understanding of structure. I would suggest you watch movies, and write out their beats. And read a lot of screenplays. As you do this, you will begin to see how these things are put together and become more familiar with screenplay structure.

I hope my comments have made the issues of your script clear. If you have any questions, feel free to fire away when we have our story meeting.

In the meantime, keep writing!

(This script evaluation was followed by a dynamic story meeting, filled with brainstorming and multiple suggestions for taking the script to the next level.)

There are many considerations that go into creating a great script, including its artistic merit and commercial potential. There are also many other aspects of a screenplay, such as "core concept," "synopsis," "treatment," "logline," and "pitch," that you may be called upon to analyze for your clients.

That's what we'll look at next.

Chapter Summary

◌ Script consulting is an art more than a science; while there are certain tools and techniques to evaluating a script, the process is more of a mystery to be explored than a mathematical problem to be solved.

◌ Giving good feedback requires a strong backbone and some "tough love"; which sometimes means telling clients the hard facts even when they hurt.

◌ To gain objectivity, you should ask pre-qualifying questions: What is your first impression of the work, its purpose/writer's intent? Do you enjoy this type of story? Do your first impressions change as you read the material?

◌ Script Reading Rules: (1) Read the entire script in one sitting; (2) Read the script until you really know it; (3) Make all written script notes legible.

◌ Make sure script is written primarily in images and sound, since that's all that can be filmed.

◌ Honor the cardinal rule: *Thou shalt not bore thy audience.*

◌ "Amateurs" turn in scripts improperly bound, with photos, drawings, wrong margins and fonts, excess camera angles, scene transitions (CUT TO, FADE TO) and parenthetical phrases under the character ("sadly," "angrily"). "Professionals" (or those who have at least read a script) turn in scripts with more white on the page than black, and don't do many of the above mistakes.

◌ Basic Analysis: Character (protagonist goal, universal appeal, stakes, obstacles, antagonist), Plot (dilemma, plot points, value changes, plain old story sense), Theme/Premise/Message, Setting, Dialogue, Description.

◌ Besides basic analysis, there are three key areas to focus on: the first page, the first ten pages, and the last few pages (or ending). If the beginning doesn't grab the reader, an otherwise great script may not get read. If the ending doesn't satisfy the reader, an otherwise solid script may get passed on.

◌ The Analysis Report can come in many shapes and sizes — including graphs, charts, and pictures — but usually consists of the following basics: Overview, Detailed Script Notes and, in some cases, page-by-page notes.

◌ As a consultant you can offer various "services" including: notes directly on script, typed reports from two to 20 pages, story meetings (in person or by phone) from a half hour to a full day, writer coaching, and script "coverage."

Chapter Three

*"The answer to any problem pre-exists.
We need to ask the right question to
reveal the answer."*
— *Jonas Salk*

*"All drama is conflict. Without conflict,
you have no action. Without action,
you have no character. Without character, you have no story. And without
story, you ain't got no screenplays."*
— *Syd Field*

Different Types of Analysis

The Artistic Evaluation

Art and commerce don't have to be mutually exclusive, but if you know the difference, it makes it easier to tune into specific elements of the script and magnify its artistic and/or commercial potential.

When I speak of "art," I don't necessarily mean "art house." Just because a movie is "small" doesn't make it more artistic. In fact, some "art house" films are no more artful than the latest *Die Hard* rip-off. By art, I'm referring to something that grows organically out of the artist. It's created from the inside-out, rather than looking outside to see what's popular, then trying to concoct something to feed that trend. In the inside-out model, the creator has an inner vision — although it might have been spurred by something external — then they take this raw material and craft it in a way that can communicate with the outer world.

On the other hand, some writers believe that just because the inspiration came from a meaningful place, or they cried when they wrote it, that it's artful. But none of that matters one wit if the raw material isn't put together in a coherent, compelling structure that hooks the audience (and reader), draws them in, connects with something meaningful and universal *in them*, and delivers a satisfying resolution.

In other words, a great story must have both art and craft. It must be both meaningful and have an inherently identifiable form (not to be confused with formula). And if they want it to sell to Hollywood, it would be a good idea to also consider its "commercial appeal."

The Commercial Evaluation

What does "commercial" mean anyway? How can you advise your client on whether or not their material is "commercial"? The truth is you really can't. (If you could, you'd be getting paid millions by the studios to help them create guaranteed hits.) But you can help your clients give their stories a strong, compelling structure that hooks the reader and doesn't let them go, without sacrificing the inherent story needs. And you can help them make it as universal as possible, so that even if it's a small story it can appeal to a large audience.

It's a good idea to have a working knowledge of the types of movies Hollywood typically buys and makes, and which ones tend to be successful. Yes, there are movies that break all the rules, that defy all explanation and expectation, and that Hollywood is rarely able to repeat. These are not our concern here.

If your client has a piece that they're passionate about, and it's well written but not typically commercial in nature, that's okay. Maybe they'll be one of the lucky ones. But it never hurts to at ask some questions that might heighten the possibility of making it more mainstream:

◦ **The Big Idea.** Is the core concept fresh or have we seen it a thousand times before? Where most well-written scripts fail (as far as selling goes) is not in their execution, but in their core concept. In the world of business, it's called a USP — Unique Selling Proposition. Before Domino's Pizza came along, there were plenty of pizza places. But then some guy came up with the concept of delivering pizzas hot and fresh to your door in thirty minutes or less — or it's free! That was unique — and a billion-dollar idea. Starbucks did the same thing. They took something we've seen all our lives — coffee — and made it not just a billion-dollar business, but a cultural phenomenon.

How does this relate to movie ideas? Writers are basically telling the same stories over and over again. So they must come up with ways to tell them that are original, offer a new perspective on familiar material, and give us something more than we've ever gotten out of it before. A truly great idea, with average execution, has a better chance of selling than a mediocre idea with brilliant execution. In this information age, the idea is king. Some additional questions to ask are:

- *Can this idea be summed up in a sentence or two? Can it be pitched in a logline that will pique the buyer's interest enough to read the script?*

- *Is it fresh, yet familiar? Hollywood suffers from the "approach-avoidance" disorder. It wants "new" ideas, but wants them derivative of past hits.*

- **A New World.** Just like we've seen every story under the sun, we've also seen — or think we've seen — every location as well. If a writer can bring us into a place or a world we've never been before — and teach us something about life in the process — they may have the workings of a big movie. *The Fast & the Furious* gave us a glimpse of the world of street racing; *A Beautiful Mind* gave us a glimpse of the world through the eyes of not only a mathematical genius, but one with schizophrenia; *Star Wars* gave us such an interesting world that we're still buying the movies, books, and toys over twenty years later! Some questions to ask here are:

- *Is this the most interesting, exciting world that this story could take place in?*

- *Have we seen this world before? If yes, how can you show it in a unique way that allows us to learn something? If no, are you taking full advantage of what this new world has to offer?*

◦ **Big Goal / Universality.** We've already discussed this concept. Basically, what the main character wants should not only be worthy of a great story, and be as difficult as hell to get, but it should also be something that we, the audience want (or would want in that situation). It should be deeply personal. The closer to home you can hit, the better. *Titanic* wasn't a massive success because of its great special effects. It was a blockbuster because young girls were so moved by the love story that they came back again and again to re-experience that emotion — and live out their own desire for love. Questions to ask here:

  ◦ *Is the main character's goal provocative enough to hold a mainstream audience's attention — and bring them back for seconds?*

  ◦ *Is the goal and theme universally appealing enough to draw a large audience across more than one demographic? Could it even be developed into a 4-Quadrant Film (appeals to all four major quadrants: male, female, older, younger)? Some examples are* Pirates of the Caribbean, National Treasure, *and* The Incredibles.

◦ **Great Characters.** We already know that you must have fully fleshed out, three-dimensional characters with strong desires and plenty of obstacles. But to create a hit movie (especially if it's character based), the characters need to be truly memorable. Think Forrest Gump, Lester Burnham (*American Beauty*), Rick (*Casablanca*), Darth Vader (and most of the cast in *Star Wars*). If the script doesn't have the Big Idea or the New World, it better have some truly unique and powerful characters. Questions to ask here:

  ◦ *Is the main character truly an original? Do we feel like we're meeting someone we've never quite met before, but can still relate to?*

  ◦ *Are these characters we'd like to watch over and over again? In other words, will people want to pay to see the movie again, rent the DVD, or buy the lunchbox?*

◦ **A Love Story.** While this doesn't always have to be there, it almost always is. I'm not just talking about male-female love. It might be the love of a boy and his dog (*My Dog Skip*), a boy and his alien (*E.T.*), or the love of brothers (*Rain*

Man). The key is to have this most basic of emotions and desires included in some meaningful way.

Interestingly, if your client has aspirations of writing an Academy Award winning script, they might want to consider having the lovers not stay together in the end. Check out the last ten Academy Award winning movies. How many of the endings are bittersweet? You'll be surprised to find out the answer.

More questions to ask here are:

⟨⟩ *Is the obstacle that keeps the lovers apart — or in conflict — seemingly insurmountable? A great love story must have a great obstacle to that love.*

⟨⟩ *Do we root for the characters to get together? Do they have crackling chemistry when they do?*

⟨⟩ **Happy Endings.** Most moviegoers want to leave the theatre feeling better than when they went in. And most of the time that means the characters get what they want in the end; the hero is victorious, the bad guy is vanquished, and the world is restored to order. This has definitely evolved over the years, however. We as an audience have become much more tolerant of, and even interested in, darker, edgier, more ambiguous endings. As I mentioned above, almost all Academy Award winning movies have bittersweet endings. *Titanic* ends with the lover dying. (But you'll notice how they ultimately end up together in the hereafter. Very clever, James.) *American Beauty* ends with Lester getting his brains blown out. (But again, the way it's depicted, he's still seemingly alive after to tell us his tale.)

For those of you (or your clients) who cringe at the thought of Happy Endings, try to think of it instead as an "optimistic" ending. A couple more questions to ponder:

⟨⟩ *Does the ending leave us feeling satisfied? Is the ending appropriate to the story or does it feel "tacked on"?*

○ *If it's a "down" ending, can it be made into a "hopeful" one, while still maintaining the story's integrity and meaning? I'm not suggesting you try to homogenize every script that crosses your desk, just that you ask the questions which might make your client's script more saleable.*

○ **The Pitch, the Poster, and the Preview.** If you really want to finesse a project's marketing potential, challenge your client to develop a *pitch* (one or two sentences that capture the core concept and conflict in a compelling way), a *poster* (virtual mock-up of what the movie poster might look like), and the *preview* (visualize or write the trailer for the movie). Besides helping your client clarify their story, this will force them to think about their script the way studios do. More and more it's the marketing department's judgment that determines whether or not a script is bought.

Additional questions:

○ *Are there some "commercial" elements that could be brought out more?*

○ *Could this movie be a franchise — something every studio desperately wants? If so, does the script clearly demonstrate it?*

Evaluating Books for Adaptation

With a million books written a year (in the U.S. and U.K.), and at least a hundred thousand published, you're going to want to tap into this market. My experience has shown me that there are many unknown authors who would like to see their novels turned into screenplays. And there's good reason for this. A casual glance at the sales of story material to the studios makes it clear that many of the purchases are novels. It's not uncommon for producers to package an unpublished novel with a treatment or screenplay adaptation, and use this to make the book and movie deal at the same time. A screenplay based on a novel (published or not) tends to get more credibility — and attention — than a screenplay written from scratch.

So how do you evaluate a book for a possible film adaptation? A complete guide on this would be beyond the scope of this work (there are great books on the art of adaptation by Linda Seger and Richard Krevolin), but there are a few things to look for when determining if a book is a good candidate for adaptation.

Does the story have a primarily external plot? Plays are great for dialogue. Movies are the playground of images. And great novels are about the inner landscape of the characters. When determining a book's adaptability, you need to peel away all the character thoughts and author commentary, and see what the basic plot is. Is there enough to create a two-hour, visually dynamic film, or are you left with a paper-thin storyline? If the plot is too simple, can you use the character's thoughts and implied action to bulk it up?

Is the book a great read because of the author's style? This is where I think some people get tricked. They read a great book that makes them laugh and cry. The writing is brilliant. They can't put it down. They're sure it will make a great movie. But when it's translated into a screenplay and then a film, it lacks the energy, the beauty and, in many cases, the humor that had them so enthralled in the book. So what happened? What happened is that they fell in love with the author's style.

A good example of this, in my opinion, is *Angela's Ashes*. Here was a book that was both sad and funny — because of the author's narrative style. But that didn't play in the movie. All you've got to work with in a script is "sight" and "sound." If you can't put the author's clever and witty words into the character's mouths, you're going to lose that whole layer in the translation. Again, you need to strip away all the commentary and clever narrative, and see what the basic bones of the story are — plot, dialogue, and visuals. That is the raw material from which the screenplay will be constructed.

Are there too many subplots and characters? A book has the luxury of being sprawling, with many tributaries branching out from the core storyline. This works, in part, because the reader can pick up, put down, and re-read sections the book — and still follow along with the story. You can't do that with a movie — at least not in the theatre. So the challenge here is to identify the 'A' Story, or main plot, and build the screenplay upon that. There are ways to refer to other subplots and weave their themes into the 'A' story so that it still contains the essence of the author's intent, but there's just no way to cram everything from a 600-page book into a 120 (or even 150) page screenplay.

Concept Analysis

Writers and producers often have several "ideas" they're interested in developing, and they can usually benefit from having an objective opinion to help them sort out which ones have the most potential, both commercially and artistically. When analyzing an idea, there are a few key things you want to look for:

○ **Which ideas is the client most passionate about?** If they're going to invest their time (and possibly money) into this for the next several months, they need to have enough excitement to stick with it.

○ **Which ideas seem too familiar?** Has it already been done, or something very close to it? Did a similar story get sold or put into production recently? (This information is available through various online sources, and it's a good idea to be up-to-date if you're going to advise clients on the viability of their stories.) If the client is still in love with the idea, can it be developed in a fresh way?

○ **Which ideas would be better suited to a medium other than film?** Do some of the concepts lack an inherent visual component? Are they more appropriate for a play (very limited locations), a novel (historical, sprawling epic, heavy in themes, and the psychology of the characters), a nonfiction book (the author's interest is to investigate a topic in great detail)?

○ **Which ideas really seem like movies?** There are some ideas that "pop" when you read them. Scenes and characters immediately begin springing to mind. You can just see it on the big screen. This is fertile soil, worthy of consideration.

Once you narrow the list of ideas down to a few, you can begin exploring them in more detail with additional questions:

○ **Is there a clear beginning, middle, and end in the idea?** Some ideas sound good at first glance, then wither upon closer scrutiny, exposing themselves to be one-beat-wonders. Sometimes, the client falls in love with a "place" or a "character" or a "concept" like "a world where nobody ever dies" — but there's no story there. That doesn't mean you can't discover or invent one, but it's going to take some serious brainstorming. If the client is willing to pay your hourly rate, go for it.

◌ **Is the central conflict strong enough?** This goes back to basics, such as "dilemma." It's important to know if the main problem can sustain an entire screenplay before the writer commits to it.

◌ **Is the main character compelling enough to attract a star?** You may think this is a purely commercial consideration, but it's really just common sense. The studios mainly buy scripts they think will attract stars. If the idea your client is considering doesn't have the potential for great characters, then it better have everything else on this list in abundance.

◌ **Is the idea High Concept?** I saved this one for last, since it's the most controversial, and not always the determining factor in a screenplay sale. We've already discussed some of the components that go into a high-concept idea, so I won't repeat them here. If the idea doesn't seem inherently commercial, and can't be boiled down and easily pitched, it needs to have very strong characters, conflict, and compelling themes. Then it's all about execution.

Query Letter Analysis

Some clients will enlist your help in creating a clear and concise query letter for their script. This is basically a sales pitch to an agent, producer, executive (and in some cases, an actor or director) to entice them to read the script. These "queries" need to be short (no more than a page in most cases), and to the point. The best ones start out with a "hook" such as a provocative question or compelling statement. For instance, if I were writing a query for *Jurassic Park*, I might have opened the letter like this:

Dear (insert name),

Did you know that dinosaur blood exists in prehistoric mosquitoes preserved in amber fossils?

What if someone discovered a way to extract that dino DNA and create a breed of living dinosaurs?

What if those dinosaurs got loose?

In my latest script, Jurassic Park, that's exactly what happens...

Then I would go into a "logline" or brief "synopsis" of the story. And finish up with some personal info (including credits, awards, etc.). Those are the basics. But this is a form of advertising, and thus requires a degree of marketing savvy to "sell" them on it. There are books on how to write great query letters. You might want to add one to your library.

Synopsis Analysis

"A brief statement or outline of a subject." That's the dictionary definition of a synopsis, but it doesn't describe the heart and soul of one. And that's what's going to sell it. Writing a great synopsis is an art form in and of itself. Just as writing a great logline, query letter, or giving a great pitch is. Unfortunately, writers need to be able to do all of the above to be competitive in today's business. And so do script consultants, if they truly want to help writers become successful.

A synopsis can range from a few paragraphs to a couple pages in length, is written in prose versus script style, and is in present tense. It needs to contain a beginning, middle and some sense of the ending — however, how much of the ending the writer reveals is up for debate. Some producers and agents demand to know the endings, even if it will ruin their read. I understand why they're so cynical, but I still try to avoid giving it to them. Writers shouldn't be afraid to fight for the best presentation of their material. You only get one chance to make a first impression.

Just remember, the purpose of a synopsis is to get someone to read the script. It's a sales pitch. Think "great ad copy."

Outline / Treatment Analysis

Some people use the terms "outline" and "treatment" interchangeably. In fact, they're quite different. An outline is usually what's called a "beat sheet." It is a skeletal rendering of the beats of a script. It allows the writer, producer, or executive to see the overall structure "at-a-glance." A treatment is usually a more thoroughly worked-out version. It's the skeleton with some meat on the bones. Treatments usually range from a few pages to twenty-plus (although less is almost always more). In the old studio days, some treatments were longer than the script. There are also two kinds of treatments, one for the writer's eyes only, and one that is used as a selling tool.

If a client comes to you with a treatment for evaluation before they go to script, your approach will be similar to analyzing a script in terms of focusing on story, structure, characters, themes, etc. If, however, the client is seeking feedback on a treatment that will be going to producers to try and procure a writing deal, or as the first stage in an existing development deal, you will treat the material like a completed piece of writing in and of itself. Besides dealing with all the basic issues of structure, character, and theme, you will need to determine if it reads like good prose. Is it clear, evocative, a page-turner? This is easier said than done.

Treatments are tricky animals. It's tough to convey a compelling, emotionally involving story in this form. And is it any wonder? If a script is a blueprint for a film, then a treatment is a blueprint for a blueprint. Yikes!

Logline Analysis

A logline is a one or two-sentence statement that sums up the basic story components: *Who* is it about, what do they *want*, and what's the *conflict*.

"When George wakes up as a dog, he must figure out a way to stay with the love of his life — who is deathly allergic to anyone of the canine persuasion."

Some clients might come to you for feedback on existing loglines, while others may ask for help in creating them from scratch. If you haven't had much experience at this, check out the "links" page at *www.scriptwritercentral.com* for websites that list screenplay sales and their loglines.

Pitch Analysis

There are many kinds of pitches. There is the Elevator Pitch, which should be about thirty seconds. There is the Phone Pitch, which shouldn't exceed two minutes. And there is the "in the room" pitch, which can last up to twenty minutes. Some writers like to memorize their pitch. Some put it on index cards. And some like to keep it loose, so it stays fresh and alive. The key to a great pitch, besides passion, is similar to a great logline. It's clear, compelling, and to the point. If you don't have a natural talent for this, check out Ken Rotcop's *The Perfect Pitch: How to Sell Yourself and Your Idea to Hollywood*.

Script "Coverage"

"Coverage" is what most agents, executives, and producers use to evaluate whether or not a script is worth their time. It's a few pages long, including a synopsis of the material, a brief evaluation of its positive and negative points, a grade in the major categories — plot, character, dialogue, structure — and a "pass," "consider," or "recommend." There are many scripts being submitted to the industry every week, and therefore an ongoing need for "readers" to "cover" them. If you can get in the loop, this is a way to make extra money and hone your skills as a script consultant. If you have aspirations of working in the studio system, this is also a potential inroad to becoming a development executive.

When you do simple script "coverage," you won't have a lot of room for comments (like in-depth analysis), so you'll need to distill them down to the basics of plot, character, dialogue, and structure. Make sure you write your comments in a clear and concise, linear fashion, starting either from the specific character, plot, structure notes, to the general overall feedback — or the other way around, from the general to the specific.

Also, think about "why" you're reading the script. Unlike In-depth script consulting, coverage is often used by different people (or companies) for different reasons. Keeping those "agendas" in mind as you read will maximize your time and words, and help you draw out more of what your client specifically needs.

Here are some reasons you may be called to do coverage on a script:

○ Casting. A talent agency needs coverage to evaluate a script for their actors. In this case, you want to skew your feedback toward the characters, clearly describing them so the agent can determine if the roles are right for their clients.

○ Packaging. A script is sent to a talent agency or director's company. Focus not only on the characters, but the style, tone, and visual potential of the piece. Remember, this is a "director's medium."

o Actor's Company. An actor may be evaluating the material to see if it's suitable. Supply feedback, based on her past projects and current interests, that will give her the details she needs to know if this part is right for her.

o Literary Agency. An agent might be doing coverage for a writing client. If they're doing this for feedback on a rewrite, don't hold anything back. If they're using the coverage to sell the project, focus on what works. Don't lie, but understand what you're writing. It's a "selling tool," so highlight the "selling points."

o Production Company. If you're reading for a specific company, make sure you understand their tastes and current needs. What's on their slate? What's missing?

o Books. Sometimes you might be asked to read a book for possible film adaptation (an abbreviated version of a full book consultation). The key here is its cinematic potential. That's what you're looking for. Think movie. You can't put someone's thoughts or an author's beautiful prose on screen. Just images and sound.

o Writers. The bulk of your "coverage" work at first will probably be from writers seeking a less-expensive version of script analysis. Be honest and forthright, but keep it constructive. Remember how it feels to be on the receiving end of criticism.

When you're writing "coverage" for a studio, talent agency, or production company, you'll include a synopsis of the script or book for them. This gives them a thumbnail sketch of the story so they can talk to the writer like they've actually read the material. This is where you hone the art of condensing. You must take this 120-page script or 300-page book and distill its story in one to three pages. It's a great exercise — but not always an easy one. If you find yourself getting stuck, just keep writing. You can always edit it later. In other words, "Don't get it right, just get it written."

If you're writing it for someone by whom you want to be taken seriously as a writer and not just as a script analyst, make sure to do your best writing on this. Use some style, some flair. Don't overdo it. Keep it simple. But also don't be afraid to let your talent show through.

The format for writing coverage can vary from one place to another, so you'll want to get some samples from the company you're working for. The components typically break down as follows:

- At the top: Title, Subject, Format, Length, Author, Reader, Date
- Logline: This is where you create a logline for the script
- Synopsis: In a page or two, you describe the major beats of the script so that someone reading it could talk as if they read it too
- Comments: In a page or less, you offer your evaluation of the script
- At the bottom: there will usually be boxes or some other graphic to "grade" the major areas of the script (plot, character, dialogue, structure) from "poor" to "outstanding"
- Finally, you offer your recommendation: Pass, Consider, or Recommend. Scripts are rarely recommended. Usually that means it is exceptional in all areas and the executive should read it over lunch.

If you're serious about pursuing this aspect of script consulting, get a free sample "coverage report" in The Script Clinic at *www.scriptwritercentral.com*.

The Writer's Coach

This is a relatively new development, a combination of the Success Coach and the Script Consultant. In this case, you are not simply reading the script, giving your evaluations, and sending the client on their way. You are working with them in a step-by-step fashion, rolling up your sleeves, and spending quantity (not just quality) time with them. This type of relationship can last for the entire development of a script, from concept to sale, during production, and throughout an entire career. There are no hard and fast rules about how to do this, it's something the client and coach create together.

A coach can work solely on the writing, alternating between playing the role of consultant and teacher, doling out critiques and exercises in equal measure. And a coach can be a writer's champion as well, pushing them past their blocks and boundaries, holding them accountable for their goals and dreams, not letting them cop out or hide. This can be especially productive for the procrastinating writer who has been rewriting the first 25 pages of their script for the last decade. "For a long time, I called myself a consultant and I would do critiques," says Michael

Hauge. "But in the last four to five years, I've really shifted that and truly consider myself a coach, because what I find more and more is the value in connecting a writer and their vision of their movie with what's commercial."

A coach can even play the role of a therapist (such as script consultant and psychotherapist, Dr. Rachel Ballon), digging deeper to uncover and exorcise the writer's demons, and assisting them in integrating more of themselves into their work. It all depends on the coach's talents and the client's needs. At "The Write System," they've developed a comprehensive program to address all the needs of a writer — from script to screen. Check it out at *www.scriptwritercentral.com*.

As more, and diverse, script consultants have entered the field, new and innovative ways of analyzing the material have emerged. One of the ways I stay on the cutting edge of this rapidly growing craft is to expose myself to as many of these professionals as possible. I encourage you to do the same.

So let's take a closer look at what some other script consultants have to say.

Chapter Summary

◊ Types of analysis: artistic, commercial, book, core concept, query letter, synopsis, outline/treatment, logline, pitch, and basic "coverage."

◊ Art and commerce aren't mutually exclusive, but if you know the difference, it's easier to tune into these specific elements of the script and magnify them.

◊ There are no rules for creating a commercial film, but it helps if the script has a universally appealing story, strong structure, and great characters.

◊ The key to evaluating a book's adaptation potential is to find the "external" story. You can't put what a character "thinks" on screen, only what she "does" — which, if done right, will illuminate what she thinks.

◊ When evaluating a story concept, makes sure it has a beginning, middle, and end, a clear conflict, a fresh idea, and at least one compelling character.

◊ When analyzing a "query letter," make sure it's short, to the point, not too cute, opens with a "hook," and leaves the reader wanting more.

◊ A synopsis is a "sales tool," written in present-tense prose, ranging from a few paragraphs to a couple pages, with a beginning, middle, and (sometimes) an end.

◊ An "outline" is a skeletal rendering of the beats in a script. A "treatment" puts some meat on its bones. If the client is using the treatment for his eyes only, focus on structure. If it's a sales tool, evaluate the quality of the prose as well.

◊ A logline is one or two sentences that sum up the basic story components — *who* is it about, what do they *want*, and what's the *conflict*.

◊ Types of pitches: elevator pitch (30 seconds), phone pitch (two minutes or less), and "in the room" pitch (up to 20 minutes). Whichever one your client is working on, make sure it's clear, compelling, and to the point.

‹› Script "Coverage" is a basic analysis, including a synopsis, brief evaluation, and a grade of "pass," "consider," or "recommend." This is the standard way agents, producers, and executives determine if a script is worth their time.

‹› The "writing coach" is part script consultant, part success coach. This relationship can last through the development of a script, or for a writer's entire career.

◊ Getting a "Second Opinion"

◊ Linda Seger

◊ Chris Vogler

◊ Michael Hauge

◊ Kathie Fong Yoneda

◊ Jeff Kitchen

◊ Dr. Rachel Ballon

◊ David S. Freeman

◊ Pamela Jaye Smith

◊ Dave Trottier

◊ Judith Searle

Chapter Four

*"Ask advice from everyone, but act with
your own mind."*
— Yiddish Proverb

Other Experts on Analysis

Getting a "Second Opinion"

While I've made a sincere attempt to provide you with a cornucopia of consulting ideas, I know that there are as many permutations on the analysis process as there are people — and, as I stated in the previous chapter, I think it's important to get information from as many sources as possible.

I also understand how difficult it can be to search out other professional opinions and extract the ideas that most pertain to you. So, in an effort to make your life a wee bit easier (see, I really am thinking about you), I have brought a few of these pros to you.

I hope you enjoy their insights as much as I have.

Linda Seger

When I read the script the first time, I'm looking for the events that make up the plot, writing down what's going on in the script — who does what to whom? I see my job as looking for the clues to what the writer wants from that script, and helping writers achieve their objective. At the same time, I understand that some stories are better stories than others, and if the writer's story needs to be re-thought, I help the writer do that.

I always try to define the script problem clearly, and then give some examples of ways to resolve it. I find that if the writer understands the concept of what got off track in the script, usually their creativity will help bring them back on track with some guidance and discussion and an example of what can work.

After I read the script and take notes, I go to my computer and create a report which is generally ten to twelve single-spaced pages if I've been asked to do the script overview, more pages for other services. The report always begins with the positive — what are the writer's strengths? What is working well in the script? I believe that if the writer is demoralized and shut down, that it will be difficult for them to do the creative work necessary for the rewrite. So I want them to see that there are good things going on in the script that they can build on. However, I don't want to water down the work that needs to be done.

Then I usually give an overview of the script where I'll discuss issues that affect the entire script. I believe that most scripts have a key that unlocks the script, and if the central issue is resolved, many of the elements will naturally fall into place. So if the motivation is unclear, or the research is inaccurate, or the genre or style is inconsistent, these issues need to be addressed before we can discuss the other elements.

Then my report turns to the elements of structure and story development, breaking down the "A" Story and the subplots into a three act structure, and discussing any places where the structure could be punched up, reinforced, strengthened, or clarified. I then discuss the theme and images. If there's a transformational arc, I'll break down the transformational arc and clarify any places where there are holes. If there are too many characters, or too few, I'll discuss who can be cut or what characters need to be added or how to make a character's function clearer. In some scripts, there needs to be a discussion of motivation, or conflict, or the goal of the character, or adding dimension to the character. Sometimes, if the script is very good already, I'll focus on small details such as scene transitions, or adding character details, or making sure that the style and tone are consistent throughout the entire script. I might look at the script in terms of its rhythm, as it moves from broad comedy to warm and sweeter moments. I will often give examples of films for writers to study that can give them more ideas.

When I worked as the script consultant for the film *Luther*, I wrote 45 single-spaced pages on the first draft. These notes dealt with all of the above elements mentioned, as well as scene transitions, the parallel journeys of the characters and how they intersected, the theology of Luther and how to integrate his theology without getting preachy, how to create maximum momentum from the story by creating movement, how to get across the clear journey of the story through visuals, rather than through a lot of talk. The writer, producers, and I set up goals for where Luther had to be in each point of the story, which meant cutting, particularly in Act One. I also looked for implied scenes, which means scenes that are mentioned, but not shown. If you watch the film, the first scene in the thunderstorm and the climactic scene where the princes refuse to worship "as Catholics" were originally implied scenes. I recommended that they show these scenes.

I also try to see any concepts about scriptwriting as fluid. Although I take the concepts of good screenwriting seriously, I'm not afraid to break the "rules" if necessary. Art and craft are supposed to serve and free the writer. And I'm always open to new ways of approaching stories. In *Luther*, the entire love story is played in Act Three, which breaks the "rule" that says a subplot should thread its way through two acts. But this rule interrupted the movement and focus of the story. So we solved the problem by making sure the love story had a strong three act structure.

Luther was not in the climactic scene of the film, even though the "rule" says that the protagonist is always in the climactic scene. We couldn't change history, so we intercut scenes with him, so we would feel his presence and his influence. As a result of working on thousands of scripts, I've found that I'm more able to break rules since I understand how to compensate for the problems that might arise.

When I began my business, almost all of my clients were from Los Angeles, so we usually met to discuss the script. Now that I live in Colorado, most of my work is through the mail, sometimes with a phone call, although I do get back to Los Angeles about six times a year and meet clients then. However, more and more, writers are coming to Colorado to work on their scripts, sometimes for a day, but sometimes for several days to rewrite, meet, rewrite some more. There are two beautiful bed-and-breakfasts across the street from me, which have been called "the perfect writer's retreat" by my clients.

Every script needs something different to make it work. My goal is to identify, analyze, and help the writer solve script problems while also being encouraging and nurturing of their creative process.

Dr. Linda Seger is a world-renowned script consultant of over 2000 scripts, (100 of them produced for film and TV), as well as a teacher (with clients from six continents), and author of seven books on screenwriting, including the classic *Making a Good Script Great*. For more info, check out *www.lindaseger.com*.

Chris Vogler

Even as a little kid, growing up in the suburbs of St. Louis, I was analytical about stories. Before I could read, when my mother and grandmother would read to me, I used to take apart the fairy tales in my head, trying to figure out which ones would make good movies, and where you would have to change or add things. When I did learn to read I devoured the classics, fairy tales, and science fiction, always thinking in terms of what would make a cool movie. This served me well decades later when I went to work as a story analyst for the Disney company, where I became known as an expert on fairy tale and mythological themes and story patterns. It's fun to get paid for re-reading and analyzing books and stories that you read for sheer pleasure when you were a kid.

On the way to Hollywood I had a wide variety of experiences that inform my approach to consulting and teaching. In my teenage years my parents bought a farm west of St. Louis and I became a farmboy with a horse and cattle and a trac- tor. Summers I worked at a local newspaper and for awhile at an iron foundry. In college I studied journalism, then joined the Air Force as an officer and made doc- umentary films on military space programs for Congress and the Pentagon. I was sent out to Los Angeles to be part of something called "the Hollywood Air Force" and later was stationed in San Antonio, Texas. I got involved in local theater there as an actor, and again found that I had a talent for analyzing stories, in this case the plays we were producing.

I went to graduate school on the GI Bill, going through the rigorous program of the USC film school. I quickly got a reputation as a guy who was good at working out story problems in other people's films. Two important things came together in film school. One, I took a class called "story analysis" and learned there was a job in Hollywood for people like me ("script reader" or "story analyst") and that there was even a union for these people. The second big thing was that a professor pointed me to *The Hero with a Thousand Faces* by mythologist Joseph Campbell. This blew my mind. I had been looking for the rules of storytelling, and had painfully pieced together a few bits of the puzzle, but here was the whole thing, laid out and labeled in ten or twelve stages, culled from Campbell's study of hundreds of folktales, legends and fairy tales from around the world.

While finishing grad school I went to work as a freelance story analyst for a string of Hollywood companies, including United Artists, Orion, and the Ladd Company. After a year or so I got into the union as a reader for Fox under Sherry Lansing. A couple of years later I moved over to Disney where they were just beginning the new regime of Michael Eisner and Jeffrey Katzenberg.

I dug myself fairly deep into the Disney culture, eventually working in various capacities for five or six different divisions of the company. I started out reading and writing reports on the routine eight to ten scripts a week and giving "development notes" on studio projects. In that job you quickly build up a huge inventory of story possibilities from reading so many scripts and stories. You see every variation. I stopped counting after I'd written reports on ten thousand screenplays.

But I got more and more into doing special research projects for the company and eventually decided to call myself a "story consultant" rather than a reader. I operated on one key principle — I was interested. I mean that I expressed a lot of interest and enthusiasm for "my" subjects, the things I like, such as science fiction, history, fantasy, children's literature, fairy tales, comic books. They knew I was the go-to guy for information on these subjects. I got to do a lot of interesting research projects on topics like ancient Egypt, the Incas and Aztecs, fairy tales of Ireland, China, Africa and Scandinavia, explorers, women adventurers, etc. A couple of times executives told me to go out and buy every comic book printed that month and tell them in a memo what was going on in the comics world and where the next hits were coming from.

I discovered there was a lucrative need for story "experts" in the legal departments of the studios. Many of us who are consultants have been called in as expert witnesses in copyright cases. I never actually testified but I wrote depositions and did research to help the studios defend against copyright infringements. Sometimes I was called in to show that a studio had not infringed someone else's copyright, by showing that their ideas were not original but derived from well-known and ancient motifs in myths and fairy tales.

A breakthrough at Disney was that I got to see Jeffrey Katzenberg's style of doing script notes and memos and pretty much adopted that. He was a big influence on me, even in how I wrote my original memo on story structure, which I wrote at Disney, inspired by Joseph Campbell's ideas. In my book, the style is very much influenced by Katzenberg's techniques. He was a good note writer and had a logical way of going about it. It was sort of a military style of writing. You know in the military the Sergeant says, "I'm gonna tell you what I'm gonna tell ya, then I'm gonna tell ya, then I'm gonna tell you what I told ya." His memos were almost like a military set of orders, but very diplomatic. He was self-effacing, not dictatorial, and very smart about communicating with the writer and respecting what the writer was trying to do. That came across in his work and had an impact on me.

Campbell's ideas lead me to formulate this "memo" while I was working for Disney, because I thought they were so much a company of memo writing and that there was value to being able to express yourself on paper in an organized way. Campbell had developed this "hero's journey" in a mythological and academic area, but I saw that it had its applications in movie structure, so I set about doing that and wrote this seven-page memo that was an influential thing in Hollywood. It became something that everybody had to have. That eventually grew into the book, *The Writer's Journey*, through stages of teaching at UCLA Extension Writer's Program and other teaching and lecture opportunities.

My life changed when the book came out. I started traveling all over the world to teach and lecture, and am now on the faculty of several international training programs. I worked for several years at Fox as a consultant and development executive but now am freelancing. I like it when consulting leads to other things, like producing and writing. This has happened a few times, like when I served as executive producer on an independent film, *P.S. Your Cat is Dead* with actor/director Steve Guttenberg, and when I got to a write the script and songs for an animated feature film, *Jester Till*, that was produced in Europe.

When I look at somebody's work, I'm doing it with two sort of parallel toolboxes or states of mind. One of them is the tool of this "hero's journey" idea — and I think this is what people expect from me — but I don't use it exclusively. It's just one of the tools in the toolbox. Let's say Disney has a direct-to-video animation feature they want me to look at and they have a script or a storyboard or something. I'll look at that, maybe find some things from the hero's journey, and say, "The mentor isn't fully doing his function here," or "there's no sense of sacrifice at the very climax of the movie," or "in the midpoint, the hero hasn't really faced death or earned new knowledge." And somehow relate all of it to that mythic idea. But another whole body of knowledge is not directly related to that or doesn't use that language, and that's the basics of Hollywood — or just basic storytelling.

So I just react to it as an audience member would. The knowledge of vaudeville, burlesque, stage drama, and all the other things that go into entertainment. I have this sort of specialized language, the hero's journey, and a set of techniques that I'm known for, but often I will just respond on the basis of good entertainment principles, like "Always leave 'em laughing."

Chris Vogler is a world-renowned script consultant, teacher, and author of the classic, *The Writer's Journey*. For more info on Chris, check out *www.thewritersjourney.com*.

Michael Hauge

For my entire career as a screenwriting instructor, author, writers' coach and script consultant, I have held a single guiding principle: the essential component of all successful movies is the hero's pursuit of a compelling desire. This sounds like a simple concept, but it's one of the most difficult principles for new screenwriters to understand and apply to their stories.

The screenwriter's primary goal is to elicit emotion in the reader and the audience. Whatever else she (or he) hopes to achieve with her script — money, fame, artistry, a celebration of humanity or an enlightened, empowered audience — she will do so only by keeping the movie or TV audience emotionally involved in the story.

If the hero has no compelling desire to pursue, the story will have no forward movement, the audience will have nothing to root for, and the reader will have no compelling reason to keep turning the pages of the script.

The hero's primary desire defines the story concept – and often the ad campaign. Ask people what *Independence Day* is about, and they'll probably say something like, "It's about a group of people trying to stop an alien invasion." Or read the log lines for movies and TV episodes in *TV Guide*. Almost all of them state or imply the desires the heroes will pursue.

One of primary objectives with my clients is to insure that their heroes' visible desires – what I call the Outer Motivation — meet the criteria for eliciting maximum emotion:

1. *The desire must be visible*. I use the term *outer* motivation because it is outwardly apparent to the audience as they watch the action on the screen. Whether it's stopping the villains in *Silence of the Lambs*, *The Incredibles* or the Harry Potter movies, reuniting with his high school dream girl in *There's Something About Mary*, or winning a boxing title in *Million Dollar Baby*, the heroes of those films are doing things to achieve their desires, not simply revealing themselves through dialogue.

Outer motivation does not involve the desire for invisible, inner qualities like success, love, belonging, greed, revenge or self-worth. Any one of these might provide a *reason* the hero is pursuing his visible goal, but they're not the goal itself.

In the movie *In the Line of Fire*, the Clint Eastwood character wants desperately to make up for a moment of cowardice and hesitation early in his career. But this need doesn't give the story a plot, it only justifies his real outer motivation: to stop the assassin from killing the current President.

2. *The desire must have a clearly implied endpoint.* Not only do we *see* the hero pursue the goal throughout the movie, we can easily envision what achieving the goal will look like. We know when we watch *Kill Bill Vol. 2* that we will ultimately see a showdown between the hero and the villain. We may not know all the details, or exactly where and how it will occur, but we know that the outcome will resolve the story.

Think of a story as a race. The hero is trying desperately to reach the finish line before some other character or force of nature can stop her. If the writer doesn't tell the audience where the finish line is, how will they know what to root for? How will they even know when the movie's over? (Yes, the credits will come on, but how exciting is that?)

It's fine if a hero wants acceptance, or success, or love, but how will the audience know he's achieved it unless it's linked to some visible outer motivation? In *Amadeus*, a jealous Salieri wants to get revenge (invisible) on God for making Mozart a musical genius. This instills in him a *visible* desire to destroy Mozart. It is murdering Mozart that drives the story forward, and gives it a clearly defined endpoint.

3. *The hero must desperately want the desire.* If the main character is only mildly interested in achieving his outer motivation, how can we expect the audience to care whether he wins it or not? It's the hero's burning passion that will draw readers into the screenplay, and will make the outcome of vital importance to them as well.

4. *The hero must actively pursue the desire.* Heroes can't simply sit around talking about how much they'd like to have money, fulfillment, or the love of a beautiful woman. They must take control of their lives and use every ounce of strength, courage and intelligence they have to rob the bank, stop the serial killer, or win the love of the prom queen.

A protagonist can be passive at the beginning of the script, but before too long, she has to declare, "I WANT THAT!" and go after her desire.

5. It must be within the hero's power to achieve her desire. A hero must never wait to be rescued, in any sense of the word. If she's pursued by a killer, trapped in a mine shaft, or encountering dinosaurs, she can't just helplessly wait for the Mounties to arrive.

6. The hero must put everything on the line to achieve the desire. The more passionate, determined and courageous a hero is in pursuit of his quest, the greater the audience's own emotional involvement and the greater its elation when he succeeds.

This principle is fairly evident in action movies and thrillers like *National Treasure, Pirates of the Caribbean* or *The Last Samurai*, where heroes put their lives on the line. But it's equally true for romantic comedies and love stories like *Sleepless in Seattle, Good Will Hunting* and *As Good as It Gets*. These heroes must take the greatest emotional risk of all: exposing themselves to rejection, fear and pain as they let go of identities that have brought them a lifetime of protection.

7. The hero's desire must be resolved at the climax of the film. A story may end with ambiguous elements, and even leave the hero with an uncertain future. But the reader has spent two hours rooting for the hero to achieve his visible goal. A script that leaves the reader hanging at the end will never advance the writer's career.

I will always focus a client's attention on the hero's Outer Motivation at the beginning of the process. When that solid foundation is in place, then we can develop the plot structure, character arc, dialogue, style and themes that will make the client's screenplay original, compelling and commercial.

Michael Hauge is a script consultant, writer's coach, and author of the best-selling *Writing Screenplays that Sell*. For more info, check out his website at *www.screenplaymastery.com*.

Kathie Fong Yoneda

No two consultants will do a consultation or critique in exactly the same way. Through the years, I've refined my method so it is more closely aligned to the way I worked with professional screenwriters whose projects had been purchased or optioned by the studio or production company.

First, I read the script or teleplay just to get an overall idea of what the story is all about. During my second read, I do margin notations directly into the script, circling lines of dialogue that don't quite work, pointing out awkward scene transitions, logic loopholes, structural problems, the need for character interaction, pacing issues, etc. Years ago, I used to do a notes memo which sometimes was quite lengthy. Most of the professional screenwriters balked at these 15–20 pages of notes. So I started doing concise notes directly into the margins of the scripts and nearly every writer seemed to prefer the more direct approach — seeing it "on the page."

The third and final read is to check things like formatting, typos, grammatical errors and to look at the project from a "buyer's" point of view for commercial potential of the project. Is it a studio movie or is the focus better for an "indie film"? Will it need star casting or a name director? Is this something that Hollywood might want to buy now?

When I've completed the three "reads," I send the script/teleplay back to my client and we set up a mutually agreeable time for the writer to call me for an uninterrupted 30-minute phone meeting. This is the perfect opportunity for the writer to go over any notes they may not understand or agree with. It's a give-and-take discussion, during which the writer and I usually end up doing a lot of "brainstorming" over ways to solve a sticky story problem or enhance the characters or come up with a possible solution to overcome a logic issue, etc. I may not always give the very best ideas possible, but usually what I'll do is give them an idea that's in the general ballpark and most of the time, it's enough to get the writer's creative juices flowing, and before you know it, they're coming up with some terrific solutions. Many writers use the meeting to "pitch their rewrite." This is a great way to ensure that the writer will be on the right track during the revision process, plus it helps them to refine their pitching skills.

It's not uncommon for a client to ask if they can call me back once they've come up with solutions to incorporate in their next draft. This is where the "teacher" in me comes in — writers often work better when you give them an "assignment" — i.e., "Let me look at a five-page outline before you start rewriting," or "Why don't we schedule a 15-minute phone meeting so you can pitch your ideas for the rewrite," etc.

Sometimes a screenplay needs a page one rewrite. The writer may have a great idea, but they might be telling it from the wrong person's point of view or maybe the story is not complex enough to sustain an audience's interest. I haven't had too many writers who didn't want to do anything at all to their project. Most of them usually end up wanting to make it a better piece of work. So much depends on the depth of the problem and the writer's willingness to tackle the job. For the few clients who decided to give up, it's probably because they really weren't meant to be writers. The most successful writers spend much more time on rewriting and refining their work and willingly accept rewriting as a very major and necessary part of the overall writing process.

With over 25 years in film and TV, Kathie is a former studio exec, international seminar leader, and author of *The Script-Selling Game: A Hollywood Insider's Look At Getting Your Script Sold and Produced*. For more info, check out *www.kathie-fongyoneda.com*.

Jeff Kitchen

The first thing I look at once I've laid out my first reaction to the script is the dilemma. The dictionary defines dilemma as "two equally unacceptable alternatives, two equally painful choices." Are you going to turn in your best friend or do the hard jail time yourself? Neither alternative is any good. Aristotle noticed that those plays that grip the audience tend to have a good strong dilemma for the protagonist, building to a crisis, which forces decision and action in the face of crisis, with a resolution that wraps it up, either for good or bad. I've found that dilemma is a truly remarkable tool because in my experience as a writer, consultant and teacher, it always improves the material, even if it's already great. And this one good strong dilemma can carry a film.

Let's take the popular film, *Training Day*, and put it through the paces, as if I were doing a consult on it. In my opinion it is a masterpiece, so I presumably won't be finding much weakness in it, but it does make a good example of my tools and process at work, and most people know the film, or can certainly go out and rent it.

Jake Hoyt (Ethan Hawke) is caught in a searing dilemma as he struggles to earn a highly coveted position on Alonzo Harris' (Denzel Washington) undercover narcotics squad. Jake is intensely driven to make this elite assignment, but when Alonzo leads him down an increasingly crooked path Jake begins to have serious doubts. It's unacceptable to not make the squad and yet it's equally unacceptable to engage in the corruption that Alonzo is leading him into. Jake has a strong moral compass and wants to fight crime, but he's also very ambitious. In the opening scene he talks with his wife about the size of the division commanders' homes. He's got a flaw and Alonzo plays on this like a seasoned predator. Jake looks up to Alonzo because he's a legendary super cop who makes the difference on the hardcore streets. He's fearless, masterful, awe-inspiring and incredibly persuasive. And yet the things Alonzo demands of Jake are often illegal, immoral, and potentially fatal. Jake will not let go of this great opportunity, but he cannot engage in the corruption in which Alonzo insists he partake.

After Alonzo robs the Sandman's house with the fake warrant, Jake has it out with him. Alonzo tells him to go back to cutting parking tickets in the valley. He says it takes a wolf to catch a wolf, and if you want to do undercover work then you have to be willing to get dirty and play dirty, all of which is absolutely true. He never lies to him about any of that, and Jake knows it. This is a complex dilemma because Jake's worst enemy is also his guru. It's the best thing that ever happened to him and the worst. He's damned if he doesn't make Alonzo's squad and he's literally damned if he does.

The dilemma is what the movie's about and we're on the edge of our seats watching it. It takes some time to set up the dilemma in a film, but it often kicks in about a third or a quarter of the way in. That one dilemma then builds in intensity and complexity until somewhere around the two-thirds or three-quarters point where the dilemma goes critical. This crisis forces decision and action about the dilemma, and now the protagonist begins to move toward the resolution, the completion of which wraps up the plot. In *Training Day* Jake's dilemma becomes a crisis when Alonzo robs and kills Roger, then demands at gunpoint that Jake claim he's the shooter. Here Jake has the chance to drop his idealism and become a part of this team. His decision is that he will not go down Alonzo's road and his action is to turn Alonzo's gun on him, saying he'll kill Alonzo rather than join. This decision and action does not resolve things at all — in fact he's in huge trouble — but he has broken the paralysis of his dilemma and started trying to move toward a resolution. He resolves it all when he unexpectedly defeats Alonzo in the final fight.

This provides a brief look at how I work with dilemma, crisis, decision and action, and resolution. It either exists in a script or you can experiment with putting one in to beef it up dramatically. A good strong dilemma creates dramatic action, a state of action that you put the audience in. It definitely takes some practice to get good at it, but my book, *Writing a Great Movie*, goes much deeper into this process and will give you a good grounding in it.

The next thing I look at is theme. A good way to put your finger on the theme of any script is to look at the way in which the protagonist resolves his or her dilemma. Not what the protagonist does but the way in which it's done. The way in which Jake resolves his dilemma is to know what's right and to fight for that with every ounce of strength. Thematically, this is what the movie is about: Doing the right thing. Articulating the theme enables me to put my finger on it, even if the writer has not seen it yet. This will often help the writer clarify and strengthen the script.

The 36 Dramatic Situations is another powerful tool that I use to isolate active elements in a script and to explore possible new ones. The 36 Dramatic Situations are a powerful set of elements like Madness, Disaster, Ambition, The Necessity of Sacrificing Loved Ones, and so on. The complete list is contained in my book or at *www.WordPlayer.com*.

The third tool that I use is the proposition of logic, which helps beef up the conflict and make the whole plot more coherent. Below is a simplified version that is applied to *Training Day*, an already completed masterpiece, but this tool, properly used, can really help a script that's under development. This is not an easy tool to explain, nor is this the full use of it, but for that look at my book because this brief format prohibits getting into it in any detail.

- Setting up the potential fight (earlier in the script)
  Jake, unable to stand by while Alonzo robs the Sandman, challenges Alonzo on his conduct.
- Touching off the fight to the finish (two thirds point)
  Now seeing how totally corrupt Alonzo is when Alonzo not only robs and murders Roger but demands that Jake claim he was the shooter, Jake threatens to kill Alonzo if he doesn't stop.

◌ Central Dramatic Question (the point at which the audience hangs unresolved) Will he stop Alonzo and end his criminal enterprise, or will Alonzo destroy him?

The fourth tool is a three-step process called Sequence, Proposition, Plot. The first section, Sequence works with reverse and effect. Starting at the end of a story, I work backwards through the material and tie it together by asking at each point, "What is the cause of the previous effect?" This helps to separate the necessary from the unnecessary, and also helps keep the plot moving forward without wandering off onto side paths and possibly losing the audience. The second and third sections deal with setting the action up into a map of the conflict, laying out the actions of the protagonist on the left and those of the antagonist on the right, paying attention to audience sympathy as well. This is not an easy tool to explain in such a limited space, but the main thing is that it is done to the whole script, then to each act, then to each sequence in the acts and to each scene. This makes each of them tight and dramatic. Applying this process to a script under development helps find holes in the storytelling, as well as lack of conflict and/or how intensely audience is gripped by the unfolding action.

This is a brief look at some of the major tools that I use to both diagnose and help fix scripts that I work with. There are many other things that I draw upon, including my story sense, my intuition, my experience and so on. On a brief consult we often do not proceed beyond dilemma, because until that's solidly in place it is hard to go much further. I always keep foremost in my mind what the writer's vision is, so as to work in alignment with the artist who has hired me to help maximize the potential of their script.

Jeff Kitchen is a script consultant, screenwriter, and author of *Writing a Great Movie: Four Advanced Tools for the Dramatist*. For more info, check out his website at *www.developmentheaven.com*.

Dr. Rachel Ballon

Many times people will come to me for script consulting and I'll make a diagnosis that the initial problem is with the writer, not the script — that's where I feel my services are unique. I don't just deal with the psychology of a script or character, but also of the writer. Often I don't even look at the script until I talk to them. For example, someone might come in and say they're having problems with their script and are blocked. At our consultation I'll start asking pertinent questions and discover that (a) the script is too close to some painful event that happened in their past or (b) they can't write because of something situational in their current circumstances. Either they're going through a divorce, or they're losing their house, their father died, or they can't get work. These are the real reasons keeping them from writing. Their problems have nothing to do with the script.

Other times I get them before the script is finished and they don't know how to write. So I don't just do script consulting but coach them throughout the entire screenwriting process. Being a former Adjunct Professor at USC Film School teaching scriptwriting and character development, and a Master Teacher for fifteen years in the Writers' Program at UCLA, I know how to guide them from idea to completed script. That's what my latest book, *Blueprint for Screenwriting* is based on — all my teaching experience.

I also use writing as a therapeutic tool, which is not script writing, but a tool to bring out stories that are residing inside the writer. It's something I came up with, called "free flow writing" or "fast flow writing" — because it's writing as fast as you can without stopping. For example, I had a woman who came to see me about her characters. She couldn't express anger in her characters, so they were all flat. I started talking to her and asked, "How do you express anger in your life?" She said "I wasn't allowed to express anger."

Now I could have given her script notes, but it wouldn't have helped — I had to work on the writer. So I had her do "fast flow writing," remembering a time when she was angry and could not express it, and writing that scene out. Then the next time, I had her write the scene again but change it so that she's allowed to get angry and does it no-holds barred. That freed up her anger, and allowed her to have much more exciting characters. Her script took leaps and bounds in its quality to become a wonderful, exciting emotional script, which it could not have been had I just said "Well, get more conflict here or have your character be angry there." She wouldn't have been able to access that emotion.

The whole basis of my book, *Breathing Life Into Your Characters*, is that you can't give anything to your characters which you can't allow yourself to experience. That does not mean you have to murder someone, I'm talking about the feelings.

Individuals send me the script with a self-addressed stamped envelope and I charge $500 for three reads, notes on the page, and a discussion either by phone or in person. We set up a time to have them call me and I tell them to give me 2 1/2 to 3 weeks to complete the analysis. When we speak, I give them broad strokes on the story structure and character goals, relationships and inner conflict. I've already written down the obvious problems and solutions about the script directly on the page. These become a blueprint for the writer to make changes exactly where they need to.

What I discuss with the writer are the larger issues. I might say, "Tell me what your intention was when you wrote this script. How do you want me to feel? What do you want to say through your characters? That life is not fair? That love conquers all?" It's imperative for writers to know what their theme or purpose is for writing what they're writing. Next, I talk about their basic story and character flaws. For example, I had a case where somebody wrote something where a guy date raped somebody and the next day he and this woman are joking. That would never happen.

So, as a script consultant, I not only give them notes on structure and character development, etc., but as a psychotherapist I also guide them in the psychology of human nature in relationship to their characters. I come from the point of view that character is action, character is story. If the characters don't work, the story won't. I especially do a lot with the main character. Many writers have the weakest character as their main character. That's usually the problem in most of the scripts I've read.

I feel that half the time I'm teaching when I do script consulting. Surprisingly, I get so many scripts from people who don't know how to write. I've been a judge several times in screenwriting contests and I can't tell you how poorly written some of the winners' scripts were. I was appalled at how many contestants did not know how to write. They would think that writing was telling their story rather then taking parts of themselves and putting it into the various complex characters with a solid story structure.

During the past 25 years of script consulting I've had people who are very defensive and unwilling to take any constructive criticism. And people who listen but still do what they want. Happily, there are those writers who are professional and willing to make the necessary changes and rewrite until their script works. Those are a delight to work with and they usually get an agent or a script deal. In all cases I feel that I give writers encouragement, and help them make their script the best it can be before they send it out. Because writers don't get a second chance to make a good first impression with their script. It's a one-shot deal.

Dr. Rachel Ballon is a script consultant, psychotherapist specializing in writers' issues, and author of four books, including *Breathing Life Into Your Characters: How to Give Characters Emotional and Psychological Depth*. For more info, check out *www.rachelballon.com.*

David S. Freeman

The following scene deconstruction (the original scene was written by a student), I give an example of how my techniques can be applied. The initial scene lacked many of the techniques which could enrich the flow, the characters, their relationship to one another, and their dialogue. In the second version, I rewrote it, using many "Beyond Structure" techniques. And in the third version, every "Beyond Structure" technique that was used is indicated."

(The following is only a small sample of each version.)

INT. ADMIRAL COLBY'S INNER OFFICE — DAY

Plush oak, immense. At his desk, ADMIRAL JASON COLBY calmly continues writing. VICE ADMIRAL MADDISON DALTON stands.

                        COLBY
            I'm not backing down, Maddy.

                        DALTON
            Women do NOT belong in MY navy.

                    COLBY
Your job is to recruit 900 potential
women officers in the next 90 days.

                    DALTON
We're in the middle of a war for
God's sake.

                    COLBY
Admiral James Madison Dalton,
are you contradicting a superior
officer?

                    DALTON
No, Sir, but...

                    COLBY
But, nothing, Maddy. You know
how to recruit and train better
than anyone and we're in a hurry
with this thing. Surely someone
named for a president can handle
training a few women.

                    DALTON
Give this to McNary. They can all
fail together.

                    COLBY
I'm a patient man, but...
(booming voice)
Get the hell out of here and
that's an order!

                    DALTON
This is an invasion.

The following is a partial rewrite of the scene:

INT. ADMIRAL COLBY'S INNER OFFICE — DAY

Plush oak, immense. At his desk, ADMIRAL JASON COLBY calmly
continues writing. VICE ADMIRAL MADDISON DALTON stands.

>   COLBY
>   I'm not backing down, Maddy.

>   DALTON
>   Ed, what do you like most about
>   the Navy?

>   COLBY
>   Like?

He thinks for a few seconds.

>   COLBY
>   Gotta be the grub.

Both he and Dalton smile.

(The following is a small sample of some of the "techniques" used in the rewrite.)

INT. ADMIRAL COLBY'S INNER OFFICE — DAY

Plush oak, immense. At his desk, ADMIRAL JASON COLBY calmly continues writing. VICE ADMIRAL MADDISON DALTON stands.

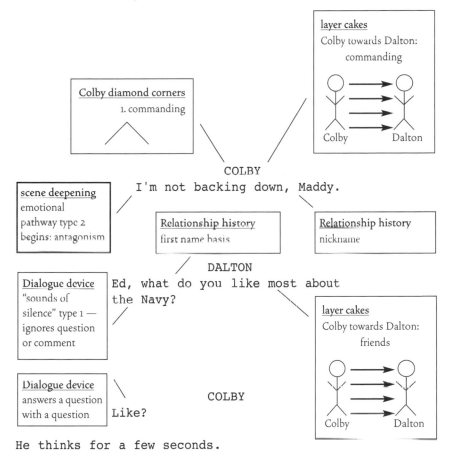

layer cakes
Colby towards Dalton:
commanding

Colby diamond corners
1. commanding

COLBY
I'm not backing down, Maddy.

scene deepening
emotional
pathway type 2
begins: antagonism

Relationship history
first name basis

Relationship history
nickname

DALTON

Dialogue device
"sounds of
silence" type 1 —
ignores question
or comment

Ed, what do you like most about the Navy?

layer cakes
Colby towards Dalton:
friends

Dialogue device
answers a question
with a question

COLBY

Like?

He thinks for a few seconds.

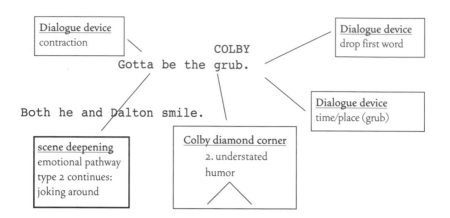

David Freeman is a script consultant and screenwriting teacher of "Beyond Structure," a popular screenwriting workshop taught around the world. For more info, check out *www.beyondstructure.com*.

Pamela Jaye Smith

What became obvious to me was that I could take the principles inherent in mythology and metaphysics and pull those out of stories, show them to people and say if you line your story up more with, say, the Prometheus myth, which is what you are intuitively telling anyway, it's going to make it that much more powerful. So I took these Wisdom Teachings, the old mythologies that you find in every time and place, in every culture's symbols and imagery — and all that stuff that had been used as communication devices for thousands of years — and began to coalesce them into a series of modules that could be used to analyze, construct and improve stories. Mostly screenplays, but I work in other media as well.

When I get the script, I read through it one time making very few notes at all. I read it straight through as though I'm reading a short story, watching a movie. Then I go back usually a day or so later and read it again. In the time between, I have begun to narrow it down to about three or four Mythic Themes and often times the problems people are having are because they are trying to tell too many stories in one. They may be doing a Wakeup Call, Prometheus Stealing Fire From Heaven, Lost Love Rescued, and the War of the Worlds. In my work I use about twenty-four different Mythic Themes. "The Hero's Journey" is not the only one, as you know.

So I go back and read it through and begin to make my notes on where the theme is coming out strongest. The main characters will have begun to reveal their archetypes, if they didn't already at the beginning. I will begin to see what it is the writer is really trying to say with those characters. Because I am a writer myself, I'm always kind of rewriting it as I go along and thinking "If they did this, that might improve this scene." So it's not just "This doesn't work," it's "Here is how I would suggest you fix it."

During that second read, I'm taking lots of notes and beginning to apply things. Then I begin to work with my templates to fill in their characters, their plot points, and the person usually ends up with three to five pages of actual script notes. "On page 13, you said so and so, but this doesn't fit with the such and such. Why did you have this car go off the cliff here?" These will be things we'll discuss, or sometimes it's just suggestions, "Gosh, you put the wrong name here." It can be as simple as that.

I usually ask for two to three weeks turnaround, because I'm working on it from a mythical, metaphysical, intuitional place. I like to let it sit for awhile and let other ideas be drawn into my mind that are in alignment with their story, because I also give suggested movies, suggested reading and other things that can get them into the mood and the mode of their particular story. Then I go back in and start putting together the profiles and the suggestions or perhaps rearranging or filling out the plot structure. I give them examples of other stories on the particular Mythic Theme that I think they should stress. I will say, "I think this is your main theme and this is your subplot and here are the plot points for this one and here are the plot points for that one. There are twelve plot points for, let's say, Prometheus. You've got five of them. If you picked up even two more, it would significantly strengthen your story and put it on that mythic theme so that it will resonate with that. So they are real specific suggestions. Not to dictate, but to suggest.

The same thing with the character profiles. I have done my analysis and my thinking about it and put down my observations and suggestions. Then I get the materials back to the person. In the high-end report, I also include a lot of artwork. Depending on the nature of the person, I might put in a Tarot Card that represents the archetype of a character, or I'll put a significant painting. "This is what your character reminds me of, this archetype, and here are some things to look at and to look for and the images and the symbols" and all that. So a lot of times there is specific imagery that goes with the notebook. Not every time. Not everybody wants or needs to get the full binder. Where we found it really helpful is for people who are actually going to be working on their story and/or going into production. You get a three-ring binder. You've got your story right there. So it's like, okay, we're going to be working on Jonathan's character today. Everybody can flip to that page and deal with that character specifically.

Also, one of the things I do for character profiles is 'the triangle.' I do a triangle of assistance and a Triangle of Resistance. So you have a character's goal and then in the Triangle of Assistance you have the wise helper and the Seductive Sidetrack where you can find conflict in a situation. In the triangle of resistance is the Inner Opposition, like you have a phobia against snakes or vertigo or claustrophobia, and then his Outer Opposition, which will be the bad guys, the antagonist or the natural disaster or whatever it is. And that can get so extensive for some clients that I've done it for every scene.

So, I try to use visual, as well as words, because people learn different ways, absorb information different ways. I put the book together and I either email it or send a hard copy. I suggest that they read it over twice before they call me, because it's a lot of information. It's more than a lot of consultants do and so they need to put in some time to make it work for them.

Pamela Jaye Smith is a Writer, Mythologist, Consultant, award-winning Producer/Director, and author of *Inner Drives: How to Create and Write Characters Using the Eight Classic Centers of Motivation*. For more info, check out *www.mythworks.net*.

Dave Trottier

My method is, I read the script and take notes. Sometimes I mark in the script and I'll have a page of notes, usually two or three words each, phrases that bring me back to the script page. Then I go back to the notes and just start writing. For me, it's creative and analytical at the same time. I organize my comments into sections, but it will be different for each writer. In other words, if you were to look at one of my evaluations, it would give you an idea of what you would get from me, but another evaluation might be organized differently. It's all personalized into what I think the writer needs. I just wrote one recently where my first item of business was page one. It was so terrible that I completely rewrote the page for him and showed him what he was doing wrong and why it was wrong and so forth. It was kind of a little mini-course in formatting. Well, you're not going to get that in every evaluation.

So, I go from the notes and write a first draft of my evaluation and things come to me. And I'm going back and forth from the script to my notes, until I finish that first draft. I guess I'm kind of doing a first and second draft at the same time. After I've done that, I go through and clean up in two ways. One is, in terms of the content, I want to make sure that I have given them everything that they need. The second thing, I want to make sure my tone is right so it'll be easily received by the reader. You can criticize someone in a way that makes them defensive and you can criticize someone in a way that makes them want to do better. That's part of the art, I think. You have to be a writer yourself and have a positive, encouraging writing tone while you're giving this criticism.

The following scene deconstruction and rewrite is an example of how I would approach a script where the writer is trying to also be the director.

```
EXT. HIGHWAY 27 - DAY - AERIAL VIEW

WE SEE the lush Florida countryside until we FIND our
subject, a dark blue van.

SLOW ZOOM IN ON VAN

VIEW ON VAN - MOVING

Two characters shout at each other while the CAMERA
MOVES beside the van until we see the child/protago-
nist looking out the window at us.

INT. VAN - BUSTER, CAROL AND ABBIE

Everyone is quiet.
```

I would not call this a riveting "reading experience." Notice in the above example that the focus is on how the story is told, not on the story itself. What is going on in the car? We don't know. Who are the "two characters"? Why is the child looking out the window? What is his or her facial expression? Is the child a boy or a girl? We aren't sure, because the writer is too involved directing her movie.

How can the writer improve this without sacrificing much in terms of the "feel" she wants to communicate? The revision that follows is not a masterpiece, but I hope you find it a better read than the original.

EXT. FLORIDA - DAY

From the Atlantic shore, the lush countryside extends for miles westward. Below, a black two-lane highway meanders through the Spring growth. A blue van scoots down the highway.

EXT. VAN - CONTINUOUS

The van rumbles along. Inside, two twenty-something parents, BUSTER and CAROL shout at each other, although their words cannot be heard.

INT. VAN - CONTINUOUS

Buster shoots an angry look to the back where ABBIE, age 6, leans away from him and stares out the window at the beautiful trees and shrubs whizzing by.

EXT. VAN WINDOW - CONTINUOUS

The child is motionless, sad, trapped. One little hand presses against the glass.

INT. VAN - CONTINUOUS

The parents are silent now — gathering steam before their next eruption.

In the revision, I have suggested almost everything the writer wanted, but my focus is on the story and the characters, not on fancy-dancy ways to tell the story.

In addition, I imply a POV shot of the child staring at the trees and shrubs. If desired, I could even describe the reflection of trees on the window glass (without using technical terms). The revision also implies that the child is the subject of the parents' shouting.

I also direct the camera (without using a camera direction) to a CLOSE UP of the child at the window. And I do that for a story reason. I want the reader to know that the child is the most important character in the scene, and that maybe she is the central character or protagonist; and I want the reader (and the movie audience) to emotionally identify with the child's situation.

I end the scene with a promise of things to come. I am trying to create some interest in what happens next while revealing the emotions of the parents.

In summary, my advice to writers is to focus on story and character; and, while they're at it, use clear, specific language.

Dave Trottier is a script consultant, teacher, and author of the best-selling, *The Screenwriter's Bible*. For more info, check out *www.keepwriting.com*.

Judith Searle

The Enneagram system is an extraordinary power tool for screenwriters. The diagram consists of a circle with nine points on it that connect with other points through interior lines. Each of the nine points on the outside of the circle has connecting lines to two other points. These two connecting lines describe what writers call a character arc.

When I was doing the research for my book, *The Literary Enneagram: Characters from the Inside Out*, I used not just modern plays and novels, but also a lot of classic works — Shakespeare, Dickens, Jane Austen and Hardy, among others — and I found that in all these the connecting lines of the Enneagram diagram inevitably matched up with the character arcs constructed by these great writers.

I gave a talk at an International Enneagram Association conference a few years ago on "Shakespeare and the Enneagram," using film clips from Mel Gibson's *Hamlet*, Lawrence Fishburne's *Othello*, and Ian Holm's *King Lear* to demonstrate how each of those characters is clearly defined in terms of the Enneagram. My conclusion was that both Shakespeare and the Enneagram system are conscious of the same essential truths about human character structures. The fact that Shakespeare's characters so clearly match the dynamics that the Enneagram describes serves as an important validation of the Enneagram system, since Shakespeare is one of the most astute observers of human nature who ever lived.

The Enneagram also helps writers with basic story construction and offers guidelines for creating more effective and economical character grids. Instead of presenting a cast of characters that contains two people of the same Enneagram type, it may be more effective to do a kind of elegant algebraic equation and cancel out duplications to achieve a more economical, compact story.

The Enneagram can help writers create character-driven plot twists that will seem both inevitable and surprising — the ultimate combination for a compelling story. If, for example, in the second act of your screenplay you're looking for a plot twist, it can often help to look at the stress point and security point of your protagonist's Enneagram type — the two lined points within the diagram — and choose some action or reaction that relates to one of these points (rather than the home point). This behavior, being rooted in the character's basic psychology, will seem inevitable but also surprising.

Some of the work I've done can also help writers understand the unwritten rules for different story genres. There is an article available on my website (*www.members.aol.com/jsearle479*) on "Story Genres and Enneagram Types" that lays out these rules. As far as I know, nobody else has gone through all the basic story genres and discussed the unwritten rules that audiences expect to see followed, and how those rules relate to the Enneagram type of protagonist in each genre. Often the protagonist of a genre story will be of the Enneagram type that is linked to that genre.

My work on story genres is also useful to help writers and directors understand why they're drawn to work in particular genres. Why do certain directors tend to do a lot of thrillers while others tend do love stories and romantic comedies? Their story choices have something to do with their habitual focus of attention.

The Enneagram is a system with so many applications for writers, directors and actors that I feel it's a major way of boosting creative power for anyone who knows it.

When I do script consulting, the first thing I do is find out the Enneagram type of the person I'm working with. If they don't know their type, I do a typing interview and then if they have an actual script, I look at that and analyze it in terms of the type of the protagonist, the types of main subsidiary characters and the genre (or combination of genres) of the story that is being told. We look at the diagram and we look at the ways the story might be enhanced.

Sometimes there will be big holes in the second act, where you need some more plot twists — and the Enneagram can be very helpful, as I was suggesting before, in coming up with those. The Enneagram offers an in-depth approach to character development, taking into account the contradictions and paradoxes that we see in all dimensional characters.

Judith Searle is a writer, teacher, script consultant, and author of several books, including *The Literary Enneagram: Characters from the Inside Out*. For more info, check out *www.members.aol.com/jsearle479*.

Pretty good stuff, huh? But it's only a taste of what these consummate pros have to offer. Take some time to let all these different perspectives soak in... then take a closer look at their websites and books. I promise it'll be well worth the effort.

Now let's look at how to give your clients feedback... that doesn't backfire.

Chapter Summary

◊ The hero's compelling "desire" is the driving force, and one of the most essential components, of a successful screenplay. When analyzing a screenplay, therefore, the consultant should be looking for several key elements:

  ◊ *The attempt to achieve the goal must elicit emotion in the reader/audience*
  ◊ *The desire must be visible*
  ◊ *The desire must have a clearly implied endpoint*
  ◊ *The hero must "desperately" want the desire*
  ◊ *The hero must actively pursue the desire*
  ◊ *It must be within the hero's power to achieve the desire*
  ◊ *The hero must put everything on the line to achieve the desire*
  ◊ *The hero's desire must be resolved at the climax of the film*

◊ As a consultant, you should work hard to create real solutions, rather than merely diagnosing problems.

◊ Stories that grip the audience tend to have a good strong "dilemma" for the protagonist, which is defined as 'two equally unacceptable alternatives, two equally painful choices.' Therefore, a consultant should look for, help define, strengthen, or even create this key element.

◊ A good way to "put your finger" on the theme of a script is to look at the way in which the protagonist resolves her dilemma; not just *what* she does, but the *way* in which it's done.

◊ The "36 Dramatic Situations" is another powerful tool to isolate active elements in a script and explore possible new ones; elements such as Madness, Disaster, Ambition, The Necessity of Sacrificing Loved Ones, etc.

◊ Another analytical tool is "Sequence, Proposition, Plot." Sequence works with reverse and effect, where you start at the end of the story and work your way backwards, asking at each point, "What is the cause of the previous effect?"

Proposition and Plot deals with setting the action up into a map that allows you to clearly see how the conflict between the characters lays out. These tools help find holes, weed out unnecessary beats, and strengthen the dramatic action.

◊ Doing script notes is a creative and analytical process, approached differently by different consultants. Some script reports cover the basics, others go into more depth and diverse topics. Some story meetings last a half hour, others can last several hours. As you work with more clients, *your* style will emerge.

◊ There are many ways to evaluate a story, from the mythological to the metaphysical. Find your unique niche and experiment with it.

◊ Speaking Your Mind, Minding What You Speak

◊ A Spoonful of Sugar

◊ Don't Fall in Love with Your Feedback

◊ Don't Make it *Your* Story

◊ Power Trippin'

Chapter Five

"Do not fear to be eccentric in opinion,
for every opinion now accepted was once
eccentric."
— Bertrand Russell

"Listen, everyone is entitled to my
opinion."
— Madonna

Giving
Good
Feedback

Speaking Your Mind, Minding What You Speak

It's easy to get so caught up in the analysis of a script — and attached to your evaluation — that you forget one of the most important principles in being an effective script consultant: *Your brilliant feedback is worthless if the Client can't receive it.*

In other words, *how* you give feedback is as important as the feedback itself. And sometimes getting a client to hear your comments and really digest them can be more challenging than analyzing *War and Peace* as a possible adaptation to a video game.

To be a truly effective script consultant, you need to be part therapist, confidante, and friend as well. You need to have excellent empathic listening skills. You need to be able to not only hear what your client is saying verbally, but read their vocal tone, rate of speech, facial expression, and overall body language (which makes up about 93% of communication) — and adjust accordingly — or risk losing them.

"Giving feedback is a tremendously complex thing," says Richard Krevolin. "I think sometimes people just need to be heard. Oftentimes, I'll spend most of the session listening. Many people have an inability to disassociate themselves from their work, so when you criticize their work they view that as a criticism of themselves and they respond accordingly. It's tricky. I think it's easy for most consultants to focus on the negative things, because that is essentially our job. When in reality, you really have to work hard to find a way to bring in the positives so the person doesn't get defensive. Because the moment they get defensive, you're in trouble. It's a real art form, being kind and gentle, supportive and inspiring, and at the same time still conveying that information. I've had some negative experiences where people have attacked me because they were unhappy that I didn't grade their material as being perfect and ready to go out when they thought it was. They didn't want to deal with the reality of the many, many hours of rewriting they had to do. So I make sure that people know this isn't about them, it's just what writers do. We have to rewrite material, it's part of the process. If you think it's difficult working with me, I'm easy compared to the people you'll deal with in the industry. When you get a script consultation, you're also getting an education in how to take notes and collaborate."

So let's take a closer look at some basic principles for giving good feedback.

A Spoonful of Sugar

"A spoonful of sugar helps the medicine go down." When it comes to giving criticism, no truer words have been spoken. As a script consultant — or "script doctor" — you'll be dealing with many ailing scripts. And if you're going to give the "medicine" in an effective way, you're going to have to learn a little "bedside manner." I know that's tough for some of you, who think it's pandering or "blowing smoke." But I suspect that's just cynicism talking. There's nothing wrong with complimenting people on what they do right — even if they're doing almost everything else wrong.

Beyond just being nice, starting with positive feedback creates trust between you and your client, and tends to make them more open to the rest of the evaluation. Writers — and most creative people — are desperate for positive reinforcement. It's like oxygen. Affirming them lets them get a nice, deep breath again. Without it, they'll have a hard time hearing anything else you say because they'll be gasping for air. This is basic stuff, but it's amazing how often it's neglected. In our head-strong rush to get to our brilliant critiques, we often forget that that person sitting across from us has labored for months to give birth to their baby — and we're about to stomp on its head right in front of them.

Even in the most god-awful script you've ever read, there's always something good you can say. And that doesn't mean complimenting them on their choice of font. Starting out your consult by saying, "You had me totally hooked, a complete page turner, right up until FADE IN," is probably not going to be a big confidence booster for your client. Just the fact that they wrote an entire script is a major accomplishment. Many pseudo-writers never get past page 25. Dig deep if you have to, but come up with some legitimate compliments and give them generous-ly. Then you can move on to the criticisms. (Never give feedback until the check has cleared though. I think it's pretty obvious why.)

Another technique is to try and sprinkle each "negative" comment with a little "sugar." I'm not saying to "sugar-coat" it. You want to tell the truth. You *have* to. That's why they hired you — whether they want to hear it or not. But there is a con-structive way to tell it, and a destructive way. And the key here is you want your client to remain *open* to your comments or the whole thing will be for naught. Pay attention to their body language. If you see them closing down, glazing over, taking a trip to la-la land, you may be hammering them a bit too roughly. Back off. Point out something that works. Change the subject. Do whatever it takes to bring them back and keep them enlisted.

Bottom line, you want to build up your client and their script, not tear them down. They get enough of that already. You want them to walk away more educated, enlightened, maybe even inspired — with a game plan to make their script better.

The sad fact is that most people walk through life bombarded by messages of inad-equacy and are rarely ever recognized for the good they do. You might be one of the few places they'll ever get positive feedback about themselves and their work. So don't be stingy. There will be plenty of time to point out the problems.

Says Linda Seger, "Basically, I'm looking at 'what does the script want to do and what is getting in the way of it doing that?' My work focuses on how to achieve the intent of the script and how to shape the script so it's workable. Naturally, sometimes you can't get the intent of the script without really re-thinking the story because the way it's designed won't work without re-conceptualizing part of it. So, there are times when I have to suggest a lot of possibilities or different directions to take, but most of the time I'm saying. 'This is the story you want to tell. This is how you can strengthen your scene. You can tighten this up, you can clarify, you can create stronger arcs.' I'm not making judgments on, 'should you be doing this story.' If the client wants to do this story, my job is to serve the client and help the client get what he/she wants. My job is to help make their story work."

Don't Fall in Love with Your Feedback

Your feedback isn't as important as your client's opinion. If you feel strongly about your point of view, and believe it will help their script, by all means make your case. But in the end, it's up to the client whether or not they'll take a word of what you say to heart. And you have to be okay with that.

Some consultants are struggling screenwriters who vicariously live through their clients' scripts, and when a client disagrees with their "take" on the script, the consultant takes it personally and fights for their position like it's their story. This is not an effective consulting technique. If you find yourself responding this way, check in and see what's really going on. Are you hungering to work on your own material? Did your material get rejected recently? Are you just having a bad day? Whatever is driving you, do what it takes to meet that inner need — because if you don't feed yourself, you'll starve your client.

Give the feedback in as positive and articulate a manner as you can. Add some clarifying points if necessary. Maybe even push back once or twice. Then let it go and move on. If you've sincerely listened to your client (not just what they say, but their body language as well), and you've done everything you can to communicate your ideas to them, then you've done your job. Hopefully, you've written the feedback in some form, or it's being taped, and if it's truly worthy the client will hear it at a later date and get it.

"I like to present things a certain way," says Chris Vogler. "Some of this comes from Jeffrey Katzenberg, but it's sort of , 'This is just my opinion, take it for what it's worth.' So you always qualify and present things as suggestions. It's like 'These are some of the reactions I had, and you're paying me for my honest opinion.' Then I point out four or five different ways to address what I see as the problem — always with the attitude that I know none of these are all that great, they're just some of the ways this could be fixed, and I trust you as the writer to see the problem and find a sixth or seventh solution that's even better.

This was a Katzenberg technique. He would say, 'I know this is a dumb idea, but you could try it and you'll probably come up with something much better.' He would always phrase things that way, which is very smart and diplomatic. It throws the writer a little challenge, but it does it in a way that acknowledges *you're* the writer. I'm not claiming to be a writer, that's your magic function and ultimately your responsibility. 'This is what I would suggest or here's some alternatives. I offer them in the spirit of hoping it'll stimulate you to think of something better.' That seems to work pretty well.

"Some people, on the other hand, need to be handheld and told exactly what to do. My favorite kinds of clients are those who can, what I would say in computer terms, globally export a single point. You show them something they're doing or a technique that they're missing on page three and you don't have to show them all the other twenty-five times when they made that mistake. They make the correction on their own and catch them all. You can just do a lot more work with somebody like that."

Don't Make It *Your* Story

As already mentioned, there is a drive for some script consultants to work out their own creative needs through their clients' stories. This is like a doctor trying to heal her patients by treating an illness *she* has.

Not very effective. And potentially deadly.

Use your tools to discover *their* story, not yours. Sometimes it's clearly on the page. Other times you have to go on an adventure to solve the mystery. This entails asking a lot of questions, giving your client homework (especially if it's more of a coaching relationship), and offering suggestions that inspire your client's muse.

"I always begin the first session by asking a lot of questions," says Michael Hauge. "The questions are geared primarily to giving me a very clear idea of what the writer's passion for the story is and what their goals for the project are. What do they love about it? Why did they pick this story to write? How do they anticipate marketing it and so on? That's the first set of questions. The next set of questions is designed to allow me to see what they think they're presenting about their hero, who they think their hero is on the page. This is important, because oftentimes a writer will think their hero is extremely sympathetic, but when you read the script it's not somebody you'd want to spend five minutes with. So, I want to know what their ideas are, what they think they have put on the page, before I start talking to them about it."

There was an original impulse that motivated your client to generate this idea, treatment, script, book, play, whatever. Find that seed. Feed it. Water it. Coax it into growing. Don't pull it up by the roots and plant your own!

This doesn't mean you can't be creative and come up with ways to solve the script's problems. That's your job. I hate it when a script consultant gives me notes on what's wrong with my script — but has no clue how to solve any of it! If they were a business consultant and all they did was point out the problems without offering solutions, they'd be fired before the ink dried on their contract.

"You want to touch people on four levels when you are trying to teach them something," says Pamela Jaye Smith. "You want to hit them on the ideal, the spiritual/metaphysical level, so you'll state that concept. You want to hit them on the mental level, so you'll give them some analytical aspect of it. You want to hit them on the emotional level, so you bring in perhaps praise or you note where they have written something that's very emotionally evocative. Then you want to do it on a physical level, talk about taking some action, like 'I think if you switch this scene and that scene, you're going to accomplish a greater emotional impact on your audience.'

"It's like kinesiology, where you come at every situation and solution from a couple of different angles. Usually, the way someone talks will tell you which way they tend to be. If you listen carefully in the first conversation, you'll know the kind of vocabulary and style with which to approach them. Maybe it's a macho kind of guy, or a chick-flick thing, so you use that approach, that vocabulary, for the communication. What works for one person who is, let's say, very logical, scientifically oriented, is not going to work with somebody who is very emotional."

Power Trippin'

Power is a strange and subtle thing. And when you're in a position of passing judgment on a person's project, and they sit before you, vulnerable, sometimes desperately needing some validation, it's tempting to become intoxicated by your authority. A single bruising critique could crush their soul and any hope of them continuing on their writing journey, while a genuine compliment could buoy them up, providing a storm shelter against the harsh weather they're buffeted by in the business.

Keep fresh in your mind the moments when you've received critiques and how fragile you were. The art and soul of people have been oppressed for so long. Let's not add to that. Let's do everything we can to support our fellow creators.

Stay humble.

Remain a student.

Check your ego at the door.

Chapter Summary

◊ One of the most important principles to remember when giving notes: "Your Brilliant Feedback is Worthless if the Client Can't Receive it."

◊ *How* you give feedback is as important as *what* feedback you give.

◊ To be an effective script consultant you need to be part therapist, confidante, and friend, with strong listening skills, and an ability to read body language.

◊ Always find something good to say about even the worst scripts, and frame criticisms as often as possible in a positive, constructive light.

◊ Be gentle on yourself. It's an art form to be kind, supportive, and inspiring, while telling a person that their script basically doesn't work.

◊ Clients need to know it's not personal. Writing is rewriting. And it's all part of their continued education in collaboration.

◊ Don't fall in love with your feedback. Give it the best you can, push back a little if needed, then *let it go.*

◊ Trying to work out your own creative needs through your client's material is like a doctor trying to heal her patients by treating an illness *she* has. Don't make it *your* story, help them realize *their* story.

◊ Look for the "intent" of the script, and help the client fulfill it.

◊ When giving suggestions on a script, give multiple choices, and acknowledge that your ideas aren't probably that good and your client could do it better.

◊ Don't pack your bags for a "power trip." Check your ego at the door.

◊ Most people are rarely recognized for the good that they do, so don't be stingy with compliments. You might be the only place they're getting any.

◊ Aren't You Special?

◊ Script Specialties

    ◊ Mythological

    ◊ Psychological

    ◊ Metaphysical

    ◊ Religious

    ◊ Science Fiction

    ◊ Police Procedural/Crime

    ◊ Military

    ◊ Legal

    ◊ Historical

    ◊ Character-based

    ◊ Comedic

Chapter Six

| "The Jack-of-all-trades seldom is good at any. Concentrate all of your efforts on one definite chief aim." — Napoleon Hill | # Specializing |

"What we need is more people who specialize in the impossible." — Theodore Roethke

Aren't You Special?

While not entirely on topic, I think that last quote is particularly resonant with the kind of work we're doing here. Writing a great script or making a great movie (just getting it made at all) often seems like a mission impossible. We're working in such a magical sphere, where talent and craft co-mingle with alchemy, psychology, mythology, and a whole lot more "ologies" to create something that can ultimately stir the mind, open the heart, and awaken the soul. As script consultants (and writers), we need to develop a "mission possible" mentality. Despite the apparent roadblocks in the business to creating truly special works of art and entertainment, we need to hold to a vision that sees that happening — and then guide our clients and our own work in that direction. "*Without vision the people perish.*" And without a bold vision of this business, the artists will perish — or become studio executives (no offense to studio execs).

Okay, enough about that...

Part of what you have to offer this alchemy of storytelling is your special knowledge and abilities, your "hook," your "Unique Selling Proposition" (USP). More and more script consultants are developing specialties to meet an increasingly diverse demand, and to stand out from the crowd. In fact, to become truly successful in today's industry, you must discover what's "special" about you and your services — and market yourself accordingly.

"You want to figure out what exactly you're bringing to the party," says Michael Hauge. "In other words, what is your strength? There are certain consultants who are extremely good with genre films; horror, western, sci-fi, and others who know a lot about family and animated films. And there are certain consultants who are very strong at the marketing process. Maybe it's not the kind of movie or the kind of principles that you're strongest in, but a certain way you work with writers. For example, if you were an agent who really liked working with writers and knew the marketplace well, you could put your shingle out based on that. You need to decide what sets you apart from everybody else."

Says Linda Seger, "I've noticed in the last ten plus years that consultants are mapping out specific specialties. So, someone like Pamela Jaye Smith and Chris Vogler consult on the mythic side of scripts. Dr. Rachel Ballon, a psychotherapist, consults on the psychology. Kathie Fong Yoneda is very good at analyzing the commercial possibilities, because of her long-time work as a studio executive. Scott Fields, out of Santa Fe, comes from both a military and FBI background, and consults with people who are doing mysteries or want to get their crime correct. Mara Purl has an acting background and can help make the characters attractive to actors. Some of us have even worked as a consulting team when the client has a variety of needs, and wants to work with a team."

So what is special about you? What unique knowledge base or life experience do you bring to the table? Are you a doctor, a lawyer, a psychologist, a detective, a retired general, a mythology professor? Or do you have a totally new technique for screenwriting, perhaps even using some ancient methodology to analyze and develop story? Maybe it's all about how you present the material. Do you make a tape of your story sessions and present the notes in a professional notebook with sections and a table of contents for easy reference? Do you offer ongoing coaching?

Do you deal with the writer's issues as well as what they've written? Do you guarantee quick turnaround? Are you a script doctor who makes house calls?

What makes you the go-to-guy (or gal) for script consulting?

Specialization is no longer an option for success, it's a requirement. There's an entrepreneurial saying, "Think big, focus small." In other words, have a grand vision, but focus it in a specialized niche. Domino's Pizza wasn't trying to be all things to all people. They weren't trying to be the best pizza or the best restaurant. They focused on the area of quick delivery and convenience and cornered the market in it. Starbucks isn't trying to get all coffee drinkers. They focus on the high-end ones, those of us who are crazy enough to pay $4.00 for a soy latte, sugar-free, half-caff.

Linda Seger is the "mother of script consulting," Syd Field is the "father of structure," John Truby focuses on "the blockbuster," Chris Vogler and Pamela Jaye Smith uncover the "mythological angle," Rachel Ballon is the "writer's therapist," Judith Searle uses the "Enneagram," and Dave Trottier is "Dr. Format" — just to name a few. And the specialization can go even further. Just as there are many kinds of doctors specializing in different parts of the body, so too can there be many kinds of "script doctors" who focus on different parts of the "body of a story." Do you have a particular knack for dialogue? Maybe you're "The Dialogue Doctor!" Do you have a flair for the funny? Maybe you're "The Script Orthopedist — Specializing in the Funny Bone!"

So what are some of the possible categories you could specialize in?

Script Specialties

○ Mythological. Do you have a love for, and in-depth understanding of, mythology? Are you able to discern the mythological structures in modern-day stories? Do you think Joseph Campbell was one sexy dude? Then this might be for you.

○ Psychological. Are you a therapist, or do you have extensive understanding of this area? Do you often find yourself analyzing the characters in stories to better understand their psychological motivations? Do you find yourself analyzing all of your family and friends? Are you convinced you know them better than they know themselves? Then you might want to consider this category.

◦ Metaphysical. Are you interested in spiritual, esoteric, or occult concepts? Do you love to discover the deeper spiritual meaning of movies? Do you believe that stories have the potential to enlighten as they entertain? Do you like to sit under a hanging pyramid, while holding crystals in your upturned palms and chanting ancient Sanskrit? Alrighty then, this might be your bag.

◦ Religious. Do you have a deep love of bible stories and religious parables? Are you a religious person (or minister) who wants to see more traditional religious values in stories? Were you as blown away as most of us by the box-office of *The Passion of the Christ* and want to get a piece of this in-demand and underrepresented market? Then hallelujah — this is the niche for you!

◦ Science Fiction. Do you have a particular interest and knowledge in science and technology — especially cutting-edge? Do you believe in aliens, flying saucers, time-travel, and remote viewing? Are you saving up to buy your own hovercraft? Do you own the boxed sets for *Star Wars*, *Star Trek*, *Lost in Space*, and the accompanying comic books — all still in shrink-wrapped mint condition? Then set your phaser to "make a killing" and beam yourself up to this category.

◦ Police Procedural / Crime. (This could include all film and TV that deals with law enforcement and crime.) Do you have a background in law enforcement (as a police officer, detective, or even an attorney)? If not, do you have a particular fascination with, and knowledge of, true-crime and other law-enforcement-related subjects? Or have you just gotten into trouble with the law a lot — and even spent some time in the slammer? Then this might be a great way to give a little something back to society.

◦ Military. Are you in the military, or have you ever been? Do you play with plastic army men? (Come on, admit it. I still love throwing those little paratroopers with the plastic parachutes off my balcony). If you have a unique knowledge, experience, or fascination with all things military — and want to get paid to play G.I. Joe — this is the specialty for you!

◦ Historical. Are you a history teacher or history buff? Are you tired of watching historical epics that completely botch — or outright mutilate — historical facts? Do you get turned on studying all the different types of spoons used throughout history? Then we need your help!

◦ Character-Driven. Are you an actor/actress with a particular passion for creating rich, complex characters? Are you tired of reading scripts with flat, cardboard cutouts posing as people? Movie stars get movies made. A script with a great role that promises plenty of scene chewing for its star, has a significant advantage over a script filled with one-dimensional stereotypes. And there's always the chance you could work in a part for yourself!

◦ Comedy. Are you a comedian, or just a funny person? Do you find yourself seeing the humor even in your own downfalls? Scripts that make people laugh will always be hot commodities. And if you can make them funnier — you'll be in demand too! One comedian I know has a consulting business where he improvises his clients' scripts to mine all of the comedic gold. It's a great way to hone your comedy skills — and make a few bucks making someone other than yourself laugh.

The list could go on and on, but I think you get the picture. The fact is, there are many roads into this business, many of which have yet to be discovered. For a more extended list of specialties, check out "The Script Consultant Institute" page at *www.scriptwritercentral.com*.

Take some time to write about your background, knowledge base, passions, obsessions, talents, and abilities. Ask friends, family members, and co-workers what they think are your unique traits and special skills.

How could these attributes be applied to the craft of story consulting?

Is a picture of your "specialty" beginning to emerge?

Don't worry if it's not clear yet, we'll be doing more work on this in the chapters on "marketing" and "mission." And lest you think you're not unique, think again. You're a one-of-a-kind, unrepeatable person. You've never happened before. And when you design your business around this uniqueness, you transcend competition — because what you have to offer has never been offered before.

Chapter Summary

() To become truly successful in today's industry, you must create your own USP (unique selling proposition), and market yourself accordingly.

() Everyone has a unique base of knowledge and experience. Discover what yours is and create your own "niche."

() One way to stand out from the crowd is to create your own cutting-edge screenwriting technique.

() Create a plan and a "brand" that makes you the "go-to guy or girl."

() Specialization is no longer an option for success — it's a requirement.

() Some possible script consultant specialties: Mythological, Psychological, Metaphysical, Religious, Science Fiction, Police Procedural/Crime, Military, Character-Driven, Comedic.

() There are many roads into this business, many of which have yet to be discovered.

() Write about your background, knowledge, passions, obsessions, talents, and abilities. Ask friends, family, and co-workers what they think is special about you. Put it all together and try to create your USP (unique selling proposition).

() Everyone is unique — including you. In fact, you are a one-of-a-kind, unre-peatable person with unique gifts to offer.

() When you design your business around your uniqueness, you transcend com-petition — because what you have to offer has never been offered in quite the same way before.

Chapter Seven

"The maker of a sentence launches out into the infinite and builds a road into Chaos and old Night."
— *Ralph Waldo Emerson*

"You write a hit play the same way you write a flop."
— *William Saroyan*

Becoming a Script Doctor

Turning an Analysis into a Writing Job

If you're a writer, being a script consultant offers a wonderful opportunity for writing work. But if you're interested in pursuing this avenue, *you have to let others know you offer it*. The most common reason that qualified script consultants don't have more script doctoring work is that they don't offer it to clients. In many cases the consultant doesn't even realize it's an option.

Don't be shy. If your client likes what you have to say, if they think your "take" on their script is a viable one, let them know that you are a screenwriter and are available to assist them in developing their script (whether it's at concept, outline, treatment, or script stage). I'm not suggesting you undermine your client's need to grow and develop as writers themselves. That is your ultimate goal. But in many cases, it's not the client's goal. Their foremost desire is to finish their script — and sell it. This is especially true when they are not primarily writers, but professionals from other fields looking to "break in." And if you can help them get a better script, one with a real chance of selling and getting made, then you've helped them take their careers to the next level.

I've helped many clients sell their movies this way.

If this is something you want, put yourself out there. Include this option on your cards, brochures, website, and at the end of each script analysis report.

First Do No Harm

There are different kinds of script doctoring jobs. You may be hired to rewrite a treatment or script, do a dialogue and/or description polish, do a "page-one" rewrite, or develop something from scratch.

If you're hired to develop a complete script, you may negotiate a "written by" credit and even a partnership in some cases. In this instance, you would have a lot of creative license on the project since it's got your name on it. However, if you're being hired to "doctor" someone else's script — don't forget it's *their* script.

Just as with consulting, your job is to fulfill their vision, not yours. This doesn't mean you can't put your creativity and imagination into it. By all means, that's what they're hiring you for. But make sure you have worked out the details of the story with them before you do — and they've signed off on it. There's nothing worse than pouring your heart into a project, only to discover that they didn't want your heart in it, they wanted theirs. They want to believe it's still their script, that it represents their talent, not yours, so that they can tell everyone they did it with a clean conscience.

And it's their right to do so.

They're paying for that privilege. If your "artistic integrity" won't allow you to do this, you might not want to be a script doctor.

Questions to Ask Your Client Before You Begin

◊ **Why are you hiring a script doctor instead of doing it yourself?** If the person is a producer, investor, or professional from some other field, the answer to this will be more obvious. But if they're a writer, try to arrange it so that their writing ability — and not just their script — improves in the process.

○ **What type of working arrangement do you envision with a script doctor?** Some clients want you sitting in front of them while you write, so they can (a) make sure you're really putting in the hours; (b) make sure you're writing up to their standards; and (c) have input so they feel like they're co-writing it with you. Other clients will actually add something of value to the writing process and can be a joy to be around. I prefer to have story meetings with the client, where we go over the script and brainstorm on the possible changes — then I go away and write the script alone.

○ **Have you worked with other script doctors or writers?** This is key, because their relationship with past writers/script doctors could be a clue to what you're in for. If someone proposed to you, you'd want to know if they were married — and divorced — before, right? It's also a good way to discern what does and doesn't work for this client, so that you don't make the same mistakes.

○ **Who do you see as the audience for this film?** You want to make sure you're on the same page with the client before you start rewriting their script. If they envision the film for Russian Octogenarians, and you're writing a teen comedy, there's going to be trouble. Like I've already mentioned, get clear with your client about the details of the story you are about to write (hopefully in outline form) — and get them to sign off on it.

○ **How much have you budgeted for the project?** In other words, how much are they willing to pay you? This can be an awkward subject for many people, especially creative types, but you must make sure the client is aware of your fees and is willing/able to pay for them.

○ **Exactly what do you want from a script doctor?** To write an entire script from scratch? Rewrite an existing script? Polish dialogue and description? Punch up the humor or other aspect of the script? Create an outline, treatment, pitch, or query letter? Do a line edit on the page? Edit the entire script for grammar and spelling? (If this is the case, refer it to a typist who does this for a living.)

"Deskside" Manner

You need to establish clear boundaries and expectations. Make sure you're both talking about the same story. Make sure the client is clear about your role. If they're hiring you as a script doctor, you are *not* their agent — and are therefore not responsible for the script selling. You might even want to include this in your contract. If, however, you plan to help the client sell their script, clearly outline this process in the agreement. Also clarify the matter of credit. Will you get some? Or is it a ghost job?

There's another challenge you'll face as a script doctor — the quality of projects you're asked to work on. You might have a standard for yourself that you'll only work on scripts that have a snowball's chance of selling. That's fine. Just know that you probably won't be doing much writing in the early years of your career. The fact is, a majority of scripts you receive — as a consultant and script doctor — will never sell. I know that's a hard one to swallow. I'm the world's biggest optimist, and I still have to admit it's true.

So how do you reconcile this fact when a client is about to hand over their hard-earned cash to have you develop something you don't think will ever see the light of dailies? The first thing I do is tell them my honest opinion, qualifying it with William Goldman's adage that nobody knows anything in this business. The truth is, I could be wrong. This could become the next Big Thing — or at least sell.

If they still want to go ahead with it, I do everything I can to add as much value as possible to the script and their life, so that by the end of the process they have the best script possible and have grown in the process. Like I mentioned in the introduction, I didn't sell any of the scripts I worked on with my first script consultant. But that experience — and subsequent ones — ultimately made it possible for me to earn hundreds of thousands of dollars as a screenwriter and script consultant.

Let's be realistic. Early on in your career, you're going to need to take just about whatever comes your way — for the experience, the exposure, and to pay the expenses. But as your business matures, you'll be able to be more selective, and choose only those projects that turn you on in some way.

Questions to Ask Yourself Before You Begin

In the event you take on a project that is less than stellar, you need to ask yourself a few questions to make sure you can fulfill your obligations with minimal anxiety:

◊ **Do I believe in the project — or the writer — enough to invest my time?** Again, you may not have the luxury early on to make these distinctions. But at some point (hopefully) you'll be in a position to choose the projects you're most passionate about. I came to a place in my career where I wasn't being fulfilled by my work anymore. I knew I had to make a decision and take a leap. That's when I decided to work primarily on projects (as a script doctor) that I believed in. That can be a scary decision. It's hard to turn away a paycheck when you have a mortgage payment. But if you want your career and creativity to evolve, you might have to take that step.

◊ **If I don't really believe in the project or think it has a chance of selling, will I still be able to sleep at night, knowing I gave the client my honest opinion?** If you accept a project you don't fully believe in, make sure you can live with yourself. Do everything you can to give the client honest and accurate information, and really determine if you can maintain a sense of peace throughout the process. In my early days, I took on projects that I had absolutely no passion for — just because it was work — and I struggled like hell to get through them. Try not to put yourself in that position if you can help it.

◊ **Can the client afford me?** This connects to the question above, as far as working on projects that your conscience can handle. In other words, think twice about taking on someone's grandma who has to dig into her retirement funds to hire you to write the story of her life — no matter how interesting it is. If you're in this long enough, you'll have a situation where someone is willing to go to extreme lengths to get the money. Unless you believe they have a blockbuster in their hands, you might want to pass.

◊ **Am I being paid enough?** This may seem like an obvious question, but it's amazing how often it can be overlooked. If you have issues with self-worth, you need to pay particular attention to this one. Otherwise, every time you take a job for less than you're worth — without at least putting up a little fight — it will leave a residue of regret and resentment that will build into burnout or meltdown. Furthermore, you will continue to attract people who can't pay you what you're worth — because that's the message you're putting out!

() **Am I able to say "no" if it's the best thing for both parties?** This ties everything else up. It's a state of character that is (understandably) difficult for some to achieve, especially early on. But for long-term success, it's imperative. The reason why this question is so loaded is because within it lie several other key questions: (1) Do I trust life to work out for the best? (2) Do I believe I can be successful being in integrity? (3) Do I have an "abundance" mentality, or a "lack" mentality? (4) Do I believe in myself? (5) Do I believe in my work? (6) Do I believe there's a "Plan"? Contemplate it for yourself and see what you discover.

Working for Free or Future "Big Paydays"

You're going to have clients come to you and offer to let you write their project — that they're sure will be a smash hit — for free. If you really believe it's the next *Titanic*, or *Matrix*, or *Lord of the Rings*, then go for it. I've had many clients make me this offer, and so far I haven't found a blockbuster in the bunch.

I have a simple rule: I work for professional-level pay.

Your definition of "professional-level pay" will grow as your business and reputation does, but it's a good practice to determine what that is — and stick to it.

You can't cover your monthly nut if you're working for peanuts.

"Getting in Bed" with Your Client

This is a term that used to be popular in Hollywood. I think it's an appropriate metaphor, since a business relationship can be very much like a marriage. If you're writing an entire script or doing a healthy rewrite, you will likely be in contact — sometimes intimately — with this person for a while. And if the relationship is a good one, it might lead to a lot more work down the road. So before you take the final plunge into this partnership, ask yourself a few more questions:

◊ How will you feel being associated with this person — and this project — if it becomes a known quantity in the industry? Imagine yourself at a gathering and an executive at Fox recognizes your name in connection with this script. Do you cringe at the thought? Do you make excuses, tell the executive you had no "creative control" over it, so you can't take credit for what's on the page? Remember, this isn't about a one-shot gig. You're building a business, and quite possibly a reputation. Begin with the end in mind, and let that guide your choices.

◊ Is your client committed to this project, to this art, to this business? Or is he just some rich dentist from Des Moines who's only interested in going to parties and picking up babes? (I realize, for some of you, that might actually be a plus.)

◊ Does the prospect of working with them excite you or fill you with a strange kind of dread? Do you want to spend the next several weeks or months working with them? Would you be afraid if you met them in a dark alley?

◊ Finally, trust your gut instinct. Close your eyes and ask yourself if this is a good deal? Is this project going to benefit you and the client in a win-win way? Listen to your inner voice, feel what your body is telling you.

A Final Note on Client Screening

I know this seems like a lot to go through for a script doctor job. But I can tell you from experience that I could have avoided some pretty stress-inducing, life-sucking situations had I heeded my inner voice instead of my outer ambitions.

Trust me, the money isn't worth it.

Believe that you can attract positive, creative, inspiring projects full of potential — and reject soul-crushing, mind-numbing, anxiety-producing ones — and you will be amazed at the opportunities that show up in your life.

The Different Services of a Script Doctor

As a script doctor, there are several additional services you will be able to provide your clients, all of which take advantage of your writing skills:

Loglines. A great logline is essential in selling scripts. The writer needs it to get a good agent or producer interested. The agent and producer need it to sell to the executives. And the executives need it to sell to their bosses. I see many writers who lack the ability to put together a compelling logline, so this is an area of need. If you fancy yourself as a wordsmith, you can offer this service. If you don't have this skill, read lots of loglines.

Synopses. More and more, writers are discovering the need to have strong synopses of their scripts in order to submit them (especially online). And as I mentioned before, this is a talent that most writers don't have in abundance. It requires a different skill that is as much about marketing and selling as it is narrative writing. As a script consultant you will offer the service of analyzing a client's synopsis. As a script doctor, you will offer the service of writing the synopsis for them. This will require you to know what a good synopsis looks and feels like, what its function is, and how to create these convincing little sales pitches. The best way to learn this skill is to read lots of synopses. Check out the "links" page at *www.scriptwritercentral.com* for online sites that have sample synopses. Study them. Master their structure.

Outlines. A clear, structurally sound story outline, where all the beats work to create a compelling narrative, is an invaluable tool in developing a good script. Unfortunately, many writers don't start with one, and thus find themselves having to rewrite 120 pages over and over — instead of five or ten pages. As a script doctor, you can help them take their initial concept and craft it into a bulletproof beat outline that lays the plot out in a clear three-act structure. But I must warn you: creating a fresh, compelling story filled with twists, turns, and all the necessary plot permutations is no easy task. In fact, that is the crux of the whole thing. A great story, with only average dialogue and description, will sell faster than a bunch of brilliant writing on a bad story. The *story* is the hardest part. So don't take these jobs lightly. Don't be fooled by the minimal page count. You may only write five pages, but it may take you several weeks to nail down the beats that will fill those blank sheets. Master this skill, however, and you could become a writer-in-demand.

Treatments. A treatment is where you add flesh and blood to the bony beats you created in the outline. Here is where you dimensionalize the characters, flesh out the theme, and find the style and tone of a piece. There are two types of treatments — one for the writer's eyes only, and one to use as a marketing tool (to sell the script to producers or sell the executive in a development deal, so they'll let the writer go to first draft). I have found this service to be of great benefit to my clients in several instances. When a writer is stuck at the development stage, or can't get past the first draft, I've been hired to create a new treatment for the project — from which the writer will be able to easily create another draft of the script. This process is a less expensive way for a client to utilize your storytelling skills (the alternative being that you write the whole script), and it also allows the writer to keep writing — and grow in the process. I have also created treatments for producers who then used them as selling tools to raise money for the screenplay development — or to sell it outright as a pitch. A good book on writing treatments is *Writing Treatments that Sell* by Ken Atchity and Chi-li Wong.

Rewrites. Whenever a client brings you a completed script and wants you to develop it in a new direction, or add or delete significant elements, that constitutes a rewrite — not a polish. I say this because some producers will try to tell you it's just a polish, pay you accordingly, then proceed to have you gut the second act. I'm sorry, that ain't gonna fly. When you "polish" something, you do not change its inherent structure. When you bring your shoes in to get "polished," you don't expect them to tear out the soles and re-size them to fit your six-year old, right? You need to be clear what it is you're being asked to do, then charge and plan accordingly. You can also offer rewrites on treatments and outlines as well.

So where do you look for rewrite jobs? My experience has been that clients who have banged their heads against the wall draft after draft, or have just run out of steam, are the ones most open to this service. And if your insights and solutions on their script are truly inspired, it will give you all the more leverage. Think of it like going into a producer to pitch your take on a story idea — in hopes of landing a writing job. When you give a client your "take" on their script, you are in a sense auditioning for a potential writing job. So give them and their script your all. That way, it's a win-win. If they hire you to rewrite their script, you both know you're on the same page and the script should improve. If they're not interested in hiring you to do a rewrite, you have at least given them massive value as a script consultant — and that will usually come back to you in the form of repeat business and referrals.

There's an ethical line that you must respect, however. If your client is a writer, and has aspirations to make their living as such, then your first obligation is helping them become a better writer. That usually entails doing the rewrite, and suffering through it, themselves. So if they're interested, ask them some probing questions to determine what the best course of action would be. Encourage them to do the rewrite, to push through the pain. Make it clear that you have their best interests in mind. Suggest that they go home, reread the notes, and "sleep on it" for a while. Then, if they are still adamant about hiring you to rewrite, you can accept the offer with a clear conscience.

I know it might be tough to tell your client something that could cost you a job, but it's good business in the long run — and it's just the right thing to do. Your client will really appreciate your honesty and integrity, and be more likely to refer other potential prospects to you.

Polishes. We've already discussed what this is *not*. A polish does not generally mess with the structure of a script. It deals primarily with juicing up the dialogue and description, clarifying or changing the tone, and sometimes developing scenes without major modifications to plot. That doesn't mean that a polish can't have a significant impact on a script. Change enough dialogue and you can radically change the meaning of a piece and the content of the characters. Add enough humor and you can make the difference between a pass or a sale. Make sure you are clear about the client's expectations. Outline exactly what you intend to do. Otherwise you can find yourself doing a rewrite or several polishes — for the price of one. You can also offer polishing services on treatments and synopses. All the same points discussed above about ethics apply equally here. Just make sure it's really the right thing to do.

Then do it to the max!

Developing a complete script. At this stage you're no longer merely a script doctor, you're a professional screenwriter — and hopefully a credited one. I never develop a complete script from scratch anymore without screenplay credit. And if I'm the one doing all the writing, I take sole screenplay credit and share story credit with the client. Not that these points aren't negotiable — it's just that no one has paid me enough yet to be a complete ghost.

Obviously, this service combines all of the others. In this instance, you will be shaping the core concept, creating the compelling outline and/or treatment, and writing the screenplay. You may be writing it solo, taking notes from a client, or writing it with your client — in which case you need to outline very clear boundaries. If you've got a client who likes to talk a lot, you could find yourself working eight hours and getting a couple pages done.

We'll talk specifically about negotiating later, but there are a couple things to keep in mind when putting together this kind of deal:

o **Credit** — Ask for what you deserve, unless they're paying you to be anonymous. There's nothing worse than watching the script you wrote give someone else the career you desire — when you could have negotiated credit.

o **Fee** — In a perfect world, you'd get WGA minimum. But alas, this is not a perfect world. Most of the writing jobs you'll get as a script doctor (at least in the beginning) will be non-union. If you're in the union, you'll probably have to write under a pseudonym (but don't tell the WGA I told you), or come up with a creative financing arrangement that gives you union rates. (Check with the WGA for the most up-to-date options.)

Book adaptations. All of the above applies here. But you now have the additional challenge of re-imagining several hundred pages of dense book material into a 120-page sparsely written screenplay. This is no easy task. Even with books that are obviously written to be movies (which is most of them nowadays), you'll still have your work cut out for you.

Giving It Your All

Writing is very subjective and many of your clients (especially those from outside of the business) wouldn't know the difference between your best writing and just average. At some point in your script doctor career, it might be tempting to slack off a little, to do just "average" work. You might even be able to get away with it — for a while. But that is truly a losing proposition. You'll not only create bad scripts that don't sell, you'll become a bad writer who doesn't work. And if you consistently give less than you know you can, it will eat away at your integrity and vitality, finally leading to cynicism and burnout.

On the other hand, if you give it your all — treating every project like it's the greatest and every client like they're the most important — you'll become a better writer, build a better business, and create better odds that your clients' scripts will sell.

And that's the best kind of satisfaction — and advertising — you could ask for.

Chapter Summary

◊ Being a script consultant offers a great opportunity for getting writing work.

◊ If you're a writer, let your client know you are a script doctor. Don't be shy!

◊ If you're "doctoring" a client's script, remember it's *their* script. If you're receiving a "written by" credit, you usually have much more creative license.

◊ Clarify your overall role in the writing process — and put it in writing. In regards to the actual writing work, clearly outline the details — and have your client sign off on that too!

◊ Make sure to ask the important, and sometimes difficult, questions of your client and yourself before beginning a project. It will save you time, save them money, and save you both headaches and heartaches.

◊ The majority of scripts you work on will never sell. Don't expect failure, but prepare yourself — and, in some cases, your client — for that possibility. This way, you can both benefit from the experience regardless of the outcome.

◊ Early on in your career, you'll probably need to take whatever job comes your way. But at some point, for your sanity and soul's sake, you may need to decide on a level of material below which you will not work on.

◊ Work for professional-level pay (based on your level of experience), unless you are sure your client's project is the next *Titanic* or *Lord of the Rings*.

◊ Before you "partner," or decide to co-write, with your client, make sure you've asked yourself the hard questions to determine if this "marriage" will work.

◊ Believe that you can attract positive, creative, inspiring projects full of potential — and reject soul-crushing, mind-numbing, anxiety-producing ones.

◊ Different services of a script doctor: loglines, synopses, outlines, treatments, rewrites, polishes, developing complete scripts, book adaptations.

◊ Give it your all — treat every project like it's the most important and every client equally well.

Chapter Eight

"...Our belief was that if we kept putting great products in front of customers, they would continue to open their wallets."
— *Steve Jobs, founder Apple, Pixar*

Marketing Clients' Work

To Market or Not to Market — That is the Question

So your client has completed her screenplay — and it's actually quite good. She doesn't have an agent, so she asks for your help. You're not an agent or a producer — maybe you're not even that connected in town. Yet here is this writer asking you to help them get representation or sell their script. What do you do?

This is a controversial subject for many, who believe script consultants shouldn't market their clients' scripts. This stems largely from the illegitimate act of some script consultants who advertise that they'll help clients get their scripts into the hands of buyers — if the script is good enough — then don't fulfill this promise. It's just a sales gimmick for them. But offering to help your clients create a marketing package and strategy, and assisting them in getting their scripts into the marketplace, is a legitimate service — as long as you are willing to do the work necessary to follow through.

Some will still disagree with me, believing that to offer marketing services is somehow unethical, an abuse of a script consultant's position in the industry (or perceived position). In my opinion, this reveals an ignorance of basic business principles. Just because marketing isn't your main focus doesn't mean you can't expand your business model to include it. Did Sam Walton (founder of WalMart) start out offering everything WalMart currently sells? Did Bill Gates start out focusing on multiple software programs and video games? Of course not. They built a core business, listened to their customers needs, and expanded to meet them. Many of the most successful organizations and entrepreneurs follow this practice.

If you do choose to add marketing to your basket of services, make sure you know what you're doing. There are many ways to market a script, besides getting an agent. Get an education on the subject. Read *Guerilla Marketing for Writers* by Jay Conrad Levinson, or *Getting Everything You Can Out of All You've Got* by Jay Abraham, considered to be the top marketing expert in the country.

The insights and information these guys offer will blow you away.

Your Reputation

Another question arises: "Do I market everyone's script that asks me, or do I select only the ones I believe could sell?" I would once again return to the Sam Walton example. Did he only sell soup to the starving, or to anyone who wanted to buy it? If your clients want the service, and you've presented it honestly and ethically — even telling them, in some cases, that you don't think the project is ready to go out — then you give your clients what they want. You're not their mother, you're their script consultant. If, however, you're planning to give the script to your own contacts, and put your name on the line, then only offer that on scripts you believe in 100 %.

The Marketing Package

We've already discussed most of the elements of a marketing package, which can include any of the following:

◦ Logline
◦ Synopsis
◦ Brief list of credits, awards
◦ Query Letter (which contains all of the above)
◦ Treatment

- The Script
- A targeted list of agents, producers, and production companies

You can offer to create these marketing tools as separate services or as part of an overall package. It all depends on the needs of the client.

Your Client's Marketing Plan

Once a client enlists your marketing services, and you have created the necessary marketing tools (as mentioned above), it is now time to create a plan of attack. This should be laid out on a timeline that lists specifically what you intend to do for the writer and when, what the writer needs to do for himself, and what any other team members should do (agent, manager, attorney). A three- to six-month plan is usually a good time frame to work with.

The following is a very skeletal example of what a four-month timeline might look like:

- January: Create marketing tools and target list
- February: Submit "package" to top third of target list, follow up, get feedback, make adjustments
- March: Submit revised package/script to second third of target list, follow up, get feedback, make adjustments, take meetings (client), make deal or secure agent
- April: Submit final revised package to bottom third of target list, follow up, get feedback, client take meetings (client), make deal, or secure an agent

As you can see, it's possible (though not probable) that a deal will be struck or an agent procured before the plan is fully executed. If a deal is made, the plan is fulfilled. If an agent is landed, the plan can be altered to include the agent's involvement (which will probably include your dismissal).

The Target List

The key word here is "target." You don't want to throw the script out to every company in town. It's more expensive and time-consuming. And it doesn't give the material the respect it deserves — which I believe has an impact on how it's received.

You should have the latest version of the *Hollywood Creative Directory* (and hopefully a warm-market list of contacts). Go through it, page-by-page, locating the companies who have done similar projects as your client's. But also include some companies who have done a lot of one thing, because they might be looking for a change. It's also a good idea to keep up to date on what companies are buying. You can get this information from the industry trades, the *Hollywood Reporter*, *Variety*, and online at sites that list spec script sales (check the "links" page at *www.scriptwritercentral.com*).

Once you have compiled this list — which is a time-consuming process, as you can imagine — break it down into an A, B, and C list, the "A's" being the top choices. Go over it with your client and make sure it reflects their "dream companies" — then have them sign off on it. I repeat, have them sign off on it. Even the most honest, decent individuals have a strange ability to forget what they've agreed to if it's not in writing.

The Physical Marketing

I must provide a word of warning here. If your client wants you to do the actual physical marketing (as opposed to just creating the marketing package), they are enlisting you to do the work of an agent. That requires a lot of grunt work (calling, submitting, follow-up) and is very time-consuming. Unless you're getting paid well for it, or have a percentage of the script (and are passionate about it), I would advise against it. The alternative is to act in an "advisory" role, hire a marketing partner, or refer your client to a company that specializes in these types of services.

If you decide to handle the physical marketing, here are some helpful hints:

Making the Calls. If you're going to do this right, you can't fire-hose the industry with your client's package and expect any kind of effective reaction. If you want a warm response, you must begin by making *cold calls*.

Make sure you have your 30-second to two-minute pitch ready to go (or written down in front of you), begin with the top third of the target list (the A-list), pick up the phone, and start dialing. If you haven't had a lot of experience in this, that's okay. It might be rough at first, but it gets easier. (You might even want to "practice" on some of the C-list before approaching your A-list.)

A few key things to keep in mind for the call:

◦ Request the agent or development exec by name, don't just ask for "someone in development." You'll probably get their secretary. That's fine.

◦ Treat everyone you speak to, from the operator to the assistant, with the utmost respect. They are the gatekeepers. They wield the power to keep you out of the tower, or let you in. And they might be running a studio some day.

◦ Tell them you are marketing your client's script, and give them the brief pitch (usually the 30-second one first). If they're interested, you can give them a longer version or answer questions about the project.

◦ ABC — Always Be Closing. It's amazing how many people pitch their project and don't ask for what they want. If the executive doesn't outright reject you, ask if you can send the script. If they hem and haw, don't back down right away. Assure them they'll enjoy the read. Remind them of some of the script's hookier elements. If they still resist, sincerely thank them for their time (they are usually so overworked) and be on your way.

◦ Keep it short and simple. Respect them and their time and they will be more likely to respect you.

If they aren't interested, you can still send them a query letter, making adjustments to deal with any objections they may have brought up. They may request a synopsis. Ask if you can send it via email. If not, get it into the snail mail ASAP.

If they tell you to send the script, you're in business.

Query Letters. For those who have rejected your phone pitch, or those you couldn't get through to, send query letters (which we've already discussed). If they accept email queries, definitely take that route. But make sure they accept them. Many agents and producers don't — and it will alienate them if you disregard their protocol.

Always submit to a specific person. Don't send letters to "development department" or "Mr. Agent." This is disrespectful and unprofessional, and will reflect poorly on your submission — if it doesn't get tossed in the round filing cabinet first.

Mailing the Script. Include a one-page cover letter, reminding them of your conversation, with a logline or brief synopsis to refresh them on the project. Make sure the script is clean, well-pressed, and not missing any pages. On the envelope, address it to a specific person, and write at the bottom "REQUESTED MATERIAL."

Keeping a Log. You can buy programs like Power Tracker, or create your own format, but keep good records of phone calls, query letters, and script submissions. This will come in handy in a variety of ways. If your client wants to know what you've been doing, you can show them the list. If your client gets an agent, the agent will want to know where the material has been. And if, god forbid, someone "steals" the material (which rarely happens), you have a paper trail that will lead to the bandit's front door.

Following Up. Some of the places you submit to will call to inform you of a "pass" or send you rejection letters. After a few weeks, you can start making follow-up calls to the companies you haven't heard from and see if they've looked at the material. Try to get specific details about why they passed. It's tough. Many development people are so buried in material, they don't remember why they passed, or have only vague answers. Probe them if it feels appropriate. But don't push too hard. You want them to read future material, you don't want to end up on their "Life Is Too Short" list.

Client Feedback Report. Keep track of the feedback, and compile a report for your client. Sit down with them and discuss the possible solutions. Can the script be rewritten or polished to deal with the issues coming up? If you're having problems getting the script read, you need to reevaluate the pitch materials (logline, synopsis).

At this point, you and your client might decide to put the marketing on hold until the necessary revisions are made on the script. That's fine. Don't rush it. Make the changes, then begin phase two.

Phase Two. This is essentially the same as the first part of the marketing campaign, only now you will be targeting the second third of the list (the "B" category). You will also most likely be continuing the follow-up process from the first phase. At this point, you can also begin to implement *alternative strategies* to bring attention to your client's material. There are many ways to market a script besides just the traditional submission route. Use your imagination. Read *Wishcraft* by Barbara Sher, who teaches some great brainstorming techniques to get you outside of the box.

If the script sells or lands representation, hallelujah! If it doesn't, don't sweat it. Just get the feedback and make the necessary changes again.

Getting the Client Meetings. In some cases, (if you're handling the physical marketing) you'll get very good feedback from the executive, but they'll still pass. Ask them if they'd be willing to refer the writer to an agent or meet the writer in person. If they're interested, set up the meeting.

This is usually an agent's job. But if you've decided to take this role, you might as well do it right. In this way, even if the script doesn't sell, you have found opportunities to add tremendous value to the client's life.

Phase Three. Compile the feedback into a Writer's Report, consult with the client on whether or not a rewrite is in order, and continue the process with the bottom third of the target list (the C-list). Follow up. Get feedback. Help the client set up meetings. Be creative. And hopefully make a deal.

There's also some wisdom in marketing the project to the C-list first, making changes to the script based on feedback, then working your way up to the A-list. The only problem is that your client might sell it to a C-list company — and never know if she could've had an A-list buyer.

If the script doesn't sell, don't dismay. Most "specs" (screenplays written speculatively) don't sell. That doesn't mean the experience can't be a positive, educational, and productive one for your client — especially if they get some meetings out of it. In rare cases, a great writing sample may even lead to "assignments" for your client.

Hiring Staff. If reading all of this gives you a headache, don't fret, you're not alone. For many creative people, this kind of work is not appealing in the least. And it may not even be fiscally efficient to invest your time in it if you could be doing more lucrative script consulting or script doctoring jobs. So, as already suggested, hire someone else to do the grunt work. You can still oversee the operation, supervise the more creative aspects, and participate in the creative meetings.

There's a saying in time management that I strive to live by, "Do only what only you can do." In other words, if someone else can do it as good as or better than you, delegate it. That's how you grow your business.

Partnerships

At some point, a project may come along that you have a genuine passion for. You just "click" with the material and the client — and decide you want to be involved in a more ongoing basis. In this case, you have an opportunity to create a partnership rather than just a work-for-hire. You may do the marketing for free — in lieu of a percentage of the project's future proceeds and/or a producer credit on it. Or you may charge less for the consulting or script doctor work, and take a percentage instead. There are many ways to form a partnership.

You'll probably want to consult with an attorney to create the agreement, but there are a few key things you can begin discussing with your prospective partner right away:

○   How much you'll get paid, when, and in what form. This is where you determine what your "up front" fees will be for working on the project, what the pay schedule will be, and what percentage of future proceeds you'll get.

○   What role you'll each take in the project's development, marketing, and production — and what credit you'll receive. Are you going to share "written by" and/or "story by" credit with your client? Do you want to be a producer on the project? Do you want to have first crack at a rewrite once it's bought?

○   The duration of the partnership, and the exit strategy (in case things don't go as planned).

Another way to assist your client in marketing their script is to refer them to an online organization that specializes in marketing scripts to the entertainment community. Check out the "links" page at *www.scriptwritercentral.com* for the best sites. Many writers have gained representation or sold their screenplays this way.

A Final Note on Marketing Your Clients' Scripts

If you sincerely believe you can help your clients get their material into the hands of buyers, by all means pursue it. Just proceed mindfully and ethically, being sure not to make false promises or build up false hope.

Bottom line, we need to do everything we can to pry open the doors of Hollywood and help quality writers gain admission.

Chapter Summary

◊ Helping your clients create a marketing package and strategy, and assisting them in getting their scripts into the marketplace, is a legitimate service — as long as you're willing to do the work necessary to follow through.

◊ Just because marketing isn't your main focus doesn't mean you can't expand your business to include it — as well as other products and services. Just make sure you get an education on the subject and can provide real value.

◊ Your reputation is one of your most important assets. If you plan on giving a client's script to your contacts, make sure that you believe in it 100%.

◊ The "Marketing Package" can include the following: logline, synopsis, brief list of credits and awards, query letter (which contains all of the above), treatment, script, targeted list of agents, producers, and production companies.

◊ Create a clear marketing plan, outlining the stages and dates of execution.

◊ Don't flood the market with the script, create a "target list" for submissions.

◊ When determining which companies are good prospects, focus on those who have done similar projects and those who may be looking for a change.

◊ Create an A, B, and C list, the "A's" being the top choices.

◊ Unless you are getting paid very well, own a percentage, or are extremely passionate about your client's script, it's probably *not* a good idea to do the actual physical marketing (which is an agent's job).

◊ If you feel particularly passionate about your client's project, and decide to form a partnership, make sure you evaluate the situation completely, outline the relationship clearly — and have your client sign off on it!

Act 2

Putting It
Into Action

◊ Creating Your Space

◊ Tools of the Trade

◊ File It Away

◊ Getting Organized

Chapter Nine

"To be prepared is half the victory."
— *Miguel de Cervantes*

"Before everything else, getting ready is the secret to success."
— *Henry Ford*

Setting Up Shop

Creating Your Space

A professional needs a "workshop" to ply her trade in. This is an important space. This is where the "magic" happens. So it must be created with care and guarded against the "lesser elements" of the outside world, which will try to break in and kidnap the muse. "Appealing workplaces are to be avoided," says writer Annie Dillard. "One wants a room with no view, so imagination can meet memory in the dark."

Your "space" can be a separate room or an external office. But it can also be a corner of a room (bedroom, living room, or garage). Whatever you can manage, make it a dedicated place for your work.

When you create such a workspace, your mind is less likely to wander and feel scattered during work hours. You tend to be more productive, more professional, and on purpose. On a slightly more "cosmic" level, when you create a space for something, it tends to attract things to fill it. When I created my official "office," new work opportunities seemed to magically manifest to make good use of that space. I was sending a message to the universe that said, in effect, "I'm ready — bring it on!" And the universe responded with, "I thought you'd never ask."

How you treat your work on every level determines in no small part how successful your business will be. Think of it like this: if your business was a relationship and you treated that person the way you treat your business, how long would they stay around? Treat your business with the utmost respect — including a respectable workspace — and it will not only "stay around," it'll be there to support you when you need it most.

Tools of the Trade

So what should you fill your new "space" with? What do you need in order to perform like a professional script consultant and/or script doctor? The good news is you don't need much.

Here's a list of the basics:

○ **Something to type with.** Typewriter, word processor, computer. Don't be cheap here. Get good quality if you can afford it. It really does pay off. Also, if you work on a computer, it's worthwhile to have a laptop for your "office away from the office." (Read: Starbucks, or whatever coffee shop you frequent.) If you work at home, you're likely to experience "cabin fever" at some point. I've found that taking a break and relocating to the nearest coffee house allows me to get a fresh perspective on the work — and remember that I'm part of the human race. And depending on where you live, it's not a bad place to meet new prospects (for business and pleasure).

○ **Desk references.** Dictionary, thesaurus, elements of style for screenplays, movie guides with plotlines, spec script marketplace, *Hollywood Creative Directory*, the trades, other scripts, and plenty of books on screenwriting, treatment writing, script marketing, etc. Nowadays, you can find most of this information on the Internet.

○ **Internet access.** For the above-mentioned references. Research. Email. Script Downloading. Get high-speed if you can afford it. Once you do, you won't believe you ever survived without it.

◊ **Fax machine.** We're moving toward a completely digital age, where eventually all paper will be transferred via the Internet. But in the meantime, it's a good idea to have a fax machine. If you can have a dedicated line, all the better.

◊ **A phone with an unlimited long-distance plan.** Get a flat-rate long-distance plan that doesn't change no matter how many calls you make. Nowadays you can get an all-inclusive plan for about $40. You don't want to be watching your minutes while you're talking to a client. And you don't want to be resisting making the necessary phone calls just because they're long-distance. If you start getting clients in other countries, get an international plan as well. This will save you a bundle. Calls that are normally $3.00 will cost you thirty cents or less instead.

◊ **Office supplies.** The basics, stapler, pens, paper clips, files, file holders, candy bars.

◊ **Book and video library.** Beyond the above-mentioned books, it's a good idea to have a thoroughly developed library at your disposal. Books on all aspects of the business, as well as those on psychology, mythology, philosophy, geography, and any other "ologies" or "ographies" that interest you. Likewise, an abundant collection of videos and/or DVDs is a must for any student of film. I can't tell you how many times it helped to be able to grab a movie off the shelf and refer to a specific scene in a script analysis or writing job. *Don't be cheap on your education — Invest in it regularly.* Anyone who has become a true success in their field understands and practices this principle.

File It Away

Create a good filing system, one for long-term reference, and one for easy access. I have a filing cabinet under my desk, which allows me to grab certain files right away. I have two other filing cabinets in my closet, which contain files I don't need to get into as often.

However you set it up, create a system that gives you maximum efficiency, organization, and ease of retrieval. You will be grateful come tax time that you have been keeping your receipts and pay stubs (or copies of checks). And you will realize the value of good filing when something comes up with a past client or an old project that requires you to access the records from that job (contracts, scripts, notes, etc.).

Getting Organized

We all have different working and living styles, and that's fine. I'm not here to make you feel guilty about that experiment in chaos theory called your office. But my experience has shown me that successful people in just about every field keep an organized, efficient workspace and lifestyle. Everything basically has its place, and is placed back when it is done being used. Things are easily found when needed. And important documents don't go missing — requiring panicked search-and-rescue missions at the eleventh hour. All of this conspires to create a generally peaceful, productive work environment, which contributes to more effective work, that finally adds up to a more prosperous business.

I know it's not easy. Our outer conditions usually reflect our inner state, so attempting to "straighten up our office" oftentimes means straightening up our lives in deeper ways. Whatever it takes, it's worth the price — even if you have to hire someone else to do it.

"Pay now or pay later." Just remember that if you pay later, you'll have to pay with interest.

Chapter Summary

- A professional needs a "workshop" to ply her trade in. It must be created with care and guarded against the "lesser elements" of the outside world, which will try to break in and kidnap the muse.

- When you create a professional workspace, your mind is less likely to wander and feel scattered, you tend to be more productive, on purpose, and attract opportunities to make good use of it.

- Think of your business like a relationship: If you treated that person the way you treat your business, how long would they stay around?

- Basic tools: something to type with, desk reference, internet, fax machine, a phone with unlimited long-distance, office supplies, book/video library.

- Create a filing system that gives you maximum efficiency, organization, and ease of retrieval. You'll be grateful come tax time if you've kept your receipts or if something comes up with a client that requires a paper trail.

- Most successful people keep an organized, efficient workspace and lifestyle. This usually contributes to more efficient and effective work, which equals a more prosperous business.

- Because the state of our "outer life" tend to reflect our "inner life," cleaning up our office usually requires us to clean up our life in a deeper way; getting rid of the inner clutter and debris that has bogged us down and hindered us from achieving our full potential.

- If you can't bring yourself to the task of getting organized — hire someone who can. Pay now or pay later!

Chapter Ten

"A market is never saturated with a good product, but it is very quickly saturated with a bad one."
— Henry Ford

"Don't bring your need to the marketplace, bring your skill... If you need money, go to the bank, not the marketplace."
— Jim Rohn

Advertising and Marketing

To Catch the Big Fish, You Need a Strong Hook

We've already touched upon this concept, but it bears repeating — because without a clear understanding and implementation of this principle, your business is almost certainly destined to underperform in today's crowded marketplace. What we're talking about here is a Unique Selling Proposition (USP). In other words, you *must* position yourself and your business in a way that hasn't been done before, in a way that makes people stand up and take notice, in a way that says you are the best in your niche of this industry.

Think of it like a great movie. It could be about something we've already seen, but if it's got a good "hook," if it's presented in a fresh and compelling way, we will plunk down our ten bucks to see it. We had pizza delivery before Domino's. But they offered something more: Hot, fresh pizza delivered to your door in thirty minutes or less, or it's free. We had mail service before FedEx, but they filled a need we didn't even know we had: *When it absolutely, positively has to be there overnight.*

And we certainly had coffee shops before Starbucks. They didn't just create a new and fresh way to serve coffee, they created an entire culture that has literally become part of the lexicon of our social conversation. Statements like "a venti latte" are as familiar to us as "please pass the salt." I'm not saying you have to create a whole new culture around script consulting. But you do need to offer something others don't, or offer the same thing in a fresh way — or you are putting yourself at a serious disadvantage.

So what differentiates you or makes you the pre-eminent script consultant in your corner of this business? After reading the chapter on "specializing" you should have some idea of what you offer that's special. Maybe it's not a specific talent or knowledge base, but rather a "process" or "service." Maybe you're an actor, or have access to actors, and can provide "script readings" and audience feedback. Many great playwrights have developed their plays through a similar workshopping for-mat. Or maybe you're an improvisational comedian and can improvise your client's script to mine the comedic gold. There are unlimited possibilities here.

Be creative.

Think innovation.

Once you develop your USP, however, you need to deliver on it. If Domino's always delivered their pizza cold and an hour late, their doors wouldn't stay open long. (They couldn't afford to give all that pizza away free!). If FedEx could no longer deliver it overnight, they'd be out of the mail delivery business. You can make all sorts of false promises and get away with it in the beginning, but with that weak foundation your business will crumble. You're a not a politician trying to get into office, where you're then free to break all your promises.

Try to live by the motto, "Under Promise, Over Deliver."

Marketing vs. Advertising

Many people will take out an ad and think they're "marketing" their business. But all they're doing is "advertising," which is only one small component of marketing.

Advertising is advertising. Marketing is the complete approach to how you let the public know about your product and/or service in a way that compels them to purchase it. Marketing can include advertising — be it print, internet, direct mail, or other more costly forms — but it can also be building strategic alliances, forming partnerships, writing articles, teaching workshops, joining networks.

Every time you connect with another human being in any way, you are engaging in a potential marketing moment.

That doesn't mean you're like a used car salesman, always hard-selling everyone. Quite the opposite. Effective marketing is about respecting your potential clients, getting their permission to introduce your product or service, creating a fiduciary relationship with them so you can discover how they can best be served — and then meeting their needs in a way that adds real value to their lives.

Free or Inexpensive Marketing

Marketing doesn't have to cost much — or anything at all in some cases. In Jay Conrad Levinson's *Guerilla Marketing* books, he gives hundreds of marketing ideas that cost little or nothing to implement. Your greatest asset in marketing is not your money but your mind. And the fact that you're naturally creative and imaginative (I'm assuming, since you're in this business) will give you an added advantage in coming up with unique ways to get the word out.

> **Write articles.** Do you have a unique angle on screenwriting or script analysis? How about writing an article — or a series of them — for the various screenwriting magazines and Internet e-zines. It's free advertising. And it's the best kind, because it doesn't feel like advertising. What's more, it positions you as an expert, an authority. And in some cases, you'll even get paid!

> **Write a book.** I read at least one new screenwriting book a year. There will never be too many of them. If you have something interesting to say about the art, craft, or business of screenwriting, try putting it into a book. If you can't find a publisher, do it yourself! There are numerous books on self-publishing that walk you through it step-by-step. It's become much easier than you think.

Contests / Giveaways. How many screenwriting networks, chat rooms, and internet sites have you stumbled across on the web? If you haven't spotted at least a dozen, you need to get out more often. Join these groups, talk about your services in the chat rooms, have a trivia contest and give away a free consultation to the winner.

Speaking. There are almost as many screenwriting events as there are writer websites. Try and get a speaking engagement at one. This is a great way to put yourself in front of potential clients. You can offer them for free or even make a few bucks doing it. If you've written some articles, or a book, this will be even easier — and you can sell some books while you're at it!

Website. A website in and of itself isn't a very effective marketing tool in the overpopulated cyberspace. But a great website, regularly updated, with products and interactive elements, can lure prospects in and keep them coming back. Create alliances with other companies in your field and create cross-marketing with hyperlinks on each other's sites.

Teaching. In all my discussions with script consultants, the number one form of marketing that built their business was teaching. Most consultants received the majority of their clients from the classes they facilitated. It makes sense. It's a great way for prospects to see what kind of script consultant they're dealing with. It takes a lot of the guesswork out. And, like some consultants, you might even find yourself building a seminar business that eclipses your consultant work — and takes you around the world!

"You have to say 'yes' to everything at an early stage," says Chris Vogler. "You don't turn down requests to go and speak here and there. You just get it out there. You develop a reputation through multiple exposures. Part of my secret was writing this whole seven page memo, which could be faxed and xeroxed and it was all over town and plagiarized and I knew that. But I knew it was also working for me. It was building this reputation. Now most people know who I am. When I go into a studio meeting, the young executive says, "Oh, yes, I used you as a footnote in my college paper" and the older executive says, "Oh, I remember you from the old days." They have seen my name on something, because I wrote so many memos. I filled several filing cabinets with research and memos and just straight up two-page analyses of ten thousand screenplays."

These are just a few of the ideas. There are hundreds, maybe thousands, more that are already widely known and used — and a virtually unlimited number of possibilities yet to be revealed.

Where to Advertise

There are the obvious places, such as screenwriting and general writing magazines (both print and online) — and it's important to create a presence here — but these are so crowded with other script consultant ads, you'll have a hard time standing out.

So where can you, as a script consultant, advertise where you won't be fighting for the reader's attention?

- ◊ **Actor forums.** Magazines, workshops, schools, online e-zines. Many actors are also writers (or are writing something as a vehicle for themselves). They need good script consultants or script doctors. And there is much less competition in these forums.

- ◊ **Entertainment executive forums.** What magazines do entertainment executives read? What organizations are they a part of? What online sites do they frequent? These are all potential platforms for advertising.

- ◊ **Professionals in other fields.** This is the most exciting one. There are thousands of professionals in other businesses (doctors, dentists, lawyers, politicians, entrepreneurs, etc.) who have aspirations to be part of this industry. A percentage of them are writers or have at least written (or attempted to write) something. And some of them just want to produce. What's more, they usually can afford to pay for your services.

So what magazines or professional journals do these people read? What organizations do they belong to? What online sites do they frequent? Tap into these networks correctly and you can grow your business into six figures in no time!

Reel Networking

We cannot walk this path alone and hope for any kind of lasting success or fulfill-ment. And the work of a script consultant or writer is primarily a solo one, so the danger of spending most of our lives as cave dwellers is strong. This is not only mentally and emotionally prohibitive, but financially as well — especially in the beginning of our business. We need to spend time cultivating relationships, building alliances, meeting others in our field and related ones. Judith Searle, known for her script consultant work using the Enneagram, says that "developing a network of others in the field is a very good idea. Linda Seger has done this brilliantly and connected me with a lot of people. I knew her through Women in Film, she came to my workshop, gave me a quote for my book. She's been really generous. Being generous to others in the field is a good thing, because it comes back to you."

I know, for some, networking is a four-letter word. But this stems largely from a limited perception of what it is. For many of us, networking is a superficial hand-slapping, elbow-rubbing, card-carrying, shmooze-a-thon that leaves us needing a good shower afterwards. But this is only one kind of networking and, in my opinion, the wrong kind. It brings out the worst in us; the needy, pushy, self-centered part that only wants to talk about itself. And it's usually not very fruitful. All those business cards you hand out usually only serve to make the trashman's load a little heavier. Think about it — how many of the cards you receive do you actually follow up on?

But it doesn't have to be this way. What if, instead of feeling like you've "sold out" while you're making others feel "sold to," you could make them feel genuinely good about themselves and about you — and in turn, feel good about yourself? The method is so easy, you might be tempted to brush it off as simplistic. But here it is, in a nutshell: *Be more interested in them, than in yourself.*

That's right, make them more important than you. Talk about them more than you talk about yourself. In fact, don't talk about yourself at all. If they ask, deflect it back to them — which is the exact opposite of what we normally do. Our natural tendency is to make everything they say about *us*. They mention how their grandma is dying and we launch into a soliloquy about how our grandma almost died too, how it drove us to drink, how we hit rock bottom, had a blinding revelation about the nature of life, then rallied our resolve to nurse poor old Nanna back from the dead and start a profitable business in the process — and by the way, here's my card! And when we look back up, our guest's eyes have either glazed over or they've long since departed — and we're left talking to an attentive, albeit unresponsive, ficus tree.

Get to know who *they* are. That is your mission, should you accept it. Then once you know what they do and what they need, ask them this question: *"How can I know if someone I meet is a good prospect for you?"* Did you catch that? It's not, *"Do you know any good prospects for me?"* Which is what they're expecting. This question might take them aback. In fact, it might be the first time anyone — even in their own family — has asked them such a thing? What you've basically just done is said that you, a relative stranger, would like to help them become more successful. Again, the complete opposite of what normally occurs.

Now if you do this, do you think this person is going to feel "sold to"? Do you think they're going to feel put upon and be looking for the nearest exit? No way. In fact, they're probably going to offer to buy you a drink. And why not? You've just spent the whole time talking about *them*, showing genuine interest in *their* success, offering to help *them* achieve their goals (without strings), and actually listening, really listening. And here's the kicker — you're not going to ask them for anything in return! In fact, once you get this information, you'll excuse yourself and move on to your next networking prospect.

After you've done this with a few people, you now have the chance to take this one step further. Let's say your first networking prospect was a writer who's in the market for an agent who likes science fiction. And as you work the party, you meet an agent who happens to be looking for some similar projects. Bingo. You introduce the two of them, instantly making good on your intention to help them become more successful. Of course, you may not find the perfect match for your networking prospects. That's okay. Any attempt you make to connect them with others will be viewed as a generous act. And as you walk away from your matchmaking moment, what do you think they'll be talking about?

You.

They may not even know what you do yet. If they do, they'll probably be telling each other how great your work is — even though they've never seen it! That's the power of good networking.

But your job isn't done yet. Once you get home, you want to create a follow-up postcard. On it, you'll include your business name and slogan and a short note that says how much you enjoyed meeting them, and that you'll keep your eye open for any potential prospects for them. In other words, you once again offer to help *them*. No hard selling. In fact, no selling at all. Then you put the card in a hand-written envelope (to give it a personal touch), and drop it in the mail.

From time to time you can drop them a line to keep the connection. For example, if they're an agent looking for a particular type of material, and you see some script listing online or in a magazine that meet their needs, you could clip out the info and send it to them. By doing this, you are establishing yourself as the "Gatekeeper." This is the person others come to when they need to find someone or something. And once you become known as the "go-to" guy or gal, you've set the ball of momentum rolling in your favor.

Now do you think they'll be likely to take your call if you should ever reach out to them? You better believe it. And when they need the kind of service you deliver, or know of someone who does, who do you think is going to get the referral?

So where can you go to network? All the online communities are a good way to warm up. But there are many more ways to meet potential prospects:

- ◌ **Union functions.** If you're part of a union, any union, there are usually events you can attend.
- ◌ **Parties.** Any party is a good party to network. Although the agenda is not usually centered on this type of activity.
- ◌ **Chamber of Commerce.** If you're a member of the chamber, they have regular events. As a script consultant or writer, you might think it's a waste of time networking with non-entertainment people. The fact is, a large percentage of my clients have come from non-entertainment fields — doctors, lawyers, and entrepreneurs.

◦ **Writer events.** The annual Screenwriter's Expo. The Maui Writers Conference. Writer panels. Film schools. Writer workshops of all kinds.

◦ **Mixers.** There are events going on all the time, with actors, writers, directors, casting directors, producers, executives, you name it. If you don't live in Hollywood, New York, or even the U.S., there are still bound to be some events you could attend. Check with your local colleges, the calendar section of the paper, and online city event schedules.

◦ **Charity events.** People at these occasions are usually in a happy, receptive mood. They're feeling good about doing something that benefits someone other than themselves, and they tend to feel more connected to others in the fraternity of the "cause."

The Magic of Referrals

The best advertising and marketing tool is free — referrals. When someone refers a friend or colleague to you, that referral is usually pre-qualified and comes already believing in you. You hardly have to sell them at all. They might even say something like, *"If Bob says you're good, you must be good."* What's more, that person is already trained in sending you referrals because that's how they came to you. So in developing your marketing strategy, make sure it has, at its center, the building of a "referral-based business" and all the activities it takes to do that.

There are many ways to generate referrals. But the most powerful way is to provide excellent service, then ask the satisfied client if they know others who could potentially benefit from your services. Usually, that client is more than happy to give you some names. The problem is that many of us rarely ask. We're either too shy, or falsely assume that our client would automatically refer people if they wanted to. Wrong. The only thing customers do automatically is complain when they receive bad service. If the service is good or even great, they may tell one or two people — if you're lucky.

"Ask and you shall receive," goes the ancient saying. This is a universal principle. *You have to ask for what you want.* If you don't ask for referrals, you probably won't get any. There's nothing greedy or selfish about it. You have something of value to offer. Ask your client if they know anyone who could *benefit* from it.

Another way to get referrals is from your "networking." Just as you brought that writer and agent together and offered to be on the lookout for their potential prospects, you also set it up so that they'll be on the lookout for you. In some cases, it won't take any more action on your part to build enough trust with this new "connection" to have them refer people to you. Other times, you'll need to work a little longer to gain their complete confidence — including them using your services.

You might be thinking that this is an awful lot of work to build a few new contacts. The fact is, it's never just "a few contacts." The average person has at least 250 contacts in their circle of influence. That means that for every new contact you create, you have effectively expanded your potential network by 250 more people. Meet ten new people, that's a potential network of 2500. Meet just ten more out of that 2500, and you're network has just expanded to 5000! If you set a goal to meet just 10 strong contacts a month, how big would your potential network be by the end of a year?

You do the math.

Strategic Alliances

There really is strength in numbers. The successful entrepreneurs of today don't reinvent the wheel, they partner with someone who already has one. They don't build new networks, they ally with someone who already has. Using this theory, your business can do in one year what it might have taken you a decade to do on your own — if ever. Remember when Burger King and Disney first partnered on the release of *The Lion King*? They both were selling very different products, but they were selling them to the *same audiences* — the tykes who ate the burgers and watched the cartoon. By pooling their resources, they were able to magnify their message by quantum leaps and get to more kids with less cash.

So how do you create these strategic alliances? Find businesses that are in complementary but non-competitive areas of your field, and partner with them. In other words, what are the businesses that need to get to the same people you do — namely writers and those who want to develop screenplays?

For example, The Writer's Store needs to connect with writers in order to sell their products. Maybe you could put on a contest or workshop, sponsored by them, offering free consultations as prizes. What about Final Draft Screenplay Software? Or computer companies (writers use computers to write on, don't they)? Or Starbucks? (Writers not only use Starbucks as an office, but they live on that rocket fuel.)

You use the partnering company's marketing machine, their built-in mailing lists, and (in some cases) their money — and they utilize your talent, knowledge, specialty, and maybe your mailing list as well.

It's a win-win, and it didn't cost you a penny!

There are many possibilities. You just need to look for them — and begin making the calls. This can be especially effective for companies looking to expand into your field, or newer companies without any public image yet. Maybe there's a new website for writers or industry professionals that you could partner with on a seminar or "webinar." Perhaps there's a new writer's magazine trying to launch. Combine a launch party with a workshop or lecture. Turn it into a national tour!

Your Marketing Plan

Once you've determined what it is you want to achieve, and the basic tools you're going to use to achieve it, it's time to put together a plan of action. There are whole books devoted to this, but let me list a few key elements you'll want to have in place:

- ◊ **Budget.** You need to know how much you can spend in both time and money, otherwise you'll get yourself in over your head and not complete the plan.
- ◊ **Clear objectives.** Know what you're going for. How many ads are you going to run? How many workshops or talks are you going to put on? How many new customers are you intending to generate? How many referrals? How much income? Is it per week, per month, per year? Be specific.
- ◊ **Timeline.** Know when you want these results by. If it's a one-year goal, break it down into a six-month, one-month, one-week, and "tomorrow" plan.
- ◊ **Accountability.** This is so important. Have someone or an entire group that can hold you accountable for doing what you say you're going to do. Having

a professional support group (mastermind group, success circle, etc.) is vital to your long-term success. And don't think it's just for beginners. Some of the most successful people in the world are still part of regular support groups. Can you imagine what it must be like to sit around the table with a bunch of multi-millionaires — or billionaires — and talk about your goals and dreams?

◌ **Flexibility.** You need to evaluate your success at various stages and determine if the plan is achieving your desired results. If it's not, you need to be willing to change — even if it's 180 degrees.

◌ **Commitment.** On the other hand, you can't be too quick to change. A good marketing plan usually takes time before it shows its fruits. It might be several months before you really begin achieving significant results.

◌ **Sustainability.** Can you keep this marketing plan up? What is its "burn rate" in both financial and emotional capital? Is it burning through resources faster than you can replenish them? Can it run itself and be duplicated? The key to a solid marketing plan is creating a system that can run like clockwork.

Working with a Marketing or Career Coach

Don't feel bad if you aren't a marketing expert and can't put together a plan to save your life. This is tough work and may require some outside help. In fact, if your USP (Unique Selling Proposition) and marketing strategy aren't inspired, you would be doing your business a disservice to *not* hire a professional. There are people who specialize in marketing, branding, and career counseling. They know all the ins and outs of what you're trying to do. This might be one of those "don't try to reinvent the wheel" moments that requires some alliances.

I know some of you are thinking, "I can't afford to hire someone else, I'm already down to my last box of mac & cheese." I understand. But there are many ways to get the help you need. If you can't get a business loan from a bank or a relative, maybe you can find a way to barter services. Maybe you can find a career coach who is also an aspiring screenwriter — or has a story they just want told. Voila! You exchange your services for theirs. Or maybe they need legal expertise and you know a lawyer who needs script consulting. Voila! You provide the lawyer with free script consulting. She in turn provides the career coach with free legal work. And the career coach then provides you with the much-needed marketing or planning help. This is called "Triangulation."

In other words, where there's a will, there's a way.

Invest in Your Success

By invest, I don't just mean the money it takes to advertise and market, but the time, the thought, and the patience that is required to create a marketing system that endures and a business model that can ultimately run itself. If you don't believe in your business and back it up with actions, you're sending yourself and the universe a message that says, *"This isn't a real business, I'm not going to be much of a success, so don't even pay any attention to little ol' me."* And that's exactly what you'll get.

You get out of life — and business — what you put into it (actually, utilizing the above-mentioned leveraging techniques, you'll get a lot more than what you put into it).

Near the end of my first full year of script consulting, I hit a dry spell. Very little business was coming in, I had one more "month" at the end of my money, and I was getting a little desperate. I couldn't understand why things had suddenly ground to a screeching halt. Then I paid a visit to a mentor. After only a few moments of dialogue, he explained that I was living in fear, making my decisions from a "scarcity mentality." Then he asked a very simple question: *"What would you do if you really believed life supported you and your dreams?"*

The question struck me deeply. As I reflected over that past year, I realized that I had been hedging my bets, playing it safe, living much smaller than I knew was possible. There was so much more that I wanted to do — begin an advertising campaign, get a real office space — but I didn't think I could afford it, I was afraid I'd fail. He explained that by not honoring the impulses inside me to expand, I was plugging up the opening through which more opportunity could flow. I was waiting for something outside of me to change, when all along the source of my success — and the obstacle to it — was within me. He challenged me to take out the ads and rent the space.

"Just do it," he said.

Bolstered by his confidence in me, I took the plunge. Within a week of the ad coming out, I had already paid for it twice over. And within a couple months, I was easily able to pay for the ads, the office, and still have more income than I did before.

Living by that principle, my life has continued to grow in an upward spiral.

Yours will do the same.

Taking the Leap

Remember in *Indiana Jones and the Last Crusade*, where Indiana had to get across that bottomless chasm to save his father's life? There was supposedly a bridge there, but it was invisible. There was no proof that the bridge existed. No guarantee that it was real. In fact, maybe it was just a trap, a hoax, a pipe dream. Maybe he would plummet to his death if he dared to cross.

That's what it might feel like right now as you embark on your marketing campaign — not to mention your business in general. It might feel like you're stepping out over a chasm with no safety net to catch you if you fall. From where you're standing, there simply ain't no bridge there.

So you wait for it to appear.

Or look around for another way to cross.

And all the while, the life is draining out of your business.

But the problem is, the bridge won't appear until *after* you step out onto it. Indiana had to take the risk *first*. He had to put his weight (commitment) into it. Only then did the bridge begin to appear. I say "begin" because he still had to take several more "small steps" out onto the "invisible" before the whole bridge materialized. That's how it works.

Make the commitment.

Take small steps.

Don't look down.

And the bridge to your destination will appear.

Chapter Summary

- Without a clear understanding and implementation of a USP (unique selling proposition), your business is almost certainly destined to underperform.

- Position your business in a way that hasn't been done before, in a way that makes people take notice, in a way that says you are the best in your niche.

- Domino's, FedEx, and Starbucks are examples of businesses with great USPs that not only dominated their fields, but transformed them.

- Try to live by the motto, "Under Promise, Over Deliver."

- Marketing is the total approach to how you inform the public of your product and/or service in a way that compels them to purchase it.

- Marketing includes advertising, strategic alliances, partnerships, writing articles, teaching, joining networks — and anything else you can dream up.

- Marketing doesn't have to cost much — or anything. Your greatest marketing asset is not your money but your mind.

- Say "yes" to everything in the early stages of your career. Accept requests to speak, teach, whatever — just get yourself and your services out there.

- Focus most of your advertising in arenas where you won't be competing against too many other consultants for the reader's attention.

- The best advertising and marketing tool is free — referrals. Make sure that your plan has, at its center, the building of a "referral-based business."

- Find businesses in complementary, non-competitive areas that need to get to the same prospects as you — and form a strategic alliance with them.

◌ Once you know what you want to achieve, create a plan (budget, objectives, timeline, accountability, flexibility, commitment, and sustainability.)

◌ We cannot walk this path alone. Spend time cultivating relationships, building alliances, meeting others in our field and related ones.

◌ What would you do if you believed life supported you and your dreams? Take the "leap of faith." And the bridge to your destination will appear.

◊ Your Meeting Space

◊ Your Fee List

◊ Hiring Other Script Consultants

◊ Keeping Good Records

◊ Getting a D.B.A.

◊ Opening a Business Account

◊ Getting a P.O. Box

◊ Stationery

◊ Phone Service, Secretary, or Answering Machine

◊ A Closing Thought About Opening Your Doors

Chapter Eleven

"The biggest chance you can take is not taking a chance at all."
— *Anonymous*

"A journey of a thousand miles begins with a single step."
— *Chinese Proverb*

Hanging Out Your Shingle

Your Meeting Space

The moment a client walks into your office, they adjust (if only unconsciously) their inner thermostat to match the environment they encounter. If the environment seems cluttered and disorganized, they will be prepared for a cluttered and disorganized experience. If the environment is hostile, they will martial their defense mechanisms and battle armaments to the frontlines.

While you can't completely control how your client will feel and react when you meet, you can significantly upgrade the possibilities of having a receptive client and a successful meeting by preparing an environment that is most likely to evoke that response in them. We will talk in a later chapter about the actual meeting. For now, it is important to make sure you have created the "space" for the meeting to take place — whether it is in your home, an external office, your client's place of business, or a coffee shop.

How you create the space is a creative act, so there are no exact rules. And depending on the client, different spaces will have different effects. Nonetheless, there are a few things you can have in place to ensure a more effective environment:

- An organized (clutter- and odor-free), professional space
- If you have posters of produced movies, awards, or credentials, having them visible (like doctors and lawyers do) can put the client at ease, feeling like they're in the hands of a pro
- Appropriate attire (not a suit necessarily, but something other than those sweats you've been in all week)
- Phone turned off, and free of other distractions and interruptions
- All necessary documents neatly arranged, with copies for the client when appropriate
- A beverage of choice for the client
- Comfortable seating
- Moderate temperature

Your Fee List

Create a list of services and rates that can be given to the client upon request. Without this, your prospect may think you're just making the prices up as you go — and this can erode trust and credibility.

When determining your fees, look at what you bring (knowledge, specialty, experience, credentials) and put a reasonable price on it. If you don't have a lot of experience yet, that's okay. All of the work you've put into building this business still has a value. Begin with inexpensive prices. As your business expands, the law of supply and demand will allow you to confidently charge more.

Whatever your fee, make sure it is within reasonable limits of current market rates. In other words, don't charge much more than the going rate (unless you have exceptional credits), and don't charge much less (because it gives the impression that you have less value). The exception to this last rule is if you're running a limited-time-only special to attract new customers.

We'll get into more specifics regarding fees in the chapter on "Dollars and Sense."

Hiring Other Script Consultants

If you plan on eventually building a script consulting firm, it's important to have that in mind from the beginning. In fact, it's a good idea to build your business as if it's a franchise — even if you never intend it to be. This will force you to systematize every aspect of it, creating a more efficient, productive, duplicable, and valuable business. And if you do hire other consultants, you will be able to easily plug them into your system and maintain a certain level of quality control.

Keeping Good Records

Professionals keep good records. Was that a groan I heard? I know you're an "arteest." But you're also a businessperson. And if you want your business to thrive, you need to honor and respect it — every aspect of it. And trust me, come tax time you'll be very happy you did.

I've already described how I keep files organized. My way is not perfect by any stretch. Find your own record-keeping system. But find one. Sooner rather than later. The habits you form in the beginning of your business are likely to stick, so form ones that will give you the results you want. It's so much harder to start keeping "the books" or "filing your receipts" after you've been in business for a while. The extra effort you put in now will pay big dividends down the road.

Getting a D.B.A.

D.B.A. stands for "Doing Business As." It allows you to establish your sole proprietorship and receive some of the benefits of business ownership. It's a good idea for tax purposes, since it legitimizes your company. It also puts your business name into the public record for proprietary purposes, giving you certain common law rights for trademarks or service marks. A "D.B.A" also allow you to open a bank account under your business name. All the info you need to accomplish this can be found online.

Opening a Business Account

This isn't absolutely necessary, but it's a good idea. It lends credibility to your business when dealing with vendors, allows you to keep records of business expenses, and legitimizes your business for tax purposes. It's clearly not just a hobby anymore. It's also cool to see your business in this official light. It adds to your sense of ownership and confidence — and probably to your bottom line as well.

Getting a P.O. Box

If you don't have an official office space, it's highly recommended that you have a post office box. It's more professional, for one thing. And safer. Once your home address gets out there, it's out there for good — unless you move. The choice is yours.

Stationery

While not essential, having nice stationery certainly adds a sense of legitimacy and professionalism. Just think how you would react if you received two advertising letters from script consultants — one black & white, the other a freshly minted, three-color, brochure-quality letter. Which one would you suspect is the most successful — and more likely to help you become successful? Which one would you call first?

Phone Service, Secretary, or Answering Machine

As your business grows, especially if you build a consultant firm, you may find the need to hire an assistant to answer the phone. At first though, a good answering machine (or message center at your local phone carrier) with a clear, crisp outgoing message will suffice. You could also get an answering service where a live person takes the calls remotely and relays the messages to you.

A Closing Thought About Opening Your Doors

This is an exciting time. You are now officially open for business. But as much as you've learned, your education has only just begun. Make space in your head and heart for the mistakes that are likely to happen — and the successes that will hopefully come your way.

Don't let the highs get too high or the lows get too low.

Don't expect to have all the answers or find overnight success. And keep growing. Study your field — and other related fields. Study business principles. Study things you don't think have anything to do with you or your business. Some of the greatest inventions and innovations have come from "left field," from areas that seemingly had no connection to the ultimate area in which they were implemented.

Remain a pioneer.

Think of your business like a laboratory where you are constantly experimenting.

Sometimes your brilliant theories are going to blow up in your face. But if you stick with it, maybe, just maybe, you'll find a cure for bad writing.

Chapter Summary

- Create a "meeting space" that is welcoming to your clients. Keep it organized, wear appropriate attire, turn off the phone, have comfortable seating, moderate temperature, and a beverage of choice.

- Create a "fee list" that can be given to clients. Without this, it can appear as if you're pricing arbitrarily.

- Create fees that reflect your level of experience, knowledge, and the going market rate for that degree of expertise. (More on this in "Dollars and Sense.")

- Systematize your business, so that it is duplicable. This will make it easier to hire staff, sell the business, or license aspects of it.

- Keep good records. And start sooner rather than later. The extra effort will pay big dividends down the road.

- Get a D.B.A. ("Doing Business As"). This legitimizes your business for tax benefits, and puts your name into the public record for proprietary purposes.

- Open a business account. This helps to keep clean books, and makes you feel like your business is more credible.

- If your office is in your home, use a P.O. box for mail. It's just a safer bet.

- Nice stationery (brochures, letterhead, cards) adds a sense of professionalism and an air of success to your business.

- If you don't have a 24-hour live phone answering service, make sure you have a nice, clean outgoing message.

o Keep learning. Study your field, related fields, and even areas that you don't think are connected at all. You may be surprised at the insights you have.

o Keep your mind and heart open for the mistakes — and successes — you will experience. Don't let the highs get too high, or the lows get too low. And be patient. This is a marathon, not a sprint.

◊ First Impressions

◊ The Elevator Pitch

◊ Asking the Right Questions, Giving the Right Answers

◊ Evaluating the Prospect

◊ Payment Policy

◊ Release Forms

◊ Closing the Deal

◊ Receiving and Organizing the Material

◊ Confirming the Commencement of Services

◊ Time to Dig In

Chapter Twelve

> *"Let us make a special effort to stop communicating with each other, so we can have some conversation."*
> — *Mark Twain*

> *"I wish people who have trouble communicating would just shut up."*
> — *Tom Lehrer*

First Contact

First Impressions

You've put the word out, marketed your business, hung out your shingle, and thrown open your doors.

And now you sit at your desk.

Waiting...

Suddenly, the phone rings. You eagerly reach for it, take a breath, and announce yourself, "The Scripter Fixer-Upper!" The prospect begins barraging you with questions. You start to sweat like Albert Brooks in *Broadcast News*. You stumble over your words. The prospect says they'll "think about it." And you lose your first fish before you can hook it. You hang up the phone, shake your head, *"I knew this would never work,"* and contemplate a profession in the food-services industry.

That pretty much describes my first encounters. Hopefully it won't describe yours. Even if it does, you can take heart. With practice and patience, you can learn how to give good phone.

Here are a few things that will help prepare you when that phone starts ringing:

- ◦ **Know your stuff.** This may seem obvious, but it's amazing how many people jump into things before they're really ready to speak authoritatively. Make sure you know what you're offering, how it will meet your various clients' varying needs, why it is a unique service that they can't get anywhere else, how much it will cost, and anything else that is pertinent to your business.

- ◦ **Practice.** Rehearse your opening lines, and your counters to the various questions you might receive. Get together with a friend and have them role-play the prospect.

- ◦ **Have a script.** If you're afraid of freezing up, have your opening salutation, possible responses, price list and service explanations written down in front of you. There's no shame in this. Soon, you'll find yourself winging it.

- ◦ **Keep at it.** Remember what I said about preparing for the eventual mistakes? You must be mentally tough for this business. If you fall, pound the floor for a few minutes, then pick yourself up, dust yourself off, and get back to work.

The Elevator Pitch

When you're networking or just out and about, you'll find yourself with many opportunities to share what you do. Have a 30-second (or less) pitch worked out that you can say in a conversational way. It should describe what you do, what's unique about you (remember the USP — Unique Selling Proposition), and any success you've recently had.

Asking the Right Questions, Giving the Right Answers

When a client calls, you're interviewing them as much as they're interviewing you. If you're going to be of excellent service, there are certain things you need to know about them. We talked about client screening as a script doctor, but these questions apply equally to script consultant prospects.

So here is a recap of the possible queries:

- Why are you hiring a script consultant?
- What is your goal for this project?
- Have you worked with other script consultants? If so, what was your experience like?
- Specifically, what do you want from a script consultant?

Evaluating the Prospect

Is this the right fit? Early on in your career, you'll likely feel that everyone is the right fit as long as they come with cash in hand. But as your business grows, and your prices follow, you will sometimes need to turn people away or refer them to other script consultants in their price range or with the right "specialty."

This is part of the ethics of the business.

I can tell you from experience that it is better to refer a prospective client to someone else than to take on a client you feel in your gut is not right for you. It belongs in the "life is too short" category. And it won't be worth the money. Do a profit and loss statement, comparing how much you'll make for the job and how much extra Prozac you'll have to buy — and see if you still turn a profit.

Here are a couple more questions to ask yourself before accepting a job:

- How much time will this project take? Is it worth the money? Is there a better, more lucrative or inspiring use of my time than this?

- If the money isn't great, is the project something that excites me? Does it have the potential of getting bought and made? Is it with an industry professional that will lead to potentially better opportunities — or at least look good on my resume?

Payment Policy

I've included this here, because in many cases you'll need to explain your "payment policy" during your first contact with a prospective client.

So what is the best policy? Full payment up front, half now, half when you've completed the work, or the full amount at the end? You can arrange it however you desire, but keep one thing in mind when determining your fee schedule: *The Up Front Money Is the Only Payment You Can Bank On.*

I don't mean to sound cynical, but the fact is there's no guarantee you'll get paid any more, even if you finish the project. I'm still owed thousands of dollars from several clients — and I will never see a penny of it. Am I angry about it? No. But I am wiser for it. You learn to live with the losses, but you also learn your lesson — hopefully.

When it comes to script consultations, I personally require full payment up front. And I don't begin work until the check has cleared (a policy that is shared by almost every consultant I've spoken to). With script doctor work, I usually require at least half up front, since I'm going to be doing at least that much work before the next scheduled payment. As I develop relationships over the course of several projects, the policy becomes more relaxed. I even have "handshake" deals with some long-term clients.

I know you're a nice, trusting individual. Maybe, like me, you're even idealistic and believe that everyone is good deep down. Perhaps you even feel a little guilty "negotiating" and creating contracts — as if it indicates a lack of trust in your client (some clients will even imply as much). But the fact is, this is a business, and the world isn't perfect.

Ask for what you need to be comfortable.

Don't accept anything less.

Release Forms

We live in a litigious society. In the entertainment industry, this shows up as writers and wannabe writers suing people for stealing their ideas. While ideas have been stolen before, it is a very rare occurrence. It's cheaper for a production company to buy the script than pay the legal fees. The truth is, if you've ever been a script reader, you know that on any given week you can receive six scripts with the same premise — and a couple of them with the identical idea and similar execution! This is why production companies no longer accept unsolicited scripts without "release forms."

And this is why you should have the same policy.

Here's an example of one:

This form is for educational purposes only. It is not intended as a legal document for actual use. Please consult with an attorney to ensure you have the proper legal protection.

Submission Release Form

1. I understand that (Your Company's Name Here) will not review any work without this signed Release Form.
2. I hereby grant (Your Company's Name Here) and its affiliates the right to read and evaluate the accompanying screenplay material (The Submission), entitled: _____
   I acknowledge that the submission was written by me (us). I also acknowledge that I (we) am (are) the sole owner(s) of this work and its copyright.
3. I understand that (Your Company's Name Here) and its affiliates are exposed to many stories, ideas, concepts and other literary materials, through this service and other means. I also understand that many stories, ideas, and concepts are similar or identical, and that different stories, ideas, and concepts frequently relate to one or more common underlying themes and may closely resemble other works.
4. I understand and agree that I will not be entitled to any compensation or other consideration because of the use of such similar or identical material, stories, ideas, and/or concepts that may have come to you or your affiliates. I hereby release (Your Company's Name Here) and its affiliate from any and all claims, liabilities and demands that may be made by me asserting that you have used or appropriated The Submission, or any portion thereof.

5. I acknowledge that (Your Company's Name Here) recommends that I copyright my screenplay submission with the United States Copyright Office and/or register my screenplay submission with the Writer's Guild of America. I also acknowledge that it is my responsibility to copyright or register the submission prior to submitting it to (Your Company's Name Here)and hereby release (Your Company's Name Here) from any claims that arise from my failure to do so.

6. I also attest that no confidential relationship is established by submitting this material to you. I understand that (Your Company's Name Here) and its affiliates are under no obligation other than to provide Literary Evaluation.

7. I understand that Literary Evaluation is a subjective process, allowing for reasonable disagreement as to the relative merits of the submission. I also understand that the evaluation may or may not be complimentary or positive in its judgment, and that the evaluation fee is non-refundable.

8. I understand that (Your Company's Name Here) may retain or destroy the submission, and I acknowledge that I possess additional copies of same.

Signed _____

Author(s) Signature & Date

Name _____

Print Author(s) Full Name

Closing the Deal

Once you've determined that the prospect is a good fit — that you can genuinely help them and that they won't take years off your life — it's time to close the deal. Sometimes you won't need to do anything other than tell the prospect to put the script and check in the mail. Other times, however, you will need to help the prospect "see" their need, "feel" the value of your services, and "desire" to invest in themselves and their career by enlisting your services. This may take some specific framing on your part. Many people don't think in terms of the future, don't invest in the future, and don't have the patience or vision to forestall immediate gratification for long-term success. Don't blame them, they were never taught to think this way (but that's another story).

Your job at this stage will be to help them see how valuable your service is and why they need it. For example, let's say it will cost them $500 to get a script analysis, but they don't think they can afford it. You might ask them, "If you had written a proposal for a multimillion dollar business, and had only one shot at selling your idea, would you invest $500 in making sure the proposal was as good as it could be?" Or, "If you had created a blueprint for a multimillion dollar building, and you were submitting it to a buyer to win the contract, would you invest $500 to make sure it was the best blueprint possible?"

Most intelligent, success-minded individuals would answer "yes" to this.

This isn't manipulation. This is sincerely framing the truth in a way that they can see it. One reason there are so many bad scripts is that there are so many writers who don't view their scripts for what they are — blueprints (or business proposals) for a multimillion dollar business venture — and invest the time and money it takes to make them the best. There's a reason why the top companies in the world hire consultants to evaluate and innovate their business — *because it makes them better*.

Qualified script consultants make scripts better.

Own it.

And don't be shy about letting your prospects know it.

Receiving and Organizing the Material

Systems really do make life easier. And if you're working on multiple projects at the same time, you need to have a way of organizing the jobs. There are various ways to do this. Some people use a filing system on their desk where each project has an easy-access folder that they can view at-a-glance, put notes into, or open and get to work on. Others have a filing system in a drawer and only have the project they're currently working on in sight. This helps them focus on one thing at a time.

Whatever system you use, try to have one. A cluttered desk with scripts piled high and paperwork scattered about is not only inefficient, it's an energy stealer. You may not even be aware of it, but every time you look at that messy desk or office, think about it, or dream about it, it is robbing several kilowatts of your precious energy.

Don't let it!

And if you're not capable of handling it yourself, hire someone who can. Pry that checkbook out of your closed fist and write a check!

It will be money well spent.

Confirming the Commencement of Services

Once you receive the material and begin work, let the client know, and give them an estimate of completion. You can even set up your first meeting or phone consult at the same time. As your schedule fills, it will be important to do these things in advance. It also establishes more credibility and professionalism and allows your client to relax, sensing that they're in the hands of a pro. This is the frame of mind you want them in. It makes them more receptive to your feedback — which equals a better finished product — and it makes them more likely to do business with you again, and refer others to you.

Time to Dig In

Once you've organized your work, notified the client that you've received the material, and cashed the check...

It's time to celebrate.

That's right. You deserve it. One of the greatest contributors to burnout is the inability — or unwillingness — to celebrate our successes.

So take the time to do it.

Then get to work.

Congratulations, you're in business!

Chapter Summary

◊ Be prepared before you start answering the phone: know your stuff, practice, have a script, and keep at it!

◊ Have a 30-second business pitch worked out for those chance encounters in elevators — and anywhere prospects may appear.

◊ When a client calls, you are interviewing them as much as they are interviewing you. Find out why they're interested in a script consultant and what they expect to get out of this experience.

◊ Early on, you will likely feel like every prospect is the right fit. But as your business grows, you will sometimes need to refer prospects to more appropriate consultants or services.

◊ When creating your fee schedule, keep one thing in mind: The Up Front Money is the Only Payment You Can Bank On.

◊ Ask for what you need to be comfortable — and don't accept anything less.

◊ Because of the possibility of receiving similar or identical material from different clients — and because of the litigious society we live in — it's a good idea to have your client's sign a release form before beginning work.

◊ Don't be afraid to help the client see the value of your services — and close the deal. If you believe in what you have to offer, then you have a right — if not an obligation — to present it in the strongest light possible.

◊ Create a system for receiving and organizing your various projects. This will increase your efficiency and effectiveness.

◊ Make sure to celebrate your success. Remember, if you don't feed yourself, you'll starve others — because you can't give away what you don't have.

Chapter Thirteen

"Meetings are indispensable when you
don't want to do anything."
— John Kenneth Galbraith

"A meeting moves at the speed of the
slowest mind in the room."
— Dale Dauten

The Meeting

Setting the Tone

We've already talked about creating the physical environment. Now let's look at establishing the emotional tone. Whether on the phone or in person, in your office or in a coffee shop, the first thing is to greet your client with a sense of enthusiasm — even if you think their script stunk! There's nothing worse for a client than walking into a meeting or answering the phone, and hearing the consultant's voice full of heaviness and burden. I know, because I've been on the receiving end. And the moment I hear that tone, my heart sinks, my defenses go up, and my positive expectations go out the window.

Needless to say, that doesn't make a client very receptive to your feedback.

I don't care if you hated their material so bad you wanted to slit your wrists with the script pages, you need to maintain a positive professional attitude. You need to immediately disarm the client and put them at ease. If the meeting is in person, it's a good idea to offer them a drink (non-alcoholic), and make sure they have a good seat.

Above all, make them comfortable.

Starting with a little small-talk is okay. But don't overdo it. Put yourself in the writer's shoes. They've labored for months over this script, then after many sleepless nights of deliberation decided to hand their baby over to you. Don't you think they're just a little bit eager to get your feedback? While you're sitting there calmly talking about the weather, there's a storm brewing inside them. And it sounds something like this: "Shut the hell up and tell me how bad my script is!" Because that's the message you're sending them. It's human psychology. After all, if you loved the script, you'd be eager to tell them.

Giving Oral Feedback

The tips on how to give written feedback pertain to your oral presentation as well. However, there are a few more things to consider when doing it face-to-face.

- When you write your ideas down, it's a one-way communication: your client can't argue every point with you — which they will most likely attempt to do in person.
- If they don't defend themselves outright, you can bet they're making a case in their mind. If they're passive-aggressive personality-types, their tactic will be to shut down — which is a wall as difficult to breach as one with cannons firing at you.

This isn't a criticism of writers. I love and respect writers. I'm one of them (and I can be as defensive or passive-aggressive about my work as anyone). If it weren't for writers, we wouldn't have books, plays, movies — or all the jobs that are created because of them. What I'm saying is that anybody can have an opinion on paper, but once you're in a room with a willful writer fighting for life and death to protect their prose, it's a whole new ball game. And it requires a whole new set of skills.

Start with the Strengths

This rule applies to written and oral presentations equally. Always say something good about the material before launching into criticisms. This puts the writer at ease. But be careful about how you present the positives — because it can backfire.

If it feels pushed, forced, or overdone, it'll just make them gear up for the "bad news" — which they know is coming.

Listen Up

When someone is talking to us, we're usually preparing our response rather than really listening. And when we're talking to someone else, we know that's what they're doing too. In other words, many of us are suffering from "recognition deprivation." We don't feel seen or heard. And as long as we're gasping for this "psychological air," we're not going to hear a word anyone else is saying.

Listen to your clients. Really listen. This simple act alone can ease their worries and concerns. Even if you don't agree with their point of view, just hearing them out can make them more receptive to your feedback. You know the cliché, "God gave us two ears and one mouth for a reason."

Don't Defend

Your ideas are only as important as your client's willingness to accept and utilize them. The moment you start defending your position, you enter into a power struggle that is no longer script consultant and writer, but ego vs. ego — a losing proposition. Present your material clearly and concisely. If the client disagrees, make your case — then move on.

Stay Objective

Keep your comments directed to the material. If you think a section isn't working, don't say, "*You* missed the point of this scene." Instead you might say, "I don't think the full potential of this scene has been realized yet." See the difference? That doesn't mean the writer won't get defensive, but it eases the blow considerably.

Stay Enthusiastic

While giving criticisms, try to frame them in a constructive light, dealing more with the potential than the pitfalls. When I explain a problem in a script, I try as often as possible to express it in the context of a possible solution. In other words, my focus isn't on what's wrong, but how to make it right. Consequently, my energy is upbeat and optimistic. And my clients usually get caught up in my enthusiasm and become excited about the possibilities for their script — even though I'm taking a machete to it!

Stay Optimistic

As I just explained, your energy as the script consultant really sets the tone in the meeting. If you're positive and passionate about the potential in your client's material, they'll generally get invested as well. Our emotional state says so much more than our words. Even when we're tearing their script apart, if we do it with the energy of an inspired artist who knows the masterpiece is in that block of marble somewhere, they will be more likely to see it as well.

You're Running the Show

I know the client hired you. And you want their future business. But don't let the client take over the meeting. If your client starts defending their material and arguing every point you make, your ability to render effective service will be compromised. And if the meeting goes too long, is fraught with friction, or gets sidetracked by tangents — you'll be the one to blame, not the client. So take responsibility. Own your authority.

How to Handle Tension

If the tension becomes too thick for the feedback to penetrate, stop right there and deal with the client's concerns. Draw them out. Ask them questions.

Listen.

Acknowledge their issues. Explain to them that this is just your opinion. Ask if you can continue. *And check in with yourself* — because *you* might be the problem. Maybe you need to take a break, excuse yourself to the restroom, or get a drink.

Response-Ability

While you can't possibly prepare for all the things a client might say to you in the heat of a meeting, it's a good idea to have a few answers worked out. If you have done your homework, given the project your all, and are there for the client's interests — not your own — you should be able to handle whatever comes up.

But just in case, here are some canned responses you can use, modify, or build on:

1. Writer: *"Why do you think you know all the answers?"*
Wrong Answer: *"Because I have a superior understanding of screenwriting than a neophyte like you."*
Right Answer: *"I don't have "the" answer, just "an" answer. It's only my opinion. And you are free to accept or reject it.*

2. Writer: *"What's the last movie you got made?"*
Wrong Answer: *"That's none of your damn business. At least I'm not making a living serving lattes."*
Right Answer (If you've had movies made, state it, but that's not what it's about):
"If you'd like to see my resume, I can supply that to you. Right now I want to help you get a movie made. If you don't agree with my feedback, that's okay. I won't take it personally. But how can we work together right now to serve you and your project the most?"

3. Writer: *"I just don't buy anything you're saying."*
Wrong Answer: *"You already bought it, sucker, and I've got the bigger bank account to prove it. Besides, I don't really give a &^%$ what you think."*
Right Answer: *"Okay. Why don't we stop for a moment, go back to what your original intent was for this script, and see how it can be realized. (Then you would proceed to ask them some probing questions to better understand why they wrote this script and what they want it to be.)*

Try coming up with some other questions a client might throw at you — and work out your possible responses. One way to get into this exercise is to imagine yourself (or your worst enemy) in the client's shoes, and see what questions come up.

The Customer Is *Not* Always Right

How do you handle abusive clients? It's one thing to take their defensiveness, and listen to their problems — to a point. But what do you do when they cross that line? The first thing you need to do is decide what "the line" is for you. The second thing you need to decide is if you're willing to lose business to honor yourself.

That's a tough one for some — especially if you need to put shoes on little Timmy. But the thing is, people treat us the way we train them to. More to the point, they treat us the way we treat ourselves. If you don't take a stand for yourself, you'll attract people who walk all over you.

And what does "taking a stand" look like? It's different for different people. I think it's a good idea to keep your emotions in check and try to remain diplomatic. But sometimes it requires a little more forceful approach. I had a client once who just couldn't hear me until I said with a *very* strong voice that he would not treat me this way anymore and I was done doing business with him. He got the point.

It's okay to give the client a chance to change. But if they aren't willing to deal honestly and honorably, you need to let them go. Simple as that.

Dealing with Cultural Differences

As your business expands, you may have the privilege of working with clients from around the globe. This is an exciting opportunity. But you need to be prepared. You need to do enough research into their culture to make sure you're communicating what you intend. Phrases and ideas that are common in our country have a very different meaning in other countries. One funny example is when Kentucky Fried Chicken launched a marketing campaign in Japan, only to discover that their slogan "Finger Lickin' Good," translated into Japanese as "Eat Your Fingers Off." Not exactly the company image they wanted to convey.

Gestures are also an important part of cultures. Some prefer to bow, others like to hug, some are very big with their hands, others might mistake your wild gesticulations as a challenge to fight. Some will not speak unless you ask them to — so you need to draw them out — and others you can't get to shut up if you try (oh, wait, that's me).

Other Roles You Might Be Expected to Play

As a script consultant or script doctor, you will likely find yourself, willing or not, filling the shoes of other roles. While there is no obligation to actively engage these, it's important to know what your client might be projecting onto you:

Therapist
Confidant
Devil's Advocate
Secretary
Psychic
Genius
Guru
Their Mother
Their Father

Recognizing Your Client's "Type"

You will also encounter many different kinds of clients with different personality types. If you can spot them, you can usually handle them:

The Control Monster. This client secretly works for the aspirin companies because they are guaranteed to give you a headache every time. A typical day might have this client calling you once to ask a question, calling you a little later to ask it again — just in case you didn't understand it the first time — then calling you a third time to ask the same question a different way. Sometimes they'll even demand that you work at their home or office where they can keep constant tabs on you.

I once had a client who insisted I work at his kitchen table — while he slept in his recliner. He'd wake up every half hour or so, hover over my shoulder to see what page I was on, throw out a few ideas, then go back to sleep. He also insisted that I hand-deliver the script pages *every day* so he could edit them (since he didn't have a fax machine and didn't know how to retrieve email).

I've since learned to create boundaries and clearly articulate them up front. While I will always strive to accommodate a client's real needs, I have a way of working that I know will get the job done — and if it doesn't work for the client I will gladly refer them to another qualified consultant.

The Talker. This individual is a walking stream of consciousness. I had one serious case of this, where I came to the conclusion that this person was more interested in having someone to talk to than working on their script. I could tell that nobody else in their life really listened. (Remember what I said about "recognition deprivation"?). So I tried to hear and acknowledge them — while also trying to get the actual work done. The result was that they thought I was one of the nicest people they'd ever met.

Still, I had to install boundaries. When their talking starting going in circles and nothing new was being said, I politely but firmly redirected their attention to the script. And when they continued to gab, I reminded them that they were paying me by the hour.

That promptly shut them up.

The Know-It-All. This client seems to have hired you just to point out how much more she knows than you. She is rarely open to actually learning anything. And if she brings her script back for a second read, she's hardly implemented any of your feedback — sometimes none of it! Best advice: don't argue with this type. You can't win. And if you do, you'll probably get fired — or at the very least never be recommended to anyone else. Just do the best work you possibly can, and move on.

The Perfectionist. This personality type is a lobbyist for the alcohol companies — because they will drive you to drink. They seem to have a built-in homing device calibrated to find every little thing wrong with something — and blind them to what's right. Have compassion for them — they must've had a pretty scary childhood to create such a defense mechanism. But don't try to get anything past them, because they have scrutinized everything about you and your work. If you're consulting with them, try to do it by the hour, because they'll always push you over your time limit. If you're script doctoring, build in a rewrite limit — or they'll have you doing drafts forever.

The Hard Head. This type of person has some similarities to the know-it-all, in that they are painfully stubborn. They want it their way and that's that. You may have brilliant feedback, but if it doesn't fit their vision of what the material is, they'll discount and discard it. That's fine, it's their script. But if you're a consultant who seeks validation for your feedback, this personality will be a major challenge to your self-esteem. If you're script doctoring a project for them, you will oftentimes feel like a secretary taking dictation. If you're not willing to do that, set your boundaries clearly up front. They may walk away. But that's better than living in hell for several weeks or months.

The Flip-Flopper. This client will change their mind when the wind blows. They're usually wracked with insecurity and are desperately struggling for something to anchor them. At the same time, they're equally afraid of making the wrong decision and losing out on something better, so the moment they're anchored, they flip out and cut loose. In psychological terms, it's called "Approach-Avoidance." You might want to utilize a little "avoidance" of your own when you see this type coming your way.

Seriously, just make sure you get everything clearly in writing. If you're script doctoring, that would include a very detailed description of what you will be writing. If you create an outline, have them sign off on it. There's nothing worse than getting a client's agreement on a project, then going off and writing exactly what you agreed on — only to have them freak out and tell you it's not at all what they asked for. At least this way, you'll have something tangible to refer them to — and you're protected.

The Plagiarist. This type isn't particularly creative — except for their ability to cleverly cut pieces from various places and paste them together as their own. If you're script consulting and you run across a scene, sequence, or line of dialogue that has been blatantly lifted from somewhere else, you'll need to take it out. Of course, you want to do it diplomatically. If the main character in their sci-fi script says, "May the Force be with you," you don't call them a big fat fraud, you just politely explain that it's been done before and it hurts their script's potential to keep it in.

I once had a client (a great guy who really meant well) who would watch a bunch of movies, copy the best lines and actions from them, and put them all together to form his screenplay. And he didn't just pick the obscure stuff. I'm talking highly visible, recognizable, Academy Award-nominated material! Needless to say, it was quite a task to rewrite all of those pieces out of the script, while still maintaining some semblance of what he had intended.

On a serious note, this could get you or your client in trouble with the law. At the very least, if it got around that you doctored the script, it could damage your career.

The Silent Partner. In some ways, this is a great type to work with. They know that they don't know, so they defer to you when appropriate. And they have respect for you, so they are open and receptive to learn and make changes. If you're script doctoring, they usually let you just go for it — and they usually love what you do! They're also usually good at paying you — and can afford it without much of a problem. The downside is that they're usually very busy professionals and are hard to get hold of. So you might actually need their feedback on a crucial story decision, but not be able to get it in a timely fashion, and be forced to complete the project without it. Sometimes this works out fine. But if you've been flying completely blind, you may end up with a result that doesn't match their vision of the project. If you sense this is the type of client you're working with, try to establish early on some kind of emergency communication system, so you can keep them in the loop on important matters.

The Real Pro. This one has the positive attributes of the Silent Partner, in that they really respect you and your work, basically let you do what you do best, and can pay your fees without complaint. They also bring a level of expertise in the area that their script deals with, which can be a huge benefit if you're script doctoring — and a whole lot of fun. Even if you're just consulting, it's a big plus. Unlike the Silent Partner, this type will make themselves and their material available for you. Treat this client very well (of course you want to treat all clients well).

This doesn't describe all the personalities you'll ever meet. In fact, these are more like archetypes. The clients you work with will probably possess various attributes that mix and match to create whole new types. And you may not even know what they're like until you're well into the work. So the best way to mitigate problems is to have your clients clearly articulate their expectations up front (particularly when you're doing script doctor work), outline what services you'll be providing — then both of you sign off on it.

If you have a problem with all this talk of "written agreements" because you think they represent a cynical society, I empathize with you. I, too, wish we lived in a society where a handshake was enough (and with long-term clients, it sometimes is). But the fact is, well-written agreements are the most efficient, effective way for both parties to get clear and feel secure. They can save time, energy, money — and even the relationship

Chapter Summary

○ Greet your clients with enthusiasm — even if you don't like their material. Otherwise they'll pick up on your tone and become unreceptive or defensive.

○ Limit the "small talk." Too much of it is usually a sign to the client that the evaluation will be negative — and it puts them on the defensive.

○ Unlike written comments, oral feedback is a two-way conversation. Be prepared for your clients to defend their material to the death.

○ Opening with positive feedback before the negative is a good idea. But don't overdo it or it can backfire, causing the client to gear up for the "bad news."

○ Listen deeply, patiently, and fully to your client. You will be amazed at how brilliant they think you are even when *they're* doing all the talking.

○ Don't defend your position. State your case clearly, concisely, then move on.

○ Keep your comments objective. It's about the material, not the writer.

○ Frame criticisms constructively, dealing more with the potential than the pitfalls. Even if you're tearing a script apart, if you do it with the energy of an inspired artist who sees the masterpiece in the marble, your client will see it as well.

○ You're running the show. If the meeting goes off track, you're to blame. If the tension gets thick, check in with yourself. *You* might be the problem.

○ Decide what your "line in the sand" is, and honor that boundary. No amount of money is worth being disrespected or abused.

○ When dealing with clients from other countries — and even other states — be aware of the cultural differences and adjust appropriately.

○ There are several roles that might be projected on you: therapist, confidante, devil's advocate, secretary, psychic, genius, guru, mother, or father.

○ There are different types of clients: the control monster, talker, know-it-all, perfectionist, hardhead, flip-flopper, plagiarist, silent partner, and real pro.

◊ Money, Money, Money!

◊ Script Consulting Fees

◊ Script Doctoring Fees

◊ A Piece of Your Mind for a Piece of the Pie

◊ Creative Negotiating

Chapter Fourteen

> *"In God we trust, all others must pay cash."*
> — American Saying
>
> *"With money in your pocket, you are wise and you are handsome and you sing well, too."*
> —Yiddish Proverb

Dollars and Sense

Money, Money, Money!

Let's face it, we didn't embark on this business venture simply out of passion. We also got into it because we thought it was a way to make some cash from our creativity.

Nothing wrong with that.

After all, the subtitle of this book is *How to Make Six Figures as a Script Consultant*. But how much can we expect, especially if we're just starting out? How do we determine what to charge and how to collect?

Script Consulting Fees

There are no hard and fast rules to pricing, except one: *"Don't price yourself out of the market."*

This has a different meaning for script consultants at different levels. If nobody knows who you are and you charge $500 for an analysis, you might be over-charging. If you're Linda Seger or Chris Vogler, you could charge several thousand and have plenty of business. "When I started out, my fee was $70," says Linda Seger. "That's what I could get. I did for $70 what I now do for $3000. New consultants have to recognize that they will occasionally do free work in order to get known. Sometimes they'll find that their work is taking far longer than they expected, so it might take a new consultant a number of scripts to figure out how long it will take for them to do their analysis. The important thing is not to become arrogant by insisting on a big fee too early."

So let's look at some examples of possible "starting" rates:

I. In-Depth Script Analysis
  ◦ With written report, notes on script, *and* one-hour story meeting $300–$700
  ◦ With written report, notes on script, *or* one-hour story meeting $250–$500
II. Script Coverage $75–$150
III. Hourly Rate $50–$150

Remember, these are just "starting" rates. As I've already stated, there are those who charge much more — up to $5000 for an analysis — with the average experienced consultant getting around $600 – $1500 per job. The key is "What can you charge and still stay in business?" That might be a process of trial and error. Says Linda Seger, "When I started my business, a sales consultant told me that my pricing should be such that I lose 10% of the people who call because I was too high, but get 90% of the clients that call — which tells me my pricing is just right. There are some consultants who say, 'well, I'm worth it, so I'm charging what I'm worth. When I started, I might have been worth $5000, but no one was going to give it to me."

You can also choose to offer a discount for clients returning with the same script after applying your notes. And of course there are various other services you could offer, as I've already outlined. To determine what to charge, research other consultants to see what the market will bear.

Script Doctoring Fees

This area is a little more difficult to determine. It's primarily a non-union gig, but that doesn't mean you can't negotiate for union prices or at least a bonus that equals WGA minimums, payable if the script sells. Bottom line: Ask for what you believe you're worth, and make sure you can return valuable services equal to or greater than what you're being paid. My motto is: *"Give more than you're being paid for."*

Here are some possible ranges of script doctor fees (notice the price range is quite broad). Obviously, at the beginning you're more likely to be on the lower end of the spectrum. I was paid $500 for my first rewriting job (and I thought I was a superstar).

⁰ Line-Edit	$500–$2,500
⁰ Outline	$500–$2,500
⁰ Treatment	$500–$10,000
⁰ Polish	$1,000–$10,000
⁰ Complete Script	$10,000–$35,000+

There are a few other elements you need to consider before determining an appropriate bid for a project:

Research. How much research will you need to do to develop or rewrite the project? Don't underestimate the need for additional research, or the time it will take to do it. This can be a shocking experience. I've hastily accepted a script doctor project, quoted my fee, and dug into it — only to discover that it would take as much time researching it as it would writing it.

Co-writing. Will you be writing alone or working closely with the client — in which case it's likely to take longer? There are pros and cons to co-writing. On the one hand, at least you know you're doing what the client wants since they're closely reviewing what you're doing while you're doing it. On the other hand, it can be a frustrating, time-consuming, labor-intensive experience that takes more creative energy than it gives. Bottom line: Think very carefully before making this kind of arrangement.

Source material. If it's a rewrite, how complete is it? Is it a page-one rewrite or can you keep some of the original material? Just because they have a completed script doesn't mean it'll be easier than writing one from scratch. In fact, often times the opposite is true.

Other expenses. Will you need to travel, make long-distance calls, or generate other above-average expenses? Make sure you think the project through and account for these things — because once the deal is struck it is much more difficult to ask for more.

A Piece of Your Mind for a Piece of the Pie

Some clients will offer you a percentage of the script sale, in return for a lower writing fee. This can sometimes be a viable option if that's all the client can afford — and you need the money. However, you should still evaluate the saleability and commercial potential of the material before determining what kind of cash/percentage deal you're willing to strike. Can you see their movie getting bought, getting made, attracting an audience, making a profit? Would you go see it? Obviously, if you don't think it has a chance of selling, let alone getting made, you'll want to weigh the deal in favor of the up front payment.

Creative Negotiating

The important thing to remember is that it's all a negotiation. Maybe you can't get the price you want for a particular project — either because you don't have the credentials or the client doesn't have the cash. That's okay. There are many ways to retain "price integrity," which you want to do as often as possible. In other words, you make it a give and take. If they want it cheaper, you ask for something else in return. If you concede their request without at least asking for something in return, your pricing loses integrity — and by association, so does your professional reputation. Maybe you can take a bigger percentage of the script sale in exchange for a portion of up front fees (as discussed above). Maybe your client has certain skills that you could barter part of your fees for.

Be creative.

Think win-win.

Expect success.

Chapter Summary

◊ Script consultants are in this business not just for the creativity — but for the cash. There's nothing wrong with that.

◊ There are no hard and fast rules about pricing except one — Don't price yourself out of the market.

◊ Script consulting fees are more subjective, unless it's a union job.

◊ Your pricing should be such that you lose 10% of the people who call because you're too high, but you get 90%.

◊ Ask for what you're worth, have a bottom line below which you will not go.

◊ Deliver services equal to or greater than what you're being paid.

◊ When determining the bid for a script doctor job, there are a key areas to consider: research, co-writing, source material, and other expenses.

◊ Some clients will offer a percentage of the script in lieu of full cash payment. When considering the details of such an agreement, you should evaluate what potential the script actually has to get bought and/or made.

◊ There are many ways to retain "price integrity" other than just with cash. Remember, it's all a negotiation.

◊ Be creative. Think win-win. Expect success.

Act 3

A Foundation for Success

◌ Working with Another Script Consultant

◌ Finding a Script Consultant

◌ Choosing the Right Script Consultant

◌ Preparing Yourself for Feedback

◌ Things to Be Wary of

◌ Getting the Most Out of Your Script Consultant

◌ Other Avenues of Mentoring

◌ See Lots of Movies

◌ Don't Go It Alone

Chapter Fifteen

> *"My chief want in life is someone who*
> *shall make me do what I can."*
> — *Ralph Waldo Emerson*
>
> *"A mentor is someone who's hindsight*
> *can become your foresight."*
> — *Anonymous*

Finding a Mentor

Working with Another Script Consultant

Many of the greatest artists and entrepreneurs had masters to apprentice under. Most champion athletes had a great coach standing on the sidelines. And in indigenous cultures, it is often an integral part of the tradition for wise elders to pass on ancient wisdom to young initiates.

But in our modern, hi-tech, low-touch society, the role of the mentor has gone sorely missing. And in the entertainment industry, an entity created to make money off creators, where there are so many apprentices in need of masters, the role of mentor has been reduced to a catch phrase. Instead of the regular guidance, direction, and training of a seasoned professional who has walked the path you are on, most "apprentices" end up instead getting some "friendly advice," enrolling in an "industry network," and receiving a monthly newsletter. This is an often painfully slow approach to learning one's craft in any "real world" sense, and likely to be filled with pitfalls that could have otherwise been avoided. And while this book is meant to serve as a sort of surrogate mentor, there's just nothing like real-time, face-to-face, in-your-face guidance from someone who will hold you accountable and point out your blind spots.

In this vacuum of real mentoring, Master Mind groups have popped up. In these gatherings, peers on relatively the same level (but sometimes of varying stature) help each other brainstorm goals, hold each other accountable for achieving them, and generally offer support and encouragement. This is a good thing. But it doesn't replace the experience of working one-on-one with a master (or at least someone who has been where you want to go). Unfortunately, finding someone who is both a working professional and has the time to mentor is a difficult task. But I have found it the least difficult in the arena of script consultants. The very nature of giving and receiving feedback on an entire script (and the subsequent rewrites) forces both parties to slow down, become more methodical, and often leads to something that resembles mentoring energy.

So when I went searching for a mentor in the arena of screenwriting, I hired a script consultant. This was a pivotal stage in my growth as a writer. But it also ended up becoming a crash course in becoming a script consultant myself — although I didn't realize it at the time. You can read and hear all the theory in the world. But that can never compare to actually sitting down and spending dozens of hours pouring over your work with a professional who's already proven themselves, then reworking the material, only to have it torn apart again and again. It not only strips the material down to its bare essence, it begins to strip you down as well. You are refined even as your material is. But what's more important, you not only learn to write better, you learn — even if by osmosis — how to judge material, how to analyze, "diagnose," and "treat" it. You also develop better "bedside manner" for your own writing "patients."

So that's why I think it's important that you invest in getting a mentor. If you can find a professional screenwriter or story consultant who will work with you for free, who will mentor you in the ways of writing and consulting, that's great. But it's rare. (These people have to pay their mortgages and feed their kids too.) So if you can't find that benevolent soul, I urge you to hire one. Anyone at first. In fact, some of my greatest lessons have come from working with bad consultants. I learned very quickly what *didn't* work, and have (hopefully) never repeated those mistakes.

If you're interested in getting some real hands-on support and training, check out the *Script Consultant Institute* (*www.scriptwritercentral.com*), where you can participate in a powerful program that will guide you, step-by-step, through the process of honing your skills, finding your niche, marketing your services, and building your business. Graduates can become "interns" and train for a possible staff position in the mentoring program, *The Write System*, or consulting firm, *The Script Clinic*.

Finding a Script Consultant

In the past, when I tried to find a qualified script consultant that met my unique needs, I would struggle for hours, searching internet sites and screenwriting magazines, compiling a stack of disparate data that had to be sorted and cross-referenced before I could even begin to make a decision. It was a frustrating experience, to put it mildly. And I know I'm not alone. That's why I created *The Script Consultant Creative Directory*. In it you will find a comprehensive listing of script consultants, script doctors, and story analysts (their services, costs, contact info, sample work, and basic writing philosophies). And be guided, step-by-step, on how to choose the right one and get the most out of your experience.

It's the only book of its kind. You can find it at *www.scriptwritercentral.com*. You can also click on "The Script Clinic" for a list of certified script consultants — and register for a chance to win a free one-on-one consultation!

Choosing the Right Script Consultant

So how do you choose the right script consultant for you? There's no hard-and-fast rule to apply. It's like choosing the right medical doctor. You look at their credentials, then make a decision based on your head, heart, wallet — or a combination of all three. Some, like Linda Seger, cost thousands. Others cost hundreds. And, while Linda Seger is worth every penny, some consultants who charge high prices aren't any more competent than those who charge a fraction of that. So do your research. Talk to them. Get a sense of their philosophy. Find out exactly what you will get for your money. Request a sample of their work if they have it available. Then sleep on it — or whatever process you need to go through to make an informed decision.

Preparing Yourself for Feedback

There's some work you can do on yourself before you submit to a script consultant's criticism. We don't need to go over it in detail, since we've already covered it in the sections dealing with your client's reactions (and in the above-mentioned guide). Nonetheless, here are some things to consider when you're in the hot seat:

- ◌ Check defensiveness at the door
- ◌ Let go of your ego
- ◌ Be open to new ideas
- ◌ Be willing to kill your babies

Things to Be Wary of

In choosing a script consultant, you want someone who is qualified, someone you feel rapport with, and someone with rates you can afford. But there are some things to be cautious about. If the consultant guarantees they can get your script to the right people in town — for a price — really consider whether or not this is a legitimate set-up. While it's true that some script consultants, and script consultant companies, do have connections and do pass along outstanding material — many of them don't have any better connections than you do.

First and foremost you are going to them to get their advice on how to improve your material. Then, if you both agree it's sellable, you can talk about using their services to help you gain representation or a sale. If you do choose this option, make sure you get a list of the people and places they are going to submit your material. One reason for this, which we've already discussed, is that you need to know where your material has been, so that you (or your agent) don't take it to the same place. Also, by having the consultant get specific, you make them accountable.

Getting the Most Out of Your Script Consultant

Okay, so you've done your homework and picked a script consultant to work with. How can you maximize this experience?

- ◌ **Write the best script you possibly can.** Don't give it to a script consultant if you know you can make it better. Only after you have exhausted *all* of your efforts should you hand it over.

◦ **Ask tough questions and be prepared for tough answers.** Ask the questions about your script (and writing in general) that you really want to know but might be afraid to ask — because of the answers you might receive.

◦ **Don't let the consultant get away with ambiguity.** If you don't understand something, ask for clarification until you do. If the script consultant seems to be sugarcoating the feedback too much, ask them to give it to you straight.

◦ **Don't chitchat.** When you get a chance to talk to them, use the time wisely. Get to work, ask questions, pick their brains.

◦ **Utilize everything they offer.** If they allow you to follow up, either by email or phone, *do it*. It's amazing how many writers never take advantage of this.

◦ **Give them feedback on their service.** If there are things you are genuinely dissatisfied with, don't keep it to yourself. How else are they going to be able to serve you and future clients better?

Other Avenues of Mentoring

If you're not a screenwriter, you don't have a script to send to a consultant. So how do you create a mentoring relationship? As mentioned above, you can enroll in the Script Consultant Institute (*www.scriptwritercentral.com*), where you'll get all the support you need. But there are a few other approaches that screenwriters and non-writers alike can utilize:

◦ Intern for talent and literary agencies
◦ Intern for script consultants or script consulting companies
◦ Be an assistant to script consultants at their seminars
◦ Read more books by script consultants
◦ Take classes with script consultants

Intern for talent and literary agencies. Talent and literary agencies get a lot of scripts. And while some of them pay readers to do "coverage," some of them can't afford to and have their assistants or "interns" read the scripts and do coverage. This can be a good way to get hands-on experience and feedback from professionals in the field. It can also lead to paying work as a script reader. And if you're a writer, you might even get representation.

Intern for a script consultant or consultant company. This is similar to working with the agencies, except in this case you're working directly with consultants. With an individual script consultant, you're not likely to be doing the "reading" and "analyzing," since that is the consultant's job. But as their business expands, it might lead to a position in their company. In the meantime, you can do other services for them: answer phones, type, file, whatever (if you're local), or do research and other services that can be done non-locally. This puts you in regular contact with a professional consultant and can lead to coaching in various aspects of the business.

Working for a script consulting company offers some potential advantages. In this case, you might have a better chance of eventually being handed some actual scripts to read — and a better chance of getting hired on staff down the road if you're good. There are several companies like this, many of which can be found in the book *The Script Consultant Creative Directory*.

Assist script consultants at seminars. Script consultants often teach workshops and seminars around the country (and the world), including the largest venue for screenwriters, *The Screenwriter's Expo*. While some of these individuals have an assistant, many of them either can't afford one or just don't have the time to find one. And there are many things they need to coordinate at a seminar, such as registration, taking tickets, selling books and tapes, passing out worksheets, working overhead projectors, charting things on boards, etc. Find out where these consultants are teaching and offer your services. It's a great way to get to know them and their methods — and you get a free class out of it as well.

Read more books by script consultants. This one is pretty obvious. Just as this book is a surrogate mentor, so are many other books on similar subjects. Read as many of them as you can stand. Take what works for you and discard the rest. Be a lifelong student. Practice what Tony Robbins calls "CANI," which is an acronym for "Constant And Never-Ending Improvement."

Take classes with script consultants. Similar to reading books, taking classes and seminars is a great way to continually expand your knowledge, work with script consultants, meet potential clients and colleagues, and prevent yourself from becoming a social zombie.

See Lots of Movies

Experiencing the works of others in your field is another form of mentoring. Painters study paintings. Musicians listen to music. Screenwriters and script consultants need to watch movies (and read scripts). This may seem obvious, yet a surprising number of professionals in this field don't watch many movies — and read even fewer screenplays.

You don't have to go to the movies alone either. Invite other writers and script consultants to come with you, then discuss it over coffee afterwards. It's a great way to build community (read: get out of your cave) and practice your film analysis skills.

Don't Go It Alone

For some of you, I know it will be very tempting to just rough it on your own. You might be introverted, shy, don't want to bother anyone, or just stubborn. But I urge you to reconsider. Without the one-on-one guidance and support of my mentors, I'd probably be flipping burgers at Mickey D's, dreaming of one day being in the movie biz. At the very least, I would have struggled much more — and never achieved this level of success.

Chapter Summary

◊ Many great artists and entrepreneurs have had masters to apprentice under, but in our modern society the role of mentor has gone sorely missing.

◊ There are no hard and fast rules to choosing a script consultant. You look at their credentials, then make a decision based on your head, heart, and wallet.

◊ When you work with a script consultant, you need to follow a few guidelines to have an effective experience: Check defensiveness at the door, let go of your ego, be open to new ideas, and be willing to kill your babies.

◊ Some consultants promise to get material to industry contacts. Few actually deliver on this. Do your homework before buying this service.

◊ Ways to get the most out of *your* consultant: Write the best script you can, ask tough questions and be prepared for tough answers, don't let the consultant get away with ambiguity, don't chitchat, utilize everything they offer, give them feedback on their service.

◊ Other avenues of mentoring: Intern for talent and literary agencies, intern for script consultants or script consulting companies, be an assistant to script consultants at seminars, read more books by script consultants, take classes with script consultants.

◊ A great form of apprenticeship is to watch movies. Study them, deconstruct them, try to improve them, talk to other writers and consultants about them.

◊ Find a mentor (or two), join a master mind group (or create your own). Whatever you do, don't go it alone.

◊ Why Do You Need a Mission Statement?

◊ What is a Mission Statement?

◊ Big Picture Perspective

◊ A Deeper Look

◊ Personal Values

◊ Creating Your "Script Consultant Credo"

Chapter Sixteen

What lies behind us and what lies
before us
are tiny matters
compared to what lies within us
— Oliver Wendell Holmes

Creating
a Mission
Statement

Why Do You Need a Mission Statement?

I have found that one of the leading causes for failure in a person's life is the lack of a clear goal, a strong "why," (a reason for doing what they're doing that is aligned with their deeper values), and a plan for accomplishing it. And since my purpose for this book is not merely to give you a bunch of information — but to guide you to success — I feel it would be remiss of me to not include this part of the process as well.

If you're reluctant to do this kind of "touchy-feely" work, I urge you to reconsider. It will only help to clarify your goals, and inspire you to accomplish them. Many business leaders at Fortune 500 companies do this kind of "visionary" work. And if you want to be successful, one of the most efficient ways to do it is to role-model those who already are.

Perhaps you don't plan to make a career out of this and are thinking, *"What's the point of creating a mission statement for it?"* The point is that once you have clarity about your core values, you can connect this work to your primary purpose in a way that supports your larger vision, rather than taking you away from it. For example, maybe what you really want to do is write screenplays. Being a script consultant/script doctor could provide an excellent training ground — and nice income — while you're developing your own scripts. Maybe you want to produce or direct films. This work will not only make your story-sense stronger — you might just find the script you're meant to make. Whatever your reasons, it can never hurt to have greater clarity and direction.

In other words, you have nothing to lose — except maybe some fear and confusion?

What is a Mission Statement?

A Mission Statement is your flight plan, your blueprint; something against which you can judge everything you do in order to keep you on track with what's most important. Without it, it's difficult to know for sure what your desired destination is, and if the steps you're taking will lead you there. Without it, it's easy to get caught up in the daily minutiae of life, the "to-do list" mentality, only to discover when the sun goes down that you haven't really accomplished anything of significance. Without it, you might climb the ladder of success only to discover it's leaning against the wrong wall.

So give this work a chance.

I promise it will be worth it.

One of the best ways to embark on this adventure of creating a personal mission statement is to set aside time when you can be alone — away from phones, friends, even family. Settle into your favorite chair, a quiet place in nature — wherever you go to get out of the fast-paced, surface-thinking mentality of the world. This will allow you clear your mind, connect with the innate harmony and order of things, and open up to your deeper thoughts and feelings.

Are you ready?

Let's begin...

Big Picture Perspective

This will be a visualization exercise. Find a comfortable place, preferably sitting up, back straight but not stiff. Close your eyes. Plant your feet firmly on the floor. Let your hands relax in your lap.

Take a moment to imagine you're a highly successful script consultant/script doctor, helping many people around the country — maybe even the world. See yourself traveling, teaching, providing excellent service and impeccable quality (whatever your vision of ultimate success looks like). See the faces of your satisfied customers as they shake your hand after a job well done.

Feel the fulfillment it brings you.

Now imagine you've been invited to a writers' conference where you will be honored. You walk down a busy hall, saying hello to fans and admirers, maybe even signing a few books. A host shows you into the large ballroom, which is packed with past clients and industry colleagues. A large poster of your most recent book (or movie) hangs on the wall with your smiling photo. You're led to the stage, take your seat, and greet the crowd — who immediately rise to their feet and give you a standing ovation. You're practically knocked out of your seat by the energy of love, appreciation, and respect coming at you.

Then, one by one, past clients, industry colleagues, friends, and family members stand up and praise your unique qualities and talents, thanking you for how you've helped them. Don't monitor their comments. Take a deep breath and let them flow. You might be surprised by what you hear. If you find it difficult to imagine what they'd say, contemplate the following questions to spur your heart and mind:

○ What qualities of character would you like them to have seen in you as a script consultant and as a person?
○ What contributions and achievements would you want them to acknowledge you for?
○ What impact would you want to have made on their lives and work?

Allow yourself to fully experience what it's like to be seen and acknowledged for what's best in you, to have your talents and abilities honored and affirmed.

As each person speaks, you may open your eyes and write down what they said. Then return to the visualization until you have gone through at least four or five tributes.

Great work!

A Deeper Look

Make sure you're in a place where you won't be disturbed or distracted for at least an hour. As you contemplate each question, allow it to sink in. Trust your intuition and don't censor your answers. Take a deep breath...

What are your personal strengths and skills (don't be humble)?

_____

_____

_____

_____

_____

What strengths have others noticed in you?

_____

_____

_____

_____

_____

What talents do you have that no one else really knows about?

_____

_____

_____

_____

_____

What natural abilities do you have, that you aren't using?

_____

_____

_____

_____

_____

What do you have to offer that would be of worth to others?

_____
_____
_____
_____
_____

What do you most admire in others (think about specific people)?

_____
_____
_____
_____
_____

Who has had the greatest impact on your life and why?

_____
_____
_____
_____
_____

When you daydream, what do you see yourself doing?

_____
_____
_____
_____
_____

What things, deep down, do you feel you really should do?

_____
_____
_____
_____
_____

What are the most important goals you want to fulfill in your work/career?

_____

_____

_____

_____

_____

If you had to teach something, what would it be?

_____

_____

_____

_____

_____

What do you get excited and passionate about?

_____

_____

_____

_____

_____

Who inspires you (artists, authors, leaders, friends) and why?

_____

_____

_____

_____

_____

Phew! You made it. That's a lot of brain strain, I know. But those synapses are firing now, even creating new neuropathways.

Personal Values

Based on all the work you've done so far, take a minute and list what you believe are your values. You can choose from the list, or write your own.

◦ Love	◦ Service	◦ Family
◦ Peace	◦ Creativity	◦ Friendship
◦ Security	◦ Recognition	◦ Contribution
◦ Health	◦ Freedom	◦ Accomplishment
◦ Wealth	◦ Spirituality	◦ Home

Go through your list of values and choose the top five.

Creating Your "Script Consultant Credo"

A mission is a reflection of your deepest values *in action*, not merely a thematic throughline for your life. So let's take all the data you've collected and craft a powerful, inspiring "call to adventure" that compels you to launch your script consultant business.

◦ Choose a few *verbs* that resonate, inspire, or excite you — and represent your core values. For example: to Play, to Serve, to Build, to Enlighten, to Help, etc.

◦ In the context of your script consultant work, decide *who* or *what* you will be *acting upon*. Will it be "Writers," "Producers," "Professionals," "The Entertainment Industry," or "All of the above"?

◦ What is your ultimate goal for the people or groups you will be serving or helping? What is the *value*, *benefit*, or *end result* you create?

◦ Now combine these three elements to create the skeleton of the mission statement, and use all the other work you've done to fill in the flesh.

Example

"As a Script Consultant, my mission is to help people around the world realize the full potential of their scripts, actualize the full capacity of their writing ability, and stay motivated and inspired. By conducting business with honesty, integrity, enthusiasm, and striving to give more than is expected, I provide a safe and productive atmosphere for people to make mistakes, take risks, create material that exceeds their expectations, and grow in ways they never thought possible."

Your mission statement doesn't have to be long. It can be one sentence if it inspires you and powerfully sums up your purpose. If you live in L.A., there's one such mission statement, painted on the side of a fleet of cars, that you've probably seen many times: *"To Protect and Serve."* Now that's clear and succinct.

Okay, time to try one yourself. Don't worry if it's not perfect. A Mission Statement is not carved in stone. It's something you "try on" at first, like a new coat, and see how it fits. If after wearing it a while, it's making you itch or sweat or feel like you showed up to the party way overdressed, then take it off and create a new one.

Once you have your Script Consultant Credo, it wouldn't be a bad idea to include it on your brochures, website, business card (if it's short enough to fit), and post it above your desk.

Chapter Summary

- One of the leading causes of failure in a person's life is the lack of a clear goal, a strong "why," and a plan for accomplishing it.

- Many business leaders at Fortune 500 companies create mission statements for their businesses and personal lives.

- One of the most efficient ways to become successful is to model those who have already achieved what you want.

- A mission statement is a "flight plan," a "blueprint," something against which you can judge everything you do to keep you on track. It's not just a thematic throughline for your life, it's a reflection of your deeper values *in action*.

- When creating a personal mission statement, it's a good idea to set some time aside to be alone, away from phone, friends, and family.

- "Visualization" is a powerful tool for imagining what your future could be like, and discovering what matters to you most — the "Big Picture."

- When considering your future achievements, there are a few key questions to ask about the people you will affect: What qualities of character would you like them to have seen in you as a script consultant and person? What contributions and achievements would you want them to acknowledge you for? What impact would you want to have made on their lives and work?

- A mission statement doesn't have to be long, but it has to inspire you to change, take action, and fulfill your potential.

- A mission statement is not carved in stone. It's something you "try on" like a new coat. If it doesn't fit well, or you outgrow it, you can always change it.

- It's a good idea to include your mission statement (or parts of it) in your marketing materials (brochures, websites, even business cards).

◊ First Things First

◊ Five-Year Vision

◊ Five-Year Vision Statement

◊ One-Year Vision

◊ Reality Check

◊ Narrowing It Down

◊ Reverse Engineering Your Goals

◊ Go With the Flow Chart

◊ One-Year Vision Statement

◊ 30-Day Vision and Action Plan

◊ One-Week Goals

◊ One-Day Goals

◊ Weekly vs. Monthly Planning

Chapter Seventeen

Things which matter most
Must never be at the mercy of things
which matter least.
— Johann Wolfgang von Goethe

Putting It Into Action

First Things First

What is something you could do that, if you did regularly, would make a huge positive difference in your life?

Your answer will give you an indication of what is truly important, a top-shelf priority, in moving your life forward. In this chapter, we'll discuss what the "top-shelf" priorities and ultimate goals are in your script consultant business and, using your Script Consultant Credo as a compass, construct a five-year, one-year, 30-day, and one-week "flight plan" to get you to your desired destination.

I know you're probably eager to get to work analyzing scripts and collecting checks, but you'll get there much quicker and with less obstacles if you have a clear road map, well-defined goals and specific action-steps to achieve them.

So let's get to it!

Five-Year Vision

What are your big goals with this business, financially, creatively, and in terms of your overall career?

Turn off your phone, get comfortable, and read your Script Consultant Credo. Reflect on it. Close your eyes and imagine where all of this could lead five years from now. Are you the preeminent script consultant or script doctor in Hollywood — in the world? Are you traveling the globe, teaching and consulting on projects? Are you making over a hundred thousand dollars a year? Two hundred thousand? What about your clients? Are they the A-list of the industry? Are the movies you're working on being produced, becoming blockbusters, or winning awards? Are you a working writer yourself, selling screenplays, stage plays, books?

Let your imagination soar. Try not to force it in any particular direction. Instead, ask yourself, quietly, over and over, *"What do I really want to accomplish with this work over the next five years?"* And see what comes to mind.

As the answers come, write them down. List your goals — financial, career, personal creativity, and whatever else comes up for you.

Look at the list.

Which goals feel in alignment with your Script Consultant Credo?

Write those on a clean piece of paper.

Which goals can you accomplish in the next five years? Pick ones that are achievable, but still a stretch. If you choose goals that feel ridiculously impossible, your mind won't engage them because deep down you'll know it's a pipe dream. If you pick goals that don't feel challenging enough, your mind will go soft and, again, will not engage with the level of passion and conviction you need.

Write these goals on a clean sheet of paper.

Study the list again.

Do these goals line up with your Credo? If not, adjust them so that they do — or consider adjusting your Credo if you feel strongly toward the goals you've articulated.

Do they feel sufficiently challenging, yet doable?

Good.

Five-Year Vision Statement

Now you're going to put these five-year goals into the form of a present-tense vision statement. Here's a mock example:

Example

"My name is John Doe. It is January 1, 2010. I am a highly sought-after Screenwriter, creating commercially successful film and TV projects. As the founder of The Script Master, a thriving organization, I continue to provide excellent service to writers, assisting them in actualizing their full potential and bringing their projects to successful fruition — creating films and TV shows of outstanding quality and substance.

I am financially secure. I have enough passive income coming in from royalties on books, scripts, and produced film and TV projects that I don't have to work at all — freeing me up to do only what I'm passionate about, and help others do the same.

I am confident and comfortable in my own skin. Everything is working as planned — and even greater than I imagined. I'm on purpose, on track, and grateful for all I have — and it's just the beginning!"

Yours doesn't have to look anything like this example. You might only need a few lines, or feel compelled to write it in iambic pentameter. Do whatever turns you on. I mean that literally. It *must* light your fire — or you'll be left out in the cold.

Okay, get comfortable, pull out your notebook, and start writing. Don't worry about grammar or spelling. After you've written it quickly, you can go back and polish it. And don't just make a dry shopping list. Let your creative energy and passion pour into this document. You might even want to turn on some music that gets your juices flowing.

Good work!

Remember, this is just a "coat" you're trying on for now. If it makes you feel like you need to call Queer Eye for the Straight Guy (or Straight Eye for the Queer Guy, depending on your preference) then take the darn thing off and try on a new one.

One-Year Vision

Now you're going to take your five-year vision, and create a one-year plan. The first step is brainstorming all the different ways you could achieve your goals — not just the way it's been done before. And not just the way the "business" says it's done. Think outside the box. There's no "right" or "wrong" here, just possibilities.

This business is full of stories of people doing all kinds of crazy things that led to their success. Many have heard the story of Spielberg. When he was starting out, he snuck onto the Universal lot, took over an abandoned office, put his name on the door, and began hanging out like he owned the place. It led to his first directing gig. He may not own the place now, but he sure could.

Make a list of at least twenty ways you can accomplish each of these five-year goals. Write until you have nothing left — then write some more. That's where the mind stops and the real magic starts.

Let's say you have a goal of becoming the top script consultant in town. Here are some ideas that might get you there:

◊ Build a strong "referral based" business that leads to more and bigger clients in the business
◊ Work on a script that becomes a major movie or garners strong word-of-mouth
◊ Offer free script consulting services to movie stars' production companies
◊ Offer to speak for free at every college, conference, coffee shop, and bookstore that will have you — and develop a following
◊ Take out ads in *Variety* and the *Hollywood Reporter*
◊ Take out billboards on Sunset Boulevard like Angelina
◊ Secretly lure Spielberg into a life-threatening situation — then save his life. When he asks how he can repay you, tell him you want to be the top script doctor in town

Reality Check

Obviously, some of these actions are more doable than others. While we would all like to be as brave as Spielberg, most of us aren't likely to break the law to "break in." (And I'm not advocating you do.)

So take a few moments and pare down your list for each five-year goal down to the things you could do without getting arrested, killed, or forced into seclusion.

Narrowing It Down

Now that you have your list of realistic, but challenging, choices, pick the one sub-goal you're going to actually go for (for each of your five-year goals). This should give you a sense of what must come "before" you can achieve your five-year goal.

Reverse Engineering Your Goals

Now work backwards from each sub-goal to the step you would need to take to accomplish it. Let's say your goal was to get a screenwriting book published. Before that, you'd need to find a publisher who wants to buy it. Before that, you'd have to find an agent who wants to represent it — or submit query letters to publishers. Before that, you'd need to write the book — or book proposal. Before that, you'd need to decide what you were going to write and outline it. Before that, you'd need to do some research to find out what kind of screenwriting books are on the market and what gap your book could fill.

Get it?

Do this until you've come up with the one-year goal.

Then repeat this process for each five-year goal you came up with.

Go with the Flow Chart

One way to organize this information is to create a *flow chart*. Take a piece of legal-size paper, turn it on its side. Make a box in the upper right hand corner, and write your five-year goal inside. (If you have several five-year goals, you should use a separate chart for each.) Then draw another box to the left of your five-year goal, and write the sub-goal inside. Draw an arrow from the left box to the right box to indicate direction. Work this backwards until you get to where you are now.

This will give you a visual "map" of how you can get from where you are to where you want to be.

One-Year Vision Statement

Just like you did with your five-year goals, you're going to put your one-year goals into a present-tense affirmative, passionate statement.

Example

"My name is John Doe. It is January 1, 2006. As a script consultant, and founder of The Script Master, I am highly sought after, working with clients around the world, helping them to write and market top-quality scripts. As a screenwriter, I am in production on my latest film, with a top star, and using that momentum to obtain more writing assignments on increasingly high-profile films.

"I am making at least six figures a year, eliminating all debt, and creating a financial freedom fund that will allow me to retire by the time I'm 40. I'm doing work that I love, creating exciting projects with amazing potential, and collaborating with other writers and artists who share my vision of excellence in entertainment.

"I am happy and secure, confident that my life is on track and on purpose."

Okay, you know what to do.

Pull out that notebook and craft your *one-year vision statement.*

Excellent!

Getting excited yet? You should be. By doing this work, you've just put yourself in the top five percent of the population. Sadly, most people don't have a clue what they're here to do or what they want. And if they do manage to muster up a vague vision of their future, they don't have a plan to achieve it.

They're like seeds upon the wind, going wherever it blows.

30-Day Vision and Action Plan

We're closing in on the starting line. We began with the end, and we're almost to the beginning. Pretty soon, you'll have a list of things to do *tomorrow*!

Just as before, you're going to brainstorm ways to achieve your one-year goals, narrow them down to the "doable" ones, then work backwards until you come up with your 30-day goals.

In addition, this time you're going to articulate the "actions" you will take to accomplish these. So if your 30-day goal is to have your first script consultant client, some of your actions might be as follows:

- Create a list of magazine and internet sites to advertise on
- Create ad copy and submit it
- Have cards made up (and maybe brochures)
- Attend writer's workshops, entertainment seminars (be specific about which ones if you can), introduce myself as a script doctor/story consultant, hand out cards
- Visit internet chat rooms for writers and entertainment people, and let them know of my services
- Offer a free talk on screenwriting at the local library, bookstore, college, coffee shop, and have my cards and brochures available
- Read a book on screenwriting
- Read a couple screenplays
- Take a workshop on screenwriting
- Send brochures to production companies, offering to do the first script free

Okay. You should now have a pretty detailed list of things you can actually do to achieve your 30-day goals which, when accomplished, will move you toward your one-year goals which, as you achieve them, will drive you with increasing momentum toward your five-year goals.

Pretty cool, huh?

But wait, there's more...

One-Week Goals

You're a pro at this by now. As you've probably already guessed, your task is to take your 30-day goals and work backwards to the things you could do in a single week.

If, when you're done, you realize you would need to work 25 hours a day to accomplish everything in a week, you'll need to re-engineer your 30-day plan to be more realistic.

Have at it!

One-Day Goals

You know the drill. Work backwards from your one-week goals to create a list of what you can actually do *tomorrow*. Don't freak out. If you've followed the process, you should have a list of doable tasks, not Herculean ones.

If your to-do list for tomorrow makes you want to start bingeing on bundt cake and pork rinds, or drink yourself to sleep, don't panic. Just go back to your previous lists and rearrange your goals until you have a one-day plan that causes maximum inspiration and minimal perspiration.

Weekly vs. Monthly Planning

Some time-management techniques advocate weekly versus monthly planning. I think you need to plan at least one week ahead to manage your time and top priorities efficiently and effectively. But the one-month overview really gives you greater perspective and allows you to track larger projects. So here's my solution: Do both. Chart your month for the bird's-eye view. But focus on it one week at a time (unless something major comes up requiring you to reevaluate your month).

So grab your calendar, daily planner, or PDA — and fill in the next month.

All right. You should have a pretty thorough plan in front of you. Now all that's left is to take Nike's advice — Just Do It!

But first, it's party time. Treat yourself tonight. Pop open a bottle of Sparkling Apple Cider and celebrate.

Because tomorrow is going to be a big day.

Chapter Summary

◊ What is something you could do that, if done regularly, would make a huge positive difference in your life? Your answer will give you an indication of what is truly important in moving your life forward.

◊ When developing your plan, pick goals that are achievable, but still a stretch.

◊ Write your vision statement in a way that really "lights your fire" — or you'll be left out in the cold.

◊ When brainstorming different ways to achieve your goals, don't just write out options that have been done before. Think outside the box.

◊ When listing different ways to achieve your goals, write until you have nothing left — then write some more. That's often when the real magic starts happening.

◊ Once you determine your major goals, use "reverse engineering" to work your way back from the accomplishment of the goal to present day. This will give you a connected road map from where you are to where you want to be.

◊ An effective way to organize your goals is with a *flow chart*. This gives you a clear, visual map from start to finish.

◊ Planning one week ahead allows you to manage your time and priorities more efficiently and effectively. Having a one-month overview gives you greater perspective and allows you to track larger projects.

◊ By doing this work, you put yourself in the top five percent of the population.

◇ If You Think You Can or Cannot, You're Right

◇ Your Mindset is More Important Than Your Typeset

◇ The Power of Intention

◇ Four Ways to Stay Fired Up When You're Fired

Chapter Eighteen

"For as he thinketh in his heart, so is he."
— *Proverbs 23:7*

"The spirit, the will to win, and the will to excel are the things that endure. These qualities are so much more important than the events that occur."
—*Vince Lombardi*

"We are what and where we are because we have first imagined it."
—*Donald Curtis*

Mindset for Success

If You Think You Can or Cannot, You're Right

Our outer life is an expression of our inner life. The things we believe, even if they're false, tend to become our experience — a "self-fulfilling prophecy." Show me a person who believes there's not enough opportunity out there, and I'll show you a person who's out of work. Show me a person who believes there's more than enough to go around, and I'll show you someone who's not only gainfully employed but has money in the bank.

While this is certainly a useful concept for all aspects of our lives, we can put it to work specifically in dealing with any limited beliefs we may have around this business, beliefs that will hinder our progress unless we consciously confront and change them.

Some of the beliefs might be: *"The market is over-saturated with script consultants competing for a handful of writers." "It's really difficult to make a good living doing script consulting." "You have to be a screenwriter." "You have to live in Hollywood." "It's going to take me years to have any success at this."*

Now you might be thinking, *"These aren't beliefs, they're the truth."* And I would both agree and disagree with you based on a mystical quote, *"A lie believed* acts *as truth, until neutralized."* In other words, it's that old self-fulfilling prophecy again. The fact is, these aren't "truths" in any ultimate sense, they're just descriptions of someone's experience, a collective "opinion." If they were "true," if they were based on natural laws or universal principles, they could *never* be defied. But, in fact, many individuals have overcome these limitations. Individuals just like you.

But here's the rub: you must *choose* a more empowering belief system consciously, and cultivate it daily, for it to have an effect in your life.

Let's just look at a couple common limited beliefs and the affirmative alternatives.

"There's not enough business out there."

I built my business on one major belief: *"There are thousands of people out there who need exactly what I have to offer, and can pay for it!"* While other script consultants I knew were struggling and railing against the economy, the business, and God, I was silently affirming this truth and reaping its fruits.

So which statement is true?

The one you believe.

The fact is, there's more than enough to go around. But it won't be going around *you* if you don't believe it exists.

"There's just too much competition."

If you're being authentic and offering your unique gifts in a unique way, you transcend competition because there's literally nobody else out there offering what you are. You only compete when you're trying to be like someone else.

Life is not a finite pie in which we must all fight to get a piece. There *is* infinite opportunity and abundance. And when we adopt that point of view, if the literal thing we need doesn't yet exist — it will be created. The boundaries of our experience are limited only by our imagination and willingness to believe in something more.

You may not agree with these concepts, but you can't escape their effects. They're principles — natural laws — not opinions. Just like the law of the farm: "*You reap what you sow.*"

Your Mindset is More Important Than Your Typeset

You can have the most beautiful font in the world, but if you don't believe there's anyone out there who wants to see it — there won't be. "*You can't make a demand on life that exceeds your belief about it.*" If you believe there's too much competition, not enough potential clients, or that all the good opportunities have already been taken — then you're right. And your experience will become an affirmation of your limited perceptions, giving you the satisfaction of saying, "*See, I told you so!*"

But if you embody the belief that there is more than enough, and that "*your own shall come to you,*" then that will become the personal law unto your life — and you will reap the rewards.

But don't take my word for it. Try it out!

The Power of Intention

Intention is like the rudder that steers your ship. Without a powerful intention, you're like a piece of driftwood upon a rough sea, tossed about until you accidentally hit land — or are smashed against the rocks.

If you've done the mission statement work, you've taken a big step *internally*. If you've hung out your shingle, you've taken a big step *externally*. These two steps are like your right and left feet — they must work together to move you forward. If you focus only on the internal step (your left foot), you'll stay stuck in place. If you focus only on the external step (your right foot), you'll fall on your face.

"I just had a sense that I would be good at this and I had something I wanted to teach," says Chris Vogler. "So I sort of made that announcement in two directions. Internally, to myself, I said, 'I want to do that, I don't know quite why, but I think that's a good path for me.' Externally, I told people in my environment at the studio, 'Yeah, I'd like to teach.' And then the opportunity came up because somebody heard me say that. A fellow analyst and junior executive there was going to teach at UCLA and didn't want to do it by himself, so he said 'Why don't we do it together?' That's how I got started. I think it's an important principle, that when you want to do something or make a change you announce it in those two directions, internally and externally. You have to let yourself know and you have to let the world know that's where you're headed.

"The other tool was enthusiasm. I was just enthusiastic about certain subjects and that's how I built my reputation in the studio. There would be a stack of scripts to be read and most people would come along and take the top ten and go off. I would go through and pull out certain ones in my area of interest. I knew what I liked and I was telling the world what I liked. Science fiction, fantasy, comic books, children's literature, history, epics, that was my thing and I declared that and claimed it and was very enthusiastic about it. And that started carving out an identity for me."

Four Ways to Stay Fired Up When You're Fired
Even with the best of intentions and a master of your craft, you will likely have the painful experience (maybe more than once) of being served your walking papers. But do not despair. Even the best among us gets the boot from time to time.

If, and when, this fate befalls you, here are some ways to deal with it:

- **Don't dwell on the negative.** Don't ask yourself, "Why me?" Because your mind will rattle off a nice laundry list of all the reasons you deserve to be fired, penniless, and on the streets. Instead ask questions like, "How is this a good thing?" "How am I going to be even more successful and effective because of this experience?" "What can I learn and how can I grow from this?" The questions you ask are so important. Ask ones that will give you inspiring, motivating, expansive answers. It's okay to take a moment to grieve the loss, but don't hang out in hell. It's hot and humid and your hair will get all flat and frizzy.

○ **Don't commiserate.** It's very tempting to tell everyone with an open ear your sad tale of woe. *Don't.* Because you'll likely get a bunch of people agreeing with how awful it is, what a jerk your client was, and how this whole world has gone to hell in a handbasket. Sure, that conversation might give you a moment of comfort, but it ultimately won't make you feel better. Keep your conversations in heaven. This is not a religious statement. It means that you want the tone of your talk to be largely optimistic and forward-looking. Don't you? I'm not saying you shouldn't talk about problems and issues — but talk about them from the perspective of *solutions, not complaints.*

○ **Wish your client the best.** In your closing comments or letter with your departing client, sincerely wish them success. This is a hard one, I know. After all, they just fired you. Here's the thing you must understand: *It's not personal.* In Hollywood, especially, writers are fired all the time — then hired back months later on the same project. You don't want to burn any bridges. Besides, it's just better to put out positive energy. It makes you — and everyone else — feel better. And it doesn't cost you anything — except your negativity.

○ **Keep your eyes on the prize.** It's the old, "you may have lost the battle, but you haven't lost the war" perspective. What is your bigger vision? Read your Script Consultant Credo and five-year plan. Pray about it. Write about it. Sacrifice a chicken over it (a rubber chicken) — whatever your groove is. Bottom line: Keep your attention on the long-term goal, re-center around your core principles and priorities — and keep moving forward.

Chapter Summary

◊ Our outer life is a reflection of our inner life; the things we believe, even if they're false, become the laws that determine our experience.

◊ There are some limited beliefs around this business that will unconsciously hinder you if you're not consciously refuting them.

◊ You must consciously choose a more empowering belief system, and cultivate it daily, for it to have an effect in your life.

◊ There is more than enough to go around — but it won't be going around you if you don't believe it.

◊ If you're being authentic and offering your unique gifts in a unique way, you transcend competition because there's nobody else out there offering what you are. You only compete when you try to be like someone else.

◊ The boundaries of our experience are limited only by our imagination and willingness to believe in something more.

◊ Intention is like the rudder that steers your ship. Without a powerful intention, you're like a piece of driftwood upon a rough sea.

◊ You must balance the "internal" steps with the "external" ones. If you focus only on the internal step, you'll stay stuck in place. If you focus only on the external step, you'll fall on your face.

◊ Four ways to stay fired up when you're fired: Don't dwell on the negative, don't commiserate, wish your client the best, keep your eyes on the prize.

◊ Juggling Too Many Balls

◊ Multitasking the Muse

◊ Finding Your Rhythm

◊ Pay Yourself First

◊ Ethics and Integrity

◊ Money-Back Guarantee

◊ Keep it Simple

Chapter Nineteen

"So divinely is the world organized that
every one of us, in our place and time, is in
balance with everything else."
— Johann Wolfgang von Goethe

"One person with passion is better than
forty people merely interested."
— E. M. Forster

Maintaining Balance and Passion

Juggling Too Many Balls

Once things get cooking in your business, and the opportunities start coming your way, it will be very tempting to take on too much. If the offers are good projects with good people for good pay, how can you say "no"? You may be able to manage several script analysis jobs at once (it's good to get away from the script after a first read, during which time you can begin work on another script analysis), but when, and if, you start doing script doctor jobs, this will become increasingly difficult. Sure, there are the Ron Bass's of the world (Academy Award winner, *Rain Man*), who can work on fifteen scripts at once — but the unfortunate fact (or fortunate, depending on how you look at it) is that the majority of us are not genetically mutated to perform like that.

Not that I haven't tried, mind you.

Says Dave Trottier, "I think one mistake that some beginning script consultants make is they think it is going to be easy, but it's intense. When I'm working on a script, I have to be really focused. And I'm tired when I'm done. Maybe it's easier for other people, I don't know, but for me, it's really hard work."

I remember one period early on in my career when I was analyzing several scripts a week, working on my own specs (scripts written speculatively), writing three full-length scripts for clients, and developing other non-writing projects — all at the same time! And I had a wife and two kids who also required ample amounts of attention. Needless to say, the time I gave them wasn't very ample. Nor was the care I gave myself.

And I paid for it.

The cost was exhaustion, soul-weariness, and a significant strain on my health (I think I gained several points on my blood pressure and lost several layers of my stomach lining).

The moral of this story: *"If you live for your work, you'll work yourself to death."*

This doesn't mean you can't be passionate about your prose, and live for a great purpose. It just means you need to keep it all in perspective. As the saying goes, "On your deathbed, you're not going to say, 'God, I wish I'd spent more time at the office.'" Seriously, you won't. I know, because I've had some "near-death" experiences myself, and I can tell you with certainty that booking that next gig was nowhere to be found on my to-do list. Having peace of mind, spending time with loved ones, and using what little life I thought I had left in service to a higher vision were what topped the list.

I don't mean to get so heavy-handed with you here. But I don't want this book, or my work, to add fuel to the already work-obsessed culture we live in (in America, anyway). So this is my plug for a more peaceful path.

Multitasking the Muse

If you do decide to take on several projects at once, here are a few tips for making it as harmonious as possible.

- Be honest with your clients about your workload, and work out a dead-line that gives you breathing room. If they're in a rush to get their project done, you can add a rush charge and put them on top of the stack. Or tell them this is the best you can do and be willing to let the project go if you can't fulfill it in a reasonable timeframe. I know this sounds hard, but you're sending a very strong message of authority and confidence with this. If they're smart, they'll realize they're in the hands of a real pro — one who's in demand and doesn't need their business — and they'll adjust to *your* schedule.

◦ **Stagger your projects in different stages.** One way to work on many projects is to have them at different phases of development; the first read on an analysis, developing a treatment from a book adaptation, writing a first draft of a script, and doing a line-edit on another.

◦ **Take plenty of vacations.** A week, a few days, even a few hours — on a regular basis. Think of it like your computer. If you keep it running and running, and never shut it down so it can reboot, its cache gets clogged, its RAM gets bogged, and it becomes slower and less efficient. We need to reboot — or we'll burn out. This is one of the hardest things for some of us. There's this terrible fear that if we walk away from our work, we'll lose our competitive edge, our careers will implode, and we'll end up broke, alone, and mentally ill, wandering down Hollywood Boulevard, mumbling the pitch to our latest script.

This couldn't be further from the truth. Taking time off actually recharges us and makes us more productive. How is it that in Europe, where they take five weeks vacation every year, and work an average of thirty-two hours a week (they're actually restricted by law to work more), their productivity levels are very close to ours? What would America look like if we all took five weeks off a year and worked thirty-two hour weeks? Maybe a few less drive-by shootings and 12-step meetings?

Finding Your Rhythm

Are you a "morning person" or a "night owl"? Do you find that no matter how late you go to bed, you still wake up early — or no matter how early you go to bed, you still wake up late? What time of the day do you feel most creative? Which time of the day do you feel most social? When is your mind the sharpest, your body the most energized? These are important questions to answer for yourself, for they are clues to what your natural rhythms are.

Knowing when you're most creative can add massive productivity to your day if you schedule your "big" projects around it. And knowing when you're *not* at your best can eliminate the frustration that comes from banging your head against the wall in a vain attempt to get it to operate — when it is clearly closed for business.

We do different kinds of things each day, requiring different parts of ourselves and different levels of energy. Writing a script or doing a script analysis requires a significant output of creative juice. Paying your bills and checking emails usually doesn't (even though it feels like it sometimes). If you fritter away your high creative time doing busy-work, it's tough to get it back. It's like watering your grass with holy water. It's a waste.

Protect your muse's energy for the most important projects. Then use the other cycles of the day for everything else. You will find yourself getting more done, at an even higher standard.

Pay Yourself First

This is a term used by financial planners when they coach their client on how to save for retirement. Most people pay everyone else first, then, if they have anything left over, they try to save it. The problem is, there is rarely anything left over. So the individual tries to work harder or smarter, spend less, and squeeze a few pennies out of what remains of their paycheck. This usually results in more frustration than financial freedom.

So what does this have to do with you and your script consulting business? In the pursuit of serving your clients (so you can pay your bills), it's easy to get so busy that you don't have anything left over to serve yourself and your bigger goals. If your ultimate dream is to be one of the top script consultants, this won't be as much of an issue for you, since everything you'll be doing will lead you in that general direction. But if your bigger goal is to be a screenwriter — as mine was — please heed this warning. It's so easy to fall prey to a false sense of fulfillment, that you lose sight of your larger vision. And before you know it, a year or two (or ten) have gone by and you haven't advanced your greater career aspirations at all.

This was the case for me. I became so busy with script consulting and script doctoring that I turned around one day and realized I hadn't written an original screenplay in two years — the one thing I needed to do to achieve my bigger dreams. Sure, I was paying my bills, feeding my family, and living a pretty abundant lifestyle — but my soul was feeling impoverished, and the big "B" word ("burnout") was right around the corner. Eventually, I found myself staring at a stack of projects for which I'd already been paid — and had basically spent the money — but had done nary a lick of work on.

I knew something was wrong.

I didn't just have writer's block, I had writer's dam. It felt like my creative juices were being held back by a wall of concrete and metal three-hundred feet thick. That's when I had an epiphany of sorts and realized I had basically sold out. In that moment, I made a decision that I would rather sleep under a bridge living my purpose than sleep in a mansion living someone else's.

This didn't mean quitting my script consulting and script doctoring, it just meant putting it into proper perspective. It meant paying myself first; making my first priority to work on my passion projects. Ironically, doing this allowed me not only to become more productive, but to give my client's even better, more attentive service than ever before.

I still struggle with balance almost daily. But at least I'm conscious of it now. And I've created a practice that enables me to become aware of when I'm out of alignment — so I can get back on track.

Ethics and Integrity

You will have clients approach you that don't know anything about the business, and it might be tempting at times to exaggerate your position in the industry, or make promises you can't keep (like telling them you can get their script to buyers when you really can't). Besides being bad karma (if you believe in that), it's bad business. It's a very small town, and it will catch up with you.

Think long-term. You're building relationships, alliances, clientele, and a reputation that will (hopefully) endure for many years. This comes at a price. It may mean sacrificing immediate gratification (getting the job) or expediency (getting the job done quickly but not doing the best job), for simply doing the right thing. But these sacrifices are like seeds you are planting that, if watered and fed with hard work, determination, and vision, will allow you to reap a bountiful harvest in this field.

"I've had a number of people say to me, 'I'd like to do what you do,'" says Linda Seger. "I say I can teach them how to do it, but it's going to take years. But many people don't want to put in the years. They want to be going over to Europe teaching, but they don't want to put in the years of doing seminars in the U.S., at colleges, and the Learning Annex, sometimes even doing speeches and seminars for free, especially in the beginning. You have to build your career — and that takes time."

Money-Back Guarantee

Risk-reversal is a powerful tool for your business, and I highly encourage you to implement it in some form. If you're an unknown, it can boost your credibility and bolster your bottom line. It gives the client some insurance, makes them more willing to make the call, and eliminates many of the barriers to sending you that check. After all, what do they have to lose?

I've talked to people who implement this strategy, and there are very few cases where customers actually ask for their money back. Says Linda Seger, "I had a client, in the last few months, who said she had come to me some years before and wasn't real happy, and I had volunteered to refund her money, but she decided not to accept. She said she was so impressed by that, so she came back to me with another script. I've consulted on over 2000 projects, and have refunded money about eight times during over 20 years in the business. If they're unhappy, I think of it as a store owner who would refund money to a dissatisfied customer. In a few instances, I refunded money because the person seemed dissatisfied, and after re-reading my notes, they sent me the money back. Another time, someone gave me the money back a year later when he realized that what I had said was reinforced by several other consultants during that year."

When it comes to script doctoring, it's a little different. In that case, you've probably put in a lot more time (weeks or months), and the client has had several opportunities to give feedback. But be open to a compromise if the client is genuinely unhappy. Maybe you can offer to give some of the money back, at least for the portion of work not yet complete. Or you can offer a free consultation on their next script.

Vying on the side of generosity and cooperation is just a good way to go. People are impressed by it. Even if they don't continue using your services, they'll usually hold your business in good regard — allowing you to maintain a positive public image.

And somehow the universe always balances out the scales.

Keep It Simple

It's important to keep studying, learning, growing, and staying involved in your field of interest. But, as we've already discussed, it's also easy to get so busy that you lose sight of the original vision, the core idea that inspired you to embark on this journey in the first place. I like to look at my life and business the way Michelangelo looked at the block of marble before he sculpted David. It wasn't about adding a bunch of stuff to make the sculpture, it was about chipping away everything that wasn't it. The perfect masterpiece was already there, Michelangelo just cleared away what was covering it up.

The masterpiece that is your life's work is already here.

You simply must keep the vision clear in your mind — uncluttered by a lot of unimportant activity — and keep chipping away.

Chapter Summary

- As your consulting/script doctoring business grows, resist the temptation to take on too much.

- If you take on several projects at once, here are a few tips to keep it harmonious: (1) Be honest with your clients about your workload, and work out a deadline that gives you breathing room ;(2) Stagger your projects in different stages; (3) Take plenty of vacations.

- When are you most creative, alert, and energized? Are you a morning person, a night person? Finding your natural rhythms and adjusting accordingly can add massive productivity to your daily schedule.

- Pay yourself first. Feed your deepest needs (creatively and otherwise) and highest priorities (passion projects, big dreams) on a daily basis, preferably *before* working on clients' material. This will actually allow you to be more productive and provide better service.

- Always tell the truth about yourself and your business, and never make a promise you can't keep. This is a small town and it will catch up to you.

- Do "the right thing," even when it means sacrificing immediate gratification. Think long term, relationship building. Think "marathon ," not "sprint."

- Risk-reversal is one of the most powerful tools for getting prospects to do business with you. Having an ironclad money-back guarantee (or "better-than-money-back-guarantee") is a great way to take advantage of this principle.

- Don't lose sight of the core reason you became a consultant. This is your source of power, your fountain of inspiration.

◊ Do Something Productive Every Day

◊ Take Frequent Breaks

◊ Get Organized

◊ Work When You Work Best

◊ Give Every Project 100%

◊ Keep Learning

◊ Act and Dress Like a Pro

◊ Honor Your Work Hours

◊ Take Care of Yourself

◊ Know Thyself

Chapter Twenty

"Bad habits are like a comfortable bed,
easy to get into, but hard to get out of."
— Unknown

"Your net worth to the world is usually
determined by what remains after your
bad habits are subtracted from your good
ones."
— Benjamin Franklin

Ten Habits of Highly Successful Script Consultants

Think of this as a quick-reference for instant inspiration.

Do Something Productive Every Day

If you're a writer, write something every day — whether it's your project or a client's. If you're strictly a consultant and you don't have any work to do at the moment, study a great script to see how it's put together. The point here is to keep exercising and refining your craft, building your knowledge, and keeping the momentum — all of which will give you a competitive edge. This isn't about becoming a workaholic. It's about breaking through the inertia of complacency. It's so easy to get comfortable, to settle for the status quo, to rationalize why you're not doing what you know you need to in order to succeed. "I don't feel like it" is not a viable excuse anymore.

Take Frequent Breaks

This may sound like a contradiction to the above habit. It's not. In fact, without this one, you won't be able to sustain the level of quality and productivity referred to above. Unless you're able to take a break (whether it's ten minutes, an hour, a day, or a week) and recharge, you'll soon be booking a room in burnout city.

Get Organized

A messy, disorganized office is an energy sapper if there ever was one. Not just because it takes longer to find that important document under that stack of unopened bills, but also because it literally pulls power from your psychic field. Every little "toleration" you put up with burns fuel that could be put to much better use in growing your business.

Work When You Work Best

Some of us are morning people. Others are struck with the muse at the stroke of midnight. If you don't already know, find out what time of day you work best, and gear your most labor-intensive activities for that time period. (Of course, if you're on a deadline, you might have to work around the clock, but that's a different issue.) If you schedule your activities based on your energy cycles, you will find your productivity take a quantum leap.

For example, I have two periods when I work the best — late morning and late afternoon. So I try to schedule the heavy-lifting (writing, analyzing) during those hours. When I first get up, I need to ease into the day's work, so I do more preparatory work, like going over the day's schedule, straightening up the office, emails. Once I'm warmed up, I crack open the script or writing file and get to work for a few hours. I break for lunch, meditation, make calls, work out, do some errands — and start my second writing period. Then it's home for family time, dinner, and bedtime stories. But not my bedtime. Because at night, my energy cycle is perfect for opening mail, paying bills, filing, doing simple research — tasks that don't take a lot of energy.

The point of this example is that if I opened my mail and paid my bills in the late morning, I would waste my most productive energy cycle (not to mention become depressed) which I couldn't make up very easily at night during my bill-paying, mail-opening time. Make sense? It may take some time to find your perfect energy-schedule, but it's worth the experimentation. I'm still making adjustments.

Give Every Project 100%

Treat every project like it's the job of your dreams — and you'll soon attract more and more of your dream jobs. Why? Because you don't get what you want in life, you get what you are. Ghandi said we must become the change we want to see in the world. Likewise, we must become the kind of person who would get the kind of jobs we want in the world. This is another one of those universal principles I keep slipping in here. If it gives you a headache to try and make sense of it, don't. Just give it a shot and see what happens.

Keep Learning

To have what others don't, you must do what others won't. The average person — and for that matter, the average script consultant — has a tendency to take the path of least resistance. So you must take the road less traveled. Stay open at the top. Maintain a Beginner's Mind. Besides continued study in related and complementary fields — read and investigate areas outside of your field — and outside of show business. Some of the most innovative ideas have come from people adapting concepts they discovered in completely unrelated fields.

Act and Dress Like a Pro

This is another relative rule. A stockbroker acts and dresses quite differently than a tennis pro. In the entertainment industry, an executive acts and dresses differently than an actor. Even more specific, different clients will have different expectations. In general, business casual seems to work best.

You also want to have an updated resume and work samples readily available. Do your homework, show up to appointments with all the right gear to get the job done, and treat each client or prospect with the utmost respect and value.

Honor Your Work Hours

During work hours, especially in a home office, you'll have plenty of opportunities for distraction from well-meaning friends and family members. In the most diplomatic tone you can muster, kindly inform them that you're at work, not at home. This is a real business, not a hobby. You'll talk to them after hours, or on your break.

Take Care of Yourself

Feed your mind and body with high quality nourishment — and exercise. I know this is obvious to most people — yet most people still don't do it. Writing and consulting is hard work that requires real endurance. If you want to be a high-performance person, you need to run on high-octane fuel.

Know Thyself

The most successful people, in this or any field, know who they are so they can be true to that. They also know their strengths — so they can play to them — and their weaknesses — so they can compensate for them.

Chapter Summary

- Exercise your craft and build your knowledge a little every day — and you will maintain a competitive advantage.

- Without regular "breaks" you won't be able to sustain the level of quality and productivity needed to remain competitive.

- A messy, disorganized office — and life — saps massive energy that could otherwise be put into growing your business and fulfilling your dreams.

- Find out what time of day you work best, and schedule your most labor-intensive activities for that time period.

- Treat every project like it's the job of your dreams — and you will attract more and more of your dream jobs.

- To have what others don't, you must do what others won't. To do what others won't, you need to know what others don't. Therefore, keep learning and keep churning.

- Operate your business like a professional, from how you answer the phone to what you wear in meetings.

- It's so easy to get distracted by friendly phone calls and unexpected visitors. Don't let that happen. When it's work time — *work*.

- If you want to be a high-performance person, you need to run on high-octane fuel. Therefore, feed your mind and body with high quality nourishment. And exercise both.

- Know Thyself. The most successful people know who they are and craft a career that compensates for their weaknesses and exploits their strengths.

Fade Out / Epilogue

Why We Need Great Script Consultants

While there are a lot of talented executives working in Hollywood today, many suits with the responsibility to shepherd a project through the maze of development have no more story sense than the typical movie-goer (even less in many cases, since movie-goers don't have the jaded perception of the movie-making process or the pressure to keep their jobs). So getting notes from some executives is like taking medical advice from the doctor's receptionist, or worse, letting her operate on your child. At least, that's how it feels to many screenwriters when they put their baby into the hands of these well-intentioned, but sometimes misguided, individuals.

But I have a dream. A dream of seeing the development process transformed so that those who are reading and evaluating scripts, doing "coverage," and guiding projects — are people who actually have a mastery of the medium. A development process populated by gifted, passionate script consultants who understand the anatomy of a good story and are dedicated not only to creating great scripts — but to seeking out the greater possibilities that this medium of movies has to offer.

It's an ambitious dream, I know.

But then any vision of real value is.

We are like foot soldiers in this battle for better movies. And the skirmishes start with our individual clients. While we can't readily control the nature of the industry or the quality of its product, we can have a hand in the development of material being submitted to fortress Hollywood. A few of the hardiest among you might even breech the outer walls (if you haven't already) and, with patience and persistence, transform the system from the inside.

It's a worthy goal.

See, I believe that movies are more than just entertainment. While one definition of "entertain" is "to divert or amuse" — and many movies certainly accomplish this — another definition is "to consider; to contemplate; to hold in mind." In other words, the stories we tell, and the ideas they contain, ultimately become the focus of mass contemplation.

And what you focus on long enough...you become.

So the question is: what do we want to become?

That's ultimately for each of us to decide.

But it's definitely a question worth "entertaining'"for a while.

See you at the movies!

About the Author

The nephew of legendary film director Don Siegel (*Dirty Harry*, *Escape from Alcatraz*, *Invasion of the Body Snatchers*), Derek Rydall has been in show business most of his life. His diverse experience as an actor, screenwriter, playwright, script consultant, and script doctor give him the unique ability to understand film (and stories in general) on many levels, and allow him to give his clients that extra edge that takes their script to the next level — the one that sells!

As an actor, Derek starred in several films and TV shows with Tom Skerritt, Charles Bronson, Elliot Gould, Tony Roberts (of Woody Allen films), Paulie Shore, director John Turtletaub (*Phenomenon*, *National Treasure*), and many others.

As a writer, script consultant, and script doctor, he has been on staff for Fox and Disney, developed projects for Saturn (Nicolas Cage's company), RKO, United Artists, Miramax, Fine Line, Deepak Chopra, the creators of *Air Force One* and *Ghost*, and worked one-on-one with many writers, independent producers, and executives from around the world.

As a playwright, he co-wrote and starred in *Welcome Home Soldier* (the longest running drama in L.A. history), which toured several cities and sponsored many Vietnam vets to go to the wall.

And as a direct result of Derek's consulting, clients have turned their novels into screenplays, made six-figure screenwriting deals, secured millions in financing, obtained major distribution, won multiple film awards, and been hired to executive produce, direct, and even star in their own movies!

Keep an eye out for Derek's next book: *There's No Business Like Soul Business: A Spiritual Path to Higher Entertainment*.

Derek currently resides just outside Los Angeles with his wife, two children, and cat.

Derek is available for speaking engagements, conferences, lectures, and workshops on script consulting and screenwriting. His presentations are both enlightening and entertaining, as he brings his audiences to a new level of understanding, inspiration, and motivation.

For more information
please contact him at:

Derek Rydall
Hollywood Studios
25852 McBean Parkway, #133
Valencia, CA 91355-3705

800.218.7182   661.296.4991

drydall@comcast.net
derek@derekrydall.com
derek@scriptwritercentral.com

Index

THE WRITER'S JOURNEY
2ND EDITION
MYTHIC STRUCTURE FOR WRITERS

CHRISTOPHER VOGLER

BEST SELLER
OVER 116,500 UNITS SOLD!

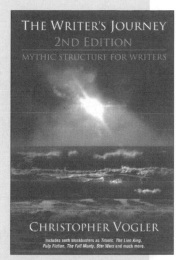

See why this book has become an international bestseller and a true classic. *The Writer's Journey* explores the powerful relationship between mythology and storytelling in a clear, concise style that's made it required reading for movie executives, screenwriters, playwrights, scholars, and fans of pop culture all over the world.

Both fiction and nonfiction writers will discover a set of useful myth-inspired storytelling paradigms (i.e., "The Hero's Journey") and step-by-step guidelines to plot and character development. Based on the work of Joseph Campbell, *The Writer's Journey* is a must for all writers interested in further developing their craft.

The updated and revised second edition provides new insights and observations from Vogler's ongoing work on mythology's influence on stories, movies, and man himself.

"This book is like having the smartest person in the story meeting come home with you and whisper what to do in your ear as you write a screenplay. Insight for insight, step for step, Chris Vogler takes us through the process of connecting theme to story and making a script come alive."

> — Lynda Obst, Producer
> Sleepless in Seattle, How to Lose a Guy in 10 Days
> *Author*, Hello, He Lied

"This is a book about the stories we write, and perhaps more importantly, the stories we live. It is the most influential work I have yet encountered on the art, nature, and the very purpose of storytelling."

> — Bruce Joel Rubin, Screenwriter
> Stuart Little 2, Deep Impact, Ghost, Jacob's Ladder

CHRISTOPHER VOGLER, a top Hollywood story consultant and development executive, has worked on such high-grossing feature films as *The Lion King*, *The Thin Red Line*, *Fight Club*, and *Beauty and the Beast*. He conducts writing workshops around the globe.

$24.95 | 325 PAGES | ORDER # 98RLS | ISBN: 0-941188-70-1

SCRIPT PARTNERS
WHAT MAKES FILM AND TV WRITING TEAMS WORK

CLAUDIA JOHNSON AND MATT STEVENS
FOREWORD BY MARSHALL BRICKMAN

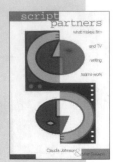

This book examines the role and the importance of collaboration, then illuminates the process of collaborative screenwriting itself. It includes revelatory interviews with such successful collaborators as Andrew Reich & Ted Cohen (*Friends*), Jim Taylor (*Election, About Schmidt*), Marshall Brickman (*Annie Hall, Manhattan*), Scott Alexander & Larry Karaszewski (*The People vs. Larry Flynt, Ed Wood*), and Larry Gelbart (*M*A*S*H*).

$24.95 | 300 PAGES | ORDER # 104RLS | ISBN: 0-941188-75-2

THE SCRIPT-SELLING GAME
A HOLLYWOOD INSIDER'S LOOK AT GETTING YOUR SCRIPT SOLD AND PRODUCED

KATHIE FONG YONEDA

Players understand that their success in Hollywood is not based on luck or nepotism; it's the result of understanding how Hollywood really works. *The Script-Selling Game* brings together over 25 years of experience from an entertainment professional who shows you how to prepare your script, pitch it, meet the moguls, talk the talk, and make the deal. It's a must for both novice and veteran screenwriters.

$14.95 | 196 PAGES | ORDER # 100RLS | ISBN: 0-941188-44-2

WHAT ARE YOU LAUGHING AT?
HOW TO WRITE FUNNY SCREENPLAYS, STORIES, AND MORE

BRAD SCHREIBER
FOREWORD BY CHRISTOPHER VOGLER AUTHOR OF THE WRITER'S JOURNEY

The definitive book on how to "write funny." Using principles developed in his popular UCLA Writers Program class on humor writing and his CBS Studio City seminars on screenwriting, Schrieber includes more than 70 excerpts from such top prose and screenwriters as Woody Allen, Steve Martin, and Kurt Vonnegut Jr.; unique writing exercises developed exclusively for this book; and vital information on writing comedy dialogue for TV, stage, and audio.

$19.95 | 278 PAGES | ORDER # 114RLS | ISBN: 0-941188-83-3

MYTH AND THE MOVIES
DISCOVERING THE MYTHIC STRUCTURE OF 50 UNFORGETTABLE FILMS

STUART VOYTILLA
FOREWORD BY CHRISTOPHER VOGLER
AUTHOR OF *THE WRITER'S JOURNEY*

BEST SELLER
OVER 15,000 UNITS SOLD!

An illuminating companion piece to *The Writer's Journey*, *Myth and the Movies* applies the mythic structure Vogler developed to 50 well-loved U.S. and foreign films. This comprehensive book offers a greater understanding of why some films continue to touch and connect with audiences generation after generation.

Movies discussed include *The Godfather, Some Like It Hot, Citizen Kane, Halloween, Jaws, Annie Hall, Chinatown, The Fugitive, Sleepless in Seattle, The Graduate, Dances with Wolves, Beauty and the Beast, Platoon,* and *Die Hard.*

"Stuart Voytilla's Myth and the Movies *is a remarkable achievement: an ambitious, thought-provoking, and cogent analysis of the mythic underpinnings of fifty great movies. It should prove a valuable resource for film teachers, students, critics, and especially screenwriters themselves, whose challenge, as Voytilla so clearly understands, is to constantly reinvent a mythology for our times."*
> — Ted Tally, Academy Award Screenwriter, Silence of the Lambs

"Myth and the Movies is a must for every writer who wants to tell better stories. Voytilla guides his readers to a richer and deeper understanding not only of mythic structure, but also of the movies we love."
> — Christopher Wehner, Web editor
> The Screenwriters Utopia *and* Creative Screenwriting

"I've script consulted for ten years and I've studied every genre thoroughly. I thought I knew all their nuances - until I read Voytilla's book. This ones goes on my Recommended Reading List. A fascinating analysis of the Hero's Myth for all genres."
> — *Lou Grantt*, Hollywood Scriptwriter Magazine

STUART VOYTILLA is a screenwriter, literary consultant, teacher, and author of *Writing the Comedy Film.*

$26.95 | 300 PAGES | ORDER # 39RLS | ISBN: 0-941188-66-3

SCREENWRITING 101
THE ESSENTIAL CRAFT OF FEATURE FILM WRITING

NEILL D. HICKS

Hicks brings the clarity and practical instruction familiar to his students and readers to screenwriters everywhere. In his inimitable and colorful style, he tells the beginning screenwriter how the mechanics of Hollywood storytelling work, and how to use those elements to create a script with blockbuster potential without falling into clichés.

"Neill Hicks makes complex writing concepts easy to grasp, in a way that only a master teacher could. And he does so while keeping his book one hell of a fun read."

– Eric Edson, Writer, Lethal Vows
Executive Director, The Hollywood Symposium

NEILL D. HICKS' screenwriting credits include *Rumble in the Bronx* and *First Strike*.

$16.95 | 220 PAGES | ORDER # 41RLS | ISBN: 0-941188-72-8

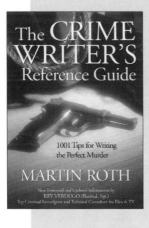

THE CRIME WRITER'S COMPLETE REFERENCE GUIDE
1001 TIPS FOR WRITING THE PERFECT CRIME

MARTIN ROTH

NEW FOREWORD AND UPDATED INFORMATION BY SGT. REY VERDUGO, TOP CRIMINAL INVESTIGATOR AND TECHNICAL CONSULTANT FOR FILM AND TV

Here's the book no writer of murder mysteries, thrillers, action-adventure, true crime, police procedurals, romantic suspense, and psychological mysteries – whether scripts or novels – can do without. Martin Roth provides all the particulars to make your crime story accurate.

"Now you don't need a friend on the force, a buddy in forensics, a contact in the D.A.'s office, or a pal in the morgue – all you need is this book."
– Lee Goldberg, Two-time Edgar Nominee

MARTIN ROTH wrote over 100 TV scripts and several best-selling books, including *The Writer's Partner*.

$17.95 | 300 PAGES | ORDER # 105RLS | ISBN: 0-941188-49-3

FILM & VIDEO BOOKS

Alone In a Room: *Secrets of Successful Screenwriters*
John Scott Lewinski / $19.95

Cinematic Storytelling: *The 100 Most Powerful Film Conventions Every Filmmaker Must Know* / Jennifer Van Sijll / $22.95

The Complete Independent Movie Marketing Handbook: *Promote, Distribute & Sell Your Film or Video* / Mark Steven Bosko / $39.95

Costume Design 101: *The Art and Business of Costume Design for Film and Television* / Richard La Motte / $19.95

Could It Be a Movie? *How to Get Your Ideas Out of Your Head and Up on the Screen* / Christina Hamlett / $26.95

Crashing Hollywood: *How to Keep Your Integrity Up, Your Clothes On & Still Make It in Hollywood* / Fran Harris / $24.95

Creating Characters: *Let Them Whisper Their Secrets*
Marisa D'Vari / $26.95

The Crime Writer's Reference Guide: *1001 Tips for Writing the Perfect Murder*
Martin Roth / $17.95

Cut by Cut: *Editing Your Film or Video*
Gael Chandler / $35.95

Cut to the Chase: *Forty-Five Years of Editing America's Favorite Movies*
Sam O'Steen as told to Bobbie O'Steen / $24.95

Digital Cinema: *The Hollywood Insider's Guide to the Evolution of Storytelling*
Thom Taylor and Melinda Hsu / $27.95

Digital Editing with Final Cut Pro 4 *(includes 45 minutes of DVD tutorials and sample footage)* / Bruce Mamer and Jason Wallace / $31.95

Digital Filmmaking 101: *An Essential Guide to Producing Low-Budget Movies*
Dale Newton and John Gaspard / $24.95

Digital Moviemaking, 2nd Edition: *All the Skills, Techniques, and Moxie You'll Need to Turn Your Passion into a Career* / Scott Billups / $26.95

Directing Actors: *Creating Memorable Performances for Film and Television*
Judith Weston / $26.95

Directing Feature Films: *The Creative Collaboration Between Directors, Writers, and Actors* / Mark Travis / $26.95

Dream Gear: *Cool & Innovative Tools for Film, Video & TV Professionals*
Catherine Lorenze / $29.95

The Encyclopedia of Underground Movies: *Films from the Fringes of Cinema*
Phil Hall / $26.95

The Eye is Quicker *Film Editing: Making a Good Film Better*
Richard D. Pepperman / $27.95

Film & Video Budgets, 3rd Updated Edition
Deke Simon and Michael Wiese / $26.95

Film Directing: *Cinematic Motion, 2nd Edition*
Steven D. Katz / $27.95

Film Directing: *Shot by Shot, Visualizing from Concept to Screen*
Steven D. Katz / $27.95

The Film Director's Intuition: *Script Analysis and Rehearsal Techniques*
Judith Weston / $26.95

Film Production Management 101: *The Ultimate Guide for Film and Television Production Management and Coordination* / Deborah S. Patz / $39.95

Filmmaking for Teens: *Pulling Off Your Shorts*
Troy Lanier and Clay Nichols / $18.95

First Time Director: *How to Make Your Breakthrough Movie*
Gil Bettman / $27.95

From Word to Image: *Storyboarding and the Filmmaking Process*
Marcie Begleiter / $26.95

The Hollywood Standard: *The Complete & Authoritative Guide to Script Format and Style* / Christopher Riley / $18.95

The Independent Film and Videomakers Guide, 2nd Edition: *Expanded and Updated* / Michael Wiese / $29.95

Inner Drives: *How to Write & Create Characters Using the Eight Classic Centers of Motivation* / Pamela Jaye Smith / $26.95

Joe Leydon's Guide to Essential Movies You Must See: *If You Read, Write About – or Make Movies* / Joe Leydon / $24.95

Myth and the Movies: *Discovering the Mythic Structure of 50 Unforgettable Films* / Stuart Voytilla / $26.95

On the Edge of a Dream: *Magic & Madness in Bali*
Michael Wiese / $16.95

The Perfect Pitch: *How to Sell Yourself and Your Movie Idea to Hollywood*
Ken Rotcop / $16.95

Psychology for Screenwriters: *Building Conflict in your Script*
William Indick, Ph.D. / $26.95

Save the Cat! *The Last Book on Screenwriting You'll Ever Need*
Blake Snyder / $19.95

Screenwriting 101: *The Essential Craft of Feature Film Writing*
Neill D. Hicks / $16.95

Script Partners: *What Makes Film and TV Writing Teams Work*
Claudia Johnson and Matt Stevens / $24.95

The Script-Selling Game: *A Hollywood Insider's Look at Getting Your Script Sold and Produced* / Kathie Fong Yoneda / $14.95

Setting Up Your Shots: *Great Camera Moves Every Filmmaker Should Know*
Jeremy Vineyard / $19.95

Shaking the Money Tree, 2nd Edition: *How to Get Grants and Donations for Film and Television* / Morrie Warshawski / $26.95

Sound Design: *The Expressive Power of Music, Voice, and Sound Effects in Cinema* / David Sonnenschein / $19.95

Stealing Fire From the Gods: *A Dynamic New Story Model for Writers and Filmmakers* / James Bonnet / $26.95

Storyboarding 101: *A Crash Course in Professional Storyboarding*
James O. Fraioli / $19.95

The Ultimate Filmmaker's Guide to Short Films: *Making It Big in Shorts*
Kim Adelman / $14.95

What Are You Laughing At? *How to Write Funny Screenplays, Stories, and More* / Brad Schreiber / $19.95

The Working Director: *How to Arrive, Thrive & Survive in the Director's Chair*
Charles Wilkinson / $22.95

The Writer's Journey, 2nd Edition: *Mythic Structure for Writers*
Christopher Vogler / $24.95

The Writer's Partner: *1001 Breakthrough Ideas to Stimulate Your Imagination*
Martin Roth / $19.95

Writing the Action Adventure: *The Moment of Truth*
Neill D. Hicks / $14.95

Writing the Comedy Film: *Make 'Em Laugh*
Stuart Voytilla and Scott Petri / $14.95

Writing the Fantasy Film: *Heroes and Journeys in Alternate Realities*
Sable Jak / $26.95

Writing the Killer Treatment: *Selling Your Story Without a Script*
Michael Halperin / $14.95

Writing the Second Act: *Building Conflict and Tension in Your Film Script*
Michael Halperin / $19.95

Writing the Thriller Film: *The Terror Within*
Neill D. Hicks / $14.95

DVD & VIDEOS

Hardware Wars: *DVD*
Written and Directed by Ernie Fosselius / $14.95

Hardware Wars: *Special Edition VHS Video*
Written and Directed by Ernie Fosselius / $9.95

Field of Fish: *VHS Video*
Directed by Steve Tanner and Michael Wiese, Written by Annamaria Murphy / $9.95